Susan M. Sheridan • Thomas R. Kratochwill

Conjoint Behavioral Consultation

Promoting Family–School Connections and Interventions

Second Edition

With contributions by Jennifer D. Burt,
Brandy L. Clarke, Shannon Dowd-Eagle, and
Diane C. Marti

 Springer

Susan M. Sheridan
Department of Educational Psychology
University of Nebraska
Lincoln, NE 68588-0345
USA
ssheridan2@unl.edu

Thomas R. Kratochwill
Wisconsin Center for
  Education Research
University of Wisconsin
Madison, WI 53706-1796
USA
tomkat@education.wisc.edu

Library of Congress Control Number: 2007928305

ISBN-13: 978-0-387-71247-5   e-ISBN-13: 978-0-387-71248-2

Printed on acid-free paper.

9 8 7 6 5 4 3 2 1

springer.com

Preface

Children learn within many systems and settings. In the United States, students spend 91% of their time from birth to the age of 18 outside of school. Once in school, they spend 70% of their waking hours outside of school. The settings, contexts, and supports provided within these systems contribute uniquely and collectively to students' educational pursuits and developmental outcomes. Continuity and congruence among systems and, in particular, integration among the expectations established for students by adults and caregivers in these systems greatly affect their learning trajectory.

It has been argued that to truly help children, service providers must paradoxically focus efforts and energies on the adults (e.g., parents and teachers) in their lives (Conoley & Gutkin, 1986; Sheridan & Gutkin, 2000). Building strengths, enhancing skills, and coalescing resources for the multiple adults in children's lives are among the key functions for school-based and school-linked service providers. That is, to enhance the lives of children, the adults who control the environments within which all are interacting must develop confidence and competence (i.e., self-efficacy and skills; Guralnick, 1989) as caregivers, supporters, and educators of children.

The purpose of this book is to provide a framework and model for interfacing the primary settings and systems in a student's life: the home and school systems. The focus is on supporting adults in their work and interactions with children for whom they are responsible. Our work in crafting this text has been guided by at least three fundamental considerations that have emerged in the field of psychology and education. These issues pertain to (a) an expanded framework for including families in a problem-solving process; (b) the integration of evidence-based interventions into prevention and intervention practices in consultation problem solving; and (c) the use of conjoint consultation problem-solving protocols as a practice guideline for the problem-solving process. Each of these issues is elaborated briefly here and then integrated throughout the text as a framework for advancing the practice and research in conjoint consultation problem-solving efforts.

Problem Solving with Families

As we have already noted, an important framework in problem solving is to involve families in the process. This decision is not simply a preference but has been supported extensively in the empirical literature as a way to improve children's social-emotional and academic performance. One of the major limitations of much of the traditional problem-solving consultation research has been the limited focus on family involvement in the problem-solving process, whether traditionally labeled prereferral intervention or the more recent work focused on response-to-intervention (RTI; see Kratochwill, 2006). Indeed, much of the work occurring within the recent RTI literature embraces the teacher as the primary and sole agent of intervention in a problem-solving process. Moreover, many of the frameworks for establishing interventions are void of family components (McKay & Bannon, 2004). When we emphasize problem solving, we refer to strategies that incorporate assessment tools as well as intervention technology into the framework of problem solving. With the exception of a few ecologically oriented assessment tools that incorporate family intervention as well as home-school collaboration (e.g., Ysseldyke & Christenson, 2003), in practice, little emphasis has been placed on this important linkage in consultation. Therefore, our message in this text and the basic conceptual framework are that we need to incorporate families into the assessment and intervention process and, specifically, the protocol for conjoint consultation.

Integration of Evidence-Based Interventions in Consultation Practice

During the past decade, tremendous emphasis has been placed on embracing evidence-based interventions in the practice of education and mental health (e.g., Kratochwill & Shernoff, 2004). Interventions with scientific support can be specifically integrated into the problem-solving process as a primary focused intervention at the individual, small group, or systems level. Conjoint consultation provides a vehicle for this integration and allows these evidence-based strategies to be integrated into intervention planning, implementation, and evaluation. In this text, we provide a framework for how this integration can occur and, specifically, indicate how a conjoint problem-solving consultation framework for children and families can be incorporated as well as link the problem-solving process to a multitiered system of prevention and intervention.

It is important to note, however, that many of the frameworks for multitiered interventions are still deficit oriented, and no compelling reason exists to focus on only these models as an effective service delivery framework for children and families or to embrace RTI as the sole model of services (Kratochwill, 2006). Nevertheless, we do provide examples of how conjoint consultation can be integrated into a framework of multilevel interventions within the school and, specifically, how conjoint consultation can be complimentary to the process of delivering effective educational and psychological services to children.

Practice Guidelines

There has been some interest in developing and using various guidelines to promote effective and evidence-based practices in educational and mental health settings. Essentially, three different frameworks have been established for potential adoption in this process (White & Kratochwill, 2005). First, many evidence-based interventions and practices can be implemented through manualized protocols that are available for various educational and mental health interventions. Most evidence-based interventions are actually accompanied by a manual that provides psychologists with guidelines to implement and monitor the effectiveness of the intervention when implemented in a practice context. Such a manual often includes the features that were part of the initial science-based evaluation of the intervention during the research process (Kratochwill & Stoiber, 2002).

A second framework that has often been used is called *intervention* or *treatment guidelines*, which refer to specific procedural protocols that assist the intervention agent or consultant in the implementation of the evidence-based interventions. Sometimes, these guidelines can be supplemented with "intervention algorithms" that assist the consultant in a step-by-step protocol for making various decisions about particular treatment targets, such as childhood academic and social-emotional disorders. Many of the traditional intervention guidelines and algorithms are focused on mental health issues and derive from the medical or clinical psychology literature. They have yet to be extensively applied within school psychology practice.

A third option is to use practice guidelines. Practice guidelines have traditionally emphasized comprehensive literature reviews (e.g., meta-analysis) to focus on treatment of a particular problem or disorder. These guidelines typically provide an intervention agent or consultant with a wide range of criteria for making decisions about a particular treatment including criteria related to diagnosis, assessment, integrity, outcome assessment, and so forth. In this context, practice guidelines represent an extension of more traditional intervention guidelines and algorithms.

In this text, we propose a somewhat different framework for defining a practice guideline and advance the notion that the protocols that accompany conjoint consultation (discussed in detail in later chapters) can be considered a practice guideline inasmuch as various components of the consultation problem-solving process have been subjected to literature reviews providing some guidance related to the specific conjoint consultation problem-solving process (see Frank & Kratochwill, 2008). Therefore, many of the topical issues that we review related to the problem-solving process—such as selection of target problems, acceptability of interventions, integrity, relationship issues, and implementation issues—establish the importance of operating with a systematic consultation problem-solving protocol in delivery of services in applied settings. In summary, the elements of integrating families into the intervention process—accompanied by evidence-based interventions and practices whenever possible—and using the protocols of conjoint problem-solving consultation as a practice guideline to implement quality services in applied settings provide a useful framework for advancing practice and research within the fields of psychology and education and, specifically, the work involving conjoint consultation.

Lincoln, Nebraska   Susan M. Sheridan
Madison, Wisconsin   Thomas R. Kratochwill

Acknowledgments

Conceptual, foundational, procedural, and empirical underpinnings of conjoint behavioral consultation have evolved over the course of several years. The current work represented herein is the product of many individuals who over the years have contributed their time, talent, effort, and ideas to enhance consultation services to children, families, and schools. We are indebted to the many colleagues, graduate students, teachers, administrators, parents, and children who have participated in research and training projects, helping us refine and improve our understanding of "what works." We appreciate the tireless efforts of Holly Sexton and Karen O'Connell for their administrative assistance. We recognize the patience of Judy Jones and Angela Burke of Springer, who continued to believe in this project and encourage its completion. We are forever grateful to our families—Steve, Erin, and Keevan, and Carol and Tyler—for their unending support and understanding.

We note with special gratitude the wisdom of Jack Bergan, whose early writings about behavioral consultation and data-based decision making have made an indelible mark on the field. His progressive thinking has inspired many generations.

Lincoln, Nebraska   Susan M. Sheridan
Madison, Wisconsin   Thomas R. Kratochwill

Contents

PREFACE v
ACKNOWLEDGMENTS ix

1. **FAMILY–SCHOOL PARTNERSHIPS IN PREVENTION
   AND INTERVENTION** 1

What Do We Mean by "Partnership"? 1
   Collaborative Relationships 2
   Shared Responsibility 4
Theories Underlying Partnerships 4
   Ecological Theory 4
   Behavioral Theory 6
   Family-Centeredness 7
   From Family-Centered to Partnership-Centered 9
Goal and Purposes of Partnerships 10
   Creating Meaningful Roles 10
   Promoting Continuity 11
   Enhancing Competencies of All Participants 12
A Framework for Developing Effective Partnerships 12
   Approach: Framework for Interaction with Families 12
   *Attitudes: Values and Perceptions Held About
      Family–School Relationships* 13
   *Atmosphere: Climate in Schools for Families
      and Educators* 14
   *Actions: Strategies for Building Shared Responsibility
      for Learning Outcomes* 14
   What Predicts Parental Involvement? 15
Evidence-Based Models of Family–School Partnerships 16
Summary 18

2. **DEFINITIONAL AND PROCEDURAL CHARACTERISTICS
   OF CONJOINT BEHAVIORAL CONSULTATION**   21

   Conjoint Behavioral Consultation   24
   Goals and Objectives of Conjoint Behavioral Consultation   26
   Characteristics/Assumptions of Conjoint Behavioral Consultation . . .   27
      *Conjoint Behavioral Consultation Is Concerned
       with Both Outcomes and Processes*   27
      *Conjoint Behavioral Consultation Is Responsive
       to Consumers' Needs*   28
      *Conjoint Behavioral Consultation Promotes
       Competency Acquisition*   28
      *Conjoint Behavioral Consultation Promotes Partnership
       and Collaboration*   29
   Description of the Conjoint Behavioral Consultation Model   29
   Conjoint Needs (Problem) Identification   30
      Prioritizing Needs   30
      Specifying and Operationalizing Target Concerns   32
      Determining Data Collection Procedures   33
      From Child Assessment to Ecological Assessment   35
   Conjoint Needs (Problem) Analysis   39
      Conducting Functional/Skills Assessments   39
      Developing Intervention Plans   42
   Plan Implementation   45
      Intervention Integrity   45
      Assessing a Child's Immediate Response to the Intervention   47
   Conjoint Plan Evaluation   47
      Assessing Intervention Effects   48
      Social Validity   49
      Assessment of Goals   50
      Planning for Maintenance of Child and Partnership   51
   Conjoint Behavioral Consultation in the Context
      of Response to Intervention   51
      Brief Overview of Response to Intervention   52
      Conjoint Problem Solving and Response to Intervention   53
   Planning and Conducting Conjoint Behavioral
      Consultation Meetings   54
   Summary   55

3. **CONJOINT BEHAVIORAL CONSULTATION IN PRACTICE:
   PROMOTING POSITIVE FAMILY–SCHOOL
   RELATIONSHIPS**   57

   Relational (Relationship-Building) Objectives in Conjoint
      Behavioral Consultation   57

*Improve Communication, Knowledge, and Understanding
    of the Child, Family, and School* 59
*Promote Shared Ownership and Joint Responsibility
    for Addressing Needs* 59
*Promote Greater Conceptualization of Needs
    and Promote Perspective Taking* 60
Strengthen Relationships Within and Across Systems 61
*Maximize Opportunities to Address Needs
    and Concerns Across, Rather than Within, Settings* 61
Increase Shared Commitment to Educational Goals 62
Increase the Diversity of Expertise and Resources Available 63
Interpersonal and Relational Skill Domains 64
Communication Strategies and Skills 64
Perspective Taking 69
Building Partnerships 70
Managing Conflict 72
Empowerment 75
Summary 75

4. **CONJOINT BEHAVIORAL CONSULTATION IN PRACTICE:
   WORKING WITH DIVERSE FAMILIES** 77
   Diane C. Marti, Jennifer D. Burt, and Susan M. Sheridan

Conceptualizing Culture and Diversity 78
Conjoint Behavioral Consultation and Diversity 79
Effective Consultant Practices for Culturally Sensitive
    Conjoint Behavioral Consultation Services 80
Practice Cultural Sensitivity 80
Build Trusting Relationships with the Family 82
Address Diversity Issues 82
Enhance Communication 83
Implement a "Family-Centered" Approach 85
Summary 85
Case Study: Donny 86
Conjoint Needs Identification 87
Problem-Solving/Content Issues 87
Process Goals and Issues 88
Conjoint Needs Analysis 89
Problem-Solving/Content Issues 89
Process Goals and Issues 90
Plan Implementation 91
Problem-Solving/Content Issues 91
Process Goals and Issues 91
Conjoint Plan Evaluation 91

    Problem-Solving/Content Issues 91
    Process Goals and Issues 95
  Summary 95

5. CONJOINT BEHAVIORAL CONSULTATION IN UNIQUE PRACTICE CONTEXTS 97

Jennifer D. Burt, Brandy L. Clarke, Shannon Dowd-Eagle, and Susan M. Sheridan

Conjoint Behavioral Consultation in a Teaming Context 97
  Team Format 98
  Team-Based Relationship Building 99
  Case Study: John 100
  Needs Identification Phase 100
  Needs Analysis Phase 101
  Plan Implementation Phase 102
  Conjoint Plan Evaluation 103
Conjoint Behavioral Consultation in Head Start Settings 105
  Case Study: Allie 107
  Needs Identification Phase 108
  Needs Analysis Phase 110
  Plan Implementation Phase 111
  Plan Evaluation Phase 112
Conjoint Behavioral Consultation in Pediatric
  Healthcare Systems 114
  Case Study: Amanda 117
  Needs Identification Phase 118
  Needs Analysis Phase 120
  Plan Implementation Phase 122
  Plan Evaluation Phase 124
Summary 126

6. RESEARCH ON CONJOINT BEHAVIORAL CONSULTATION 129

Brandy L. Clarke, Jennifer D. Burt, and Susan M. Sheridan

Review of Outcome Research 129
Reviews and Meta-Analyses 129
Review of Experimental Studies 136
Review of Case Studies 139
Review of Process Research 142
Relational Communication Patterns 142
Social Context 145
Review of Social Validity Research 146
Acceptability Research 149

Goal Attainment 150
Helpfulness Research 151
Summary 152

REFERENCES 153

APPENDIX A 167

APPENDIX B 171

APPENDIX C 175

APPENDIX D 177

APPENDIX E 181

APPENDIX F 185

APPENDIX G 186

APPENDIX H 187

APPENDIX I. 201

APPENDIX J 204

APPENDIX K 208

INDEX. 215

1
Family–School Partnerships in Prevention and Intervention

Children and youth exist in multiple contexts that both separately and together affect their functioning. These contexts include immediate settings of classrooms, home environments, peer groups, neighborhoods, and other important ecological settings. They also include the interconnected relationships among settings and individuals who participate in these settings. The relationships between children and adults, and between adults who control these contexts, are critically important for children's ultimate development.

An essential system interacting with children and families is that of the school. Schools and classrooms represent significant contexts for development, and teachers are meaningful individuals in a child's life (Sheridan & Gutkin, 2000). The establishment of partnerships between families and schools can be critical for maximizing the growth potential of a child. Positive, constructive relationships between primary systems (i.e., home and schools) can be instrumental in helping families develop competencies and utilize resources on behalf of their child's development. Indeed, cross-system partnerships and the formation of relationships and support systems are key (Dunst, Trivette, & Deal, 1988). The purposes of this chapter are to define a partnership approach in educating and socializing children; explore theories contributing to a partnership orientation; describe goals and purposes of partnerships; establish a framework for effective partnerships; and briefly review the empirical support for home–school–community partnerships.

What Do We Mean by "Partnership"?

According to Merriam-Webster (2004), a partner is "one that shares; one associated with another especially in an action." Within the context of families and schools, a partnership is a relationship involving close cooperation between parties that have clearly specified and joint rights and responsibilities. The focus of home–school partnerships is improving experiences and outcomes for children, including those that are academic, social, emotional, and behavioral in nature (Christenson & Sheridan, 2001). Operating from a traditional orientation, the

1

TABLE 1.1. Partnership versus traditional orientations toward home–school relationships.

Partnership orientation	Traditional orientation
Commitment to working together on behalf of the child's performance or achievement is clear	Emphasis on what schools do to promote learning
Communication is frequent, positive, bidirectional	Infrequent, one-directional, or problem-centered communications (school → home)
Relationship is characterized by cultural sensitivity; cultural differences are respected, appreciated, and recognized as contributing to positive learning climates	"One size fits all" orientation; cultural differences are perceived as challenges to overcome
Different perspectives are valued as important	Different perspectives are seen as barriers
Roles are clear, mutual, and supportive	Separate roles distance participants
Goals for students are mutually determined and shared	Goals determined by school personnel and sometimes shared with parents
Plans are co-constructed, with agreed upon roles for all participants	Educational plans devised and delivered by teachers

Source: From Sheridan, S.M. (2004). *Family–school partnerships: Creating essential connections for student success.* Keynote presented at the Resource Teacher: Learning and Behaviour Conference, Christchurch, New Zealand.

learning goals, activities, strategies, and desired outcomes tend to be school-determined. From a partnership perspective, however, there are mutual, bidirectional shared influences that affect learning and as such, are jointly determined. Specific differences between partnership and traditional orientations are given in Table 1.1.

Defining characteristics of home–school partnerships are presented in Table 1.2. We emphasize two characteristics as particularly salient in guiding effective partnerships. Specifically, effective home–school relationships (a) are collaborative and interdependent and (b) embrace shared responsibility for educating and socializing children.

Collaborative Relationships

Family–school partnerships place priorities on collaborative relationships. Collaboration has been defined in several ways. West (1990) defined collaboration as "an interactive planning or problem-solving process involving two or more team members . . . characterized by mutual respect, trust, and open communication; consideration of each issue or problem from an ecological perspective; consensual decision-making; pooling of personal resources and expertise; and joint ownership of the issue or problem being addressed" (p. 29). According to Welch and Sheridan (1995), collaboration is "a dynamic framework that endorses collegial, interdependent, and coequal styles of interaction between at least two partners working jointly together to achieve common goals in a decision-making process" (p. 11). The manner in which families, educators, and specialists work together (i.e., "co-labor"; Webster,

TABLE 1.2. Defining characteristics of family–school partnerships.

Characteristics	Key indicators
Relationships among partners are *collaborative, interdependent,* and *balanced*	Diverse individuals and vantage points work together as coequal parties, share in the identification of goals and solution of problems, and forge trusting relationships
	More than simply working together, the notion of partnerships involves a fundamental restructuring of how individuals work together across home and school systems
	Roles are complementary – each partner makes a unique contribution that is mutually beneficial
	All have generally equal opportunity in decision making
Responsibilities for educating and socializing children are shared	Resources, power, and responsibilities are shared
	Goals are mutually determined
	Outcomes achieved in the context of the partnership are uniquely superior to those achieved by any one party in isolation
Maintenance of a *positive relationship* is a priority	Failure to develop relationships can undermine the formation of successful partnerships
	Personal needs are put aside to allow the needs and goals of the partnership to take precedence
	To be successful, partners must believe that the other person is trustworthy, is working toward a mutually held goal, and holds positive regard toward the other
	All believe that the partnership and the anticipated outcomes are worthy of the expenditure of time and energy necessary for its maintenance
Services are *flexible, responsive,* and *proactive*	Unique family–school contexts define the form the partnership takes
Differences in perspectives are seen as strengths	A range of diverse experiences, skills, and views are brought to bear on the solution of problems
	Unique knowledge, resources, talents, and expertise brought by parents and educators enhance the potential outcomes for students
There is a commitment to *cultural competence*	Cultural values and traditions of the family and school are respected
	Services that are sensitive to important cultures and traditions of schools and families are most likely to be effective
Emphasis is on *outcomes* and *goal attainment*	Partnerships have clearly specified goals, and progress is monitored through data-based decision-making processes
	Programs are not offered because they are available; rather, they are considered fully with attention to the degree to which they *fit* within the overarching priorities of the partnership

Source: From Sheridan, S.M. (2004). *Family–school partnerships: Creating essential connections for student success.* Keynote presented at the Resource Teacher: Learning and Behaviour Conference, Christchurch, New Zealand.

1981) to promote the academic and social development of students is paramount in strengthening the integrated and continuous supports that must be provided to maximize learning and development.

Collaboration involves both *equality* — the willingness to listen to, respect, and learn from one another, and *parity* — the blending of knowledge, skills, and ideas to enhance the relationship and outcomes for children. Thus, families and schools "share joint responsibilities and rights, are seen as equals, and can jointly contribute to the process" (Vosler-Hunter, 1989, p. 15).

Shared Responsibility

Central to the home–school partnership philosophy is a belief in shared responsibility for educating and socializing children. Both families and educators are essential for children's progress in school. Neither alone can achieve what is possible when parents and educators share in the responsibility for and engage in actions designed to enhance students' success. Parents and educators contribute unique perspectives, resources, and values that support and enrich learning and development in complementary ways.

The notion of shared responsibility is particularly important when challenges or barriers to learning exist. Oftentimes in the face of difficulties, there is a tendency to place blame on another individual who may be perceived as being solely responsible for creating problems. However, when a student fails, it is often the case that the partnership has failed to live up to its potential. An alternative, more constructive approach is one wherein individuals share responsibilities for promoting growth and addressing concerns.

Theories Underlying Partnerships

Ecological Theory

Ecological theory provides a conceptual vantage point for home–school partnerships. Ecological theory is concerned with the multiple systems, environments, and contexts within which children function and the interactions and interconnections among them. These various systems are inseparable and embedded within a framework wherein each influences and is influenced by the other. A graphic depicting the ecological conceptual model is shown in Figure 1.1.

The primary, immediate system within which a child functions is the *microsystem*. The main microsystems in a child's life are the home and school. The microsystem is concerned with the relationship of the child with the immediate ecosystem and setting (e.g., home *or* classroom). An example of a microsystemic influence in the child's immediate context is support for the child's learning within the home (e.g., reading with a parent; helping prepare a meal). Microsystems are interrelated and exert bidirectional influence on each other. For example, experiences and events within the home setting

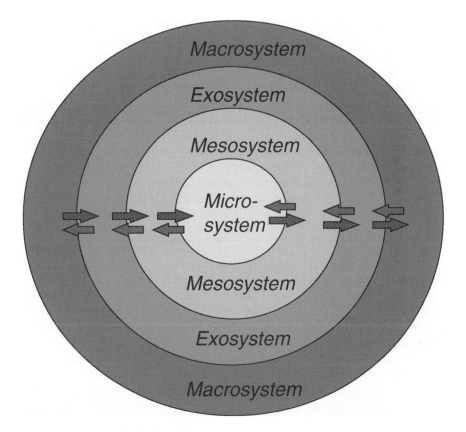

FIGURE 1.1. The ecological model.

influence the manner in which a child functions in the classroom. These interconnections among microsystems represent the *mesosystem*, which affects the child through relationships, communication patterns, and other bidirectional influences. For example, obtaining support and assistance with homework at home contributes to the child's academic functioning as demonstrated at school.

The *exosystem* is concerned with events in settings in which the child does not directly participate, but that impinge on the immediate microsystems. These are influences from other contexts, such as the degree to which parental work environments support their involvement in school-day activities. The *macrosystem* is the overall cultural or subcultural patterns and forces that subsume all other systems and subsystems, such as federal policy (e.g., No Child Left Behind, IDEA), that influence school curriculum, homework, and home–school practices (Bronfenbrenner, 1977).

Important to this discussion is the appreciation of the mesosystem as an important developmental context that is critical to children's learning (Weissberg & Greenberg, 1998). Relationships among home, school, and other primary systems are amenable to intervention and procedures for strengthening the mesosystem can produce tremendous influence on a child's learning and achievement.

Ecological theory is not without its limitations. One notable omission within ecological theory is a practical framework for service delivery. That is, until the introduction of conjoint behavioral consultation (CBC; Sheridan, Kratochwill, & Bergan, 1996), clear and operational guidelines for ecological consultation were lacking. Further, CBC research notwithstanding (e.g., Sheridan, Kratochwill, & Elliott, 1990), little empirical evidence existed attesting to the efficacy of ecologically oriented service models. Behavioral theory provides an evidence-based, technologically sophisticated template for working within and between systems to effect change (Sheridan et al., 1996).

Behavioral Theory

There are many underlying assumptions of behavioral theory. First, behavioral theory rests firmly on the assumption that behaviors are learned as a function of their interaction with the environment. Approaches that derive from behavioral theory rely on specific techniques that use learning principles to constructively change human behavior. Likewise, behavioral approaches focus on observable behaviors of a child, parent, and teacher, rather than only on some underlying cause. Especially within social learning theory, reciprocal interactions among individuals and the environmental variables that maintain specific behavior patterns are emphasized. Rather than being concerned with underlying causes of a behavior or "personality traits," the emphasis is on the "here and now" and identifying relevant environmental conditions that may be contributing to a given situation. Given the emphasis on specific behaviors, behavior therapy involves setting specific and clearly defined intervention goals. Finally, there is a great deal of emphasis placed on obtaining empirical support for various treatment techniques, including objective documentation of treatment effects for individual participants.

Over the years, some limitations of behavior therapy have been identified, and this process has set the stage for the expansion of the theory and practice. For example, behavioral consultants have traditionally considered only those stimulus events that immediately precede and follow the target behavior. This temporal constriction can cause difficulties in both the functional analysis and the measurement of behavior (Cataldo, 1984). It is desirable to investigate events that are temporally or contextually distal to a target behavior, yet functionally related to its occurrence. Setting events refer to temporally or contextually removed stimuli that bear a functional relation to behavior (Wahler & Fox, 1981). These setting events may be of a physical, social, or affective nature. Contemporary behavioral assessment frameworks go beyond immediate conditions and consider a more holistic view of a situation, including ecological considerations and setting events (Kratochwill & Shapiro, 2000; Sheridan & McCurdy, 2005; Ysseldyke & Christenson, 2002).

We support an ecological–behavioral approach to consultation that blends the strengths of both ecological and behavioral theories. With this approach, children's learning and behavior are conceptualized as a function of ongoing interactions between the characteristics of the individuals and the multiple environments within which they function (Sheridan & Gutkin, 2000). Ecological behavioral theory demands attention to the child and his or her behaviors, but only in relation to the systemic influences that surround the child when assessing concerns and developing interventions. Complex interactions and interdependencies among individual, classroom, culture, family, and community in the educational process are all considered important in assessment and intervention (Ysseldyke & Christenson, 2002). This focus requires evaluating not only variables inherent in the child (e.g., skills), but also environmental variables and the degree to which there is a "match" between the child and his or her environment (e.g., instruction, demands).

The main objectives of consultation from an ecological–behavioral approach are to (a) collect and use data that facilitate the development of solutions, (b) implement effective plans and programs to meet child-focused goals, and (c) sustain positive change long after the formal consultation procedures have been concluded (Sheridan & McCurdy, 2005). Effective services within this paradigm build ecological systems that can support children, youth, schools, and families. This task is accomplished by linking assessment to intervention, addressing a mixture of ecological and contextual variables, using a problem-solving framework, and focusing on outcomes.

Family-Centeredness

Beyond ecological and behavioral theories, elements of family-centeredness and family-centered services (FCS; Dunst et al., 1988; McWilliam, Tocci, & Harbin, 1998) contribute to the conceptual framework for family–school partnerships. FCS "place major emphasis on supporting and strengthening family functioning" in assessment and intervention (Dunst & Deal, 1994, p. 73). Services are focused on assessing a family's needs and strengths from that family's perspective, with a positive and proactive rather than deficit-based or categorical approach.

Family-centeredness is based on several premises or principles that together form the basis of service delivery. Ultimately, the dual goals of FCS are family empowerment and enhanced functioning on the part of family members (including children). In addition, there is a focus on family-identified (rather than professionally determined) needs, the use of existing family strengths, and strengthening social supports. The key principles are explored here.

Family Empowerment

Family-centered approaches to working with families promote "empowerment," which involves proactively promoting an individual's sense of control through their ability to use existing strengths (Dempsey & Dunst, 2004). For our purposes, we borrow from Dunst et al.'s (1988) notion of empowerment as a helping model that supports families in proactively identifying needs, mobilizing resources, and accomplishing goals through the development of personal capacities, strengths, and abilities. According to Dunst et al. (1988), "it is not just an issue of whether needs are met but rather that [sic] manner in which mobilization of resources and support occurs that is a major determinant of . . . empowering families" (p. 44). The emphasis is on family members' acquisition of competencies necessary for problem solution and goal attainment. As such, there is a focus on growth-producing behaviors among parents, children, and educators, rather than simply treating existing problems.

Empowerment models are in stark contrast to approaches that emphasize the professional as the sole expert (with a goal of imparting knowledge and wisdom), leading potentially to non-growth-producing outcomes. Expert models of "helping" often lead to dependency on the professional, fail to produce personal resources and positive belief systems, and result in limited skills in assessing personal needs and mobilizing familial resources in the future. According to Hobbs (1975), "The foresighted professional person knows that it is the parent who truly bears the responsibility for the child, and the parent cannot be replaced by episodic professional service" (pp. 228–229).

Acquisition of New Skills and Competencies

FCS uses helping behaviors (professional roles) focused on developing capacities, based on an understanding and appreciation for "where the family is." Rather than utilizing strategies to "treat" problems or remediate deficiencies, FCS approaches strive to promote the acquisition of family and child competencies. Models based on "correcting a problem" result in a limited, often short-term resolution of one presenting concern. Alternatively, FCS attends proactively to growth-producing behaviors. The development of strengths, assets, and skills is expected to lead to generalization of resources to address a range of presenting challenges in the future. In sum, it is necessary but not sufficient to simply "solve" an identified "problem"; it is also necessary to provide assistance to a family so its members develop increased skills and resources (Sheridan, Warnes, Cowan, Schemm, & Clarke, 2004).

Family-Identified Rather than Professional-Determined Needs

FCS is responsive to the needs of the client (i.e., family and child) and focuses assessment efforts on those needs that are most essential for the family to continue to grow. FCS models assume that families are in the best position to identify their most important needs, and commitment to change may be greatest when families' needs are self-determined. Professionals are in a position to assist families in determining those needs that are most essential in attaining short- and long-term goals and can use collaborative consultation strategies to help discern immediate and proximal foci for intervention.

Use of Existing Family Strengths

FCS is founded on the belief that all families have strengths and abilities, but ecological or systemic conditions may present difficulties in accessing or using those strengths. The help-provider is in a position to assist family members identify, access, and mobilize their strengths and use them to attain their self-determined goals. The ability of family members to use existing strengths for meeting their needs leads to positive changes in their functioning (Garbarino, 1982).

Strengthening Social Supports

FCS models are structured around intra- and intersystemic collaborations and partnerships, which access formal and informal supports for family members. The development of positive, proactive linkages and networks helps family members mobilize resources that are available to them but that they may have perceived as inaccessible. Furthermore, the notion of "partnership" implies that family members are coequal partners in the identification of needs and goals, determination of strategies and plans, and evaluation of outcomes as programs and resources are utilized (Christenson & Sheridan, 2001; Welch & Sheridan, 1995). Thus, services are not delivered "to" or "for" families, but "with" family members as active partners and participants.

From Family-Centered to Partnership-Centered

The work of Carl Dunst and colleagues has promoted a family-centered orientation in service delivery. We have adopted many of the principles of FCS in extended, reconceptualized discussions of CBC (Sheridan, Clarke, & Burt, 2008; Sheridan, Eagle, & Dowd, 2005; Sheridan, Erchul, et al., 2004; Sheridan, Warnes, et al. 2004). However, it is important to recognize that family systems represent just one component within home–school partnerships; educators and other specialists are coequal contributors in multisystem consultation. Thus, each of the main principles that focuses on "family" can be extended to "teacher," "educator," "support personnel," or any other key system supporting the child's learning and development. For example, discussions of family empowerment can be extended to considering means by which family members, educators, and the partnership to be empowered. From a *partnership-centered* orientation, attention to the development of skills and competencies extends from family members to educators and all others acquiring new abilities. Needs are jointly determined by members in the partnership (i.e., families, educators, consultants) and are not solely professionally or family determined. As a strength-based model, focusing on strengths of the *partnership* and not simply individual strengths (e.g., of the parent or teacher) can enhance outcomes. Finally, strengthening of social supports includes the support networks shared by educators and family members, who derive support from the partnership itself.

Goals and Purposes of Partnerships

Partnering with families around children's learning represents an important framework for promoting educational success. The goals of family–school partnerships address at least three important areas: creating meaningful roles for family members to support their child's learning; promoting continuity across systems; and enhancing competencies of all participants.

Creating Meaningful Roles

Parents, regardless of educational level, income status, or ethnic background, want their children to be successful in school. Across groups, parents also generally want information about how schools function, children's development and learning, and parents' roles in supporting their children. Whereas social class or family configuration predicts up to 25% of variance in achievement, family process variables predict up to 60% of variance (Kellaghan, Sloane, Alvarez, & Bloom, 1993). Family process variables (specific things families *do* to facilitate learning and educational success) have been shown to be more than status variables (who families *are*, including demographic variables such as ethnicity; Christenson & Sheridan, 2001). Process variables are amenable to change and modifiable; thus, identifying the specific factors that families can control is important.

Collective research findings support various ways for families to implement important processes conducive to student success. These strategies include ensuring school attendance; limiting television viewing; providing reading materials in the home (Barton & Coley, 1992); communicating strong, consistent values about education; demonstrating a willingness to help children and to intervene at school; and demonstrating an ability to become involved (Mitrsomwang & Hawley, 1993). In a study by Peng and Lee (1992), four variables were identified, which demonstrated a strong relationship with student learning. These family process variables were parental educational expectations, talking with students about school, providing learning materials, and providing learning opportunities outside of school (Peng & Lee, 1992).

Family process variables, and ecological conditions within the home that create opportunities for learning, have been coined the "curriculum of the home" (Walberg, 1984). The curriculum of the home includes many parent–child actions and activities that promote positive and healthy development. It recognizes the critical role of the natural home and community as important contexts for learning and opportunities to extend and generalize what children learn and do within the school day. Examples are conversations about everyday events, encouragement and discussion of leisure reading, joint analysis and monitoring of television viewing, expression of affection, and interest in children's academic and personal growth. Indeed, recognizing and creating opportunities for learning within the natural environments of home and community, modeling lifelong learning, providing structure and routine, and other positive learning conditions may be created when constructing a parent's role as a supporter and active player in learning and development.

Parents' construction (or beliefs) of their role related to their child's education contributes to choices they make (Hoover-Dempsey & Sandler, 1997). The manner in which parents perceive their own role in their child's education establishes a range of activities that they consider appropriate, necessary, and important. Through structured and planful partnership activities, it may be possible to promote role conceptions specific to learning.

Promoting Continuity

An objective of family–school partnerships is "not merely to get families involved, but rather to connect important contexts for strengthening children's learning and development" (Christenson & Sheridan, 2001, p. 7). Relationships across home, school, and other primary systems constitute mesosystemic influences and represent important developmental contexts that are amenable to intervention. Quality relationships among caregivers may be considered a primary protective factor (Weissberg & Greenberg, 1998) or "safety net" (Pianta & Walsh, 1996) for children.

Students who experience congruent worlds (i.e., where similar values, expectations, and ways of behaving are evident among family, school, and peers) make easy and smooth transitions across these environments. Continuity across home and school as experienced by students is important to support effective learning transitions. In a comprehensive ethnographic study of diverse adolescents, Phelan, Davidson, and Yu (1998) reported that students who experienced discontinuity across their home, school, and peer worlds had the most difficulty in making transitions among these different contexts and were at greatest risk for poor school performance and mental health concerns. Accordingly, low-achieving students reported extreme difficulty when they experienced "borders" among these contexts (i.e., aspects of cultural differences where the values, beliefs, knowledge, skills, and actions of one group are more valued than those of another). They saw borders, whether sociocultural, socioeconomic, or linguistic in nature, as insurmountable. In contrast, students who experienced congruent worlds (i.e., where similar values, expectations, and ways of behaving are evident among family, school, and peers) made easy and smooth transitions across these environments. The challenges posed by family diversity do not represent deficits in the child, the school, or the family, but are evidence of a lack of synchrony within the child–family–school system (Pianta & Walsh, 1996). Children at risk can succeed "against the odds" when they experience congruent messages, expectations, goals, values, priorities, and supports from families, schools, and communities (Bempechat, 1998).

Enhancing Competencies of All Participants

Seminal reviews of the literature on home–school partnerships, and benefits for students, parents, teachers, and schools are available (Henderson & Mapp, 2002). It is clear from these reviews that involving parents meaningfully and actively in their children's learning and working jointly across home and school yield ample benefits. In the presence of effective home–school partnerships, students have been shown to demonstrate improvement in grades, test scores, attitudes, self-concept, behavior, and social skills. Greater study habits, improved homework completion rates, more engagement in classroom learning activities, higher attendance rates, and a reduction in suspension rates and discipline problems are associated with meaningful parent involvement. In the presence of home–school partnerships, teachers have been shown to become more proficient in professional activities, allocate more time to instruction, become more involved with curriculum, develop more student-oriented rather than task-oriented activities, receive higher ratings on teaching performance evaluations by principals, indicate greater satisfaction with their jobs, and request fewer transfers (Christenson, 1995).

Parent benefits are also associated with home–school partnerships. For example, parents have been shown to demonstrate greater understanding of the work of schools and positive attitudes about school; report increased contacts and communication with educators and a desire for more involvement; report improved parent–child relationships and communication with their children; develop effective parenting skills; and become more involved in learning activities at home. Schools have been shown to receive higher effectiveness ratings and implement more successful school programs when parents are meaningfully involved.

A Framework for Developing Effective Partnerships

Partnering with families is an intentional process (Christenson, 2004), which is most readily accomplished when working from a framework reflecting four A's: Approach, Attitude, Atmosphere, Actions (Christenson & Sheridan, 2001). This framework, depicted in Figure 1.2, illustrates the relational prerequisites (i.e., *approach, attitudes,* and *atmosphere*) for successful, collaborative *actions* to occur. In other words, actions or activities will not reach their maximal benefit in the absence of a meaningful approach, constructive attitudes, and a positive atmosphere.

Approach: Framework for Interaction with Families

The approach that schools assume vis-à-vis family participation sets the stage for meaningful and effective involvement. When schools adopt an approach of *shared responsibility for educational outcomes*, they are recognizing the

Prerequisite Conditions:
These "3A's" must be in place for
Actions to be accepted and effective

FIGURE 1.2. The "four A's of partnerships": Approach, attitudes, and atmosphere are prerequisite conditions for the successful implementation of partnership actions.

significance of families and contributions of schools to the success of students (Christenson & Sheridan, 2001). When the responsibility for learning is shared, parents are viewed as essential, not merely desirable, for children's optimal performance in school. Both family *and* school contexts are learning environments, and each has responsibilities to promote student learning. Students are best positioned to learn in the context of integrated links between home, school, and community – links that are reinforced when each partner plays a role and when collectively they share in supporting the relationship on behalf of the student.

Attitudes: Values and Perceptions Held About Family–School Relationships

A critical attitude, or belief, that must be held by parents and educators is that home *and* school together can accomplish more than either home *or* school can accomplish alone. Children's earliest learning and development occurs in the context of the family, which is further supported when they transition across systems and enter the school and other learning environments. Recognizing families, schools, and other settings as contexts for children's learning and development, and believing that interventions should encompass the family and other support systems, may be the difference between considering families as "essential partners" versus "desirable extras" (Christenson, 2004).

An attitude that respects differences among families facilitates the development of constructive relationships. Families and children are unique with respect to their connection to schooling and ability to partner; some families deal with individual situations that may make it difficult for them to be involved and available. Constructive attitudes allow educators to accommodate parents by beginning "where they are," not where educators think parents "should" or "could" be. Such attitudes convey a willingness to learn about a family's uniqueness, while also establishing opportunities to learn with and from them (Christenson & Sheridan, 2001).

Atmosphere: Climate in Schools for Families and Educators

The atmosphere or climate of a school comprises the predominant beliefs and values of a school community (Welch & Sheridan, 1995). When related to home–school partnerships, it communicates an important message related to the value of families in schools and schooling. In general, schools should strive to become welcoming, "family-friendly" communities. Of particular importance is that the school climate is welcoming to and inclusive of input from *all* families; openness to differences is important to establish an atmosphere that is comfortable, friendly, and approachable for all families. If a school determines a priori the "right way" or "best way" of involving particular families or forming relationships, there may be little openness to differing viewpoints characteristic of some cultural groups (Christenson, 2004).

A positive atmosphere that promotes partnerships around learning is built on a foundation of trust. When family members feel welcome and wanted at school, and know what their role is or can be, generally they will be better able to participate meaningfully and actively in the education of their child. Importantly, when family members recognize the school as a place (and schooling as a process) in which they belong, and the meaningful role they play, they may increase their beliefs that their efforts make a difference for their child. Unless parents feel connected, their ability to recognize the essential nature of their role is limited. Parents' connection to schools is enhanced with invitations to partner, clearly articulated benefits for their involvement, and options for being engaged with their children's learning (Hoover-Dempsey & Sandler, 1997).

Actions: Strategies for Building Shared Responsibility for Learning Outcomes

Actions are the strategies or practices engaged in to promote partnerships in schools. If the approach, attitude, and atmosphere are intact and supportive of partnerships, home–school strategies are more likely to succeed. In addition, administrative support and guidance, home–school teams, and a school–community philosophy or mission statement holding all parties responsible are important (Christenson & Sheridan, 2001).

There are many possible actions that are appropriate for establishing meaningful and effective partnerships. In general, the action chosen must be responsive to the family and school contexts that define the nature of the relationship. There is no one action that will meet the needs of all situations, and no road map that provides solutions to all concerns. Rather, the strategy chosen should be driven by evidence supporting positive outcomes (i.e., it should have demonstrated empirical support attesting to its effectiveness) and by its responsiveness to the needs of the child, family, and school. CBC is one evidence-based practice guideline that is individualized to meet the needs of students, families, and teachers. Other models for home–school partnerships are reviewed in Carlson and Christenson (2005) and presented later in this chapter.

What Predicts Parental Involvement?

Hoover-Dempsey and colleagues (Hoover-Dempsey, Bassler, & Brissie, 1992; Hoover-Dempsey & Sandler, 1995, 1997) have advanced a theoretical model identifying variables that promote meaningful parental involvement. In ongoing investigations of this model (Walker, Wilkins, Dallaire, Sandler, & Hoover-Dempsey, 2005), they have begun to specify empirical relationships between these theoretical variables and parents' involvement behaviors. *Psychological variables* related to parental behaviors include (a) parents' motivational beliefs (parental role construction and parental self-efficacy), (b) parents' perceptions of invitations for involvement from others (including invitations from their child, their child's teacher, and the school), and (c) parents' perceived life context (perceptions of their available time and energy and specific skills and knowledge for involvement).

The manner in which parents construct their own role (i.e., role construction) contributes to their motivation for involvement. *Role construction* concerns general principles guiding a parent's definition of the parenting role, beliefs about child development and child-rearing, and beliefs about appropriate home-support roles in education. Role constructs establish a range of activities that parents will consider important, necessary, and permissible for their own actions on behalf of their child (Hoover-Dempsey & Sandler, 1997). Within family–school partnerships, there are opportunities to establish role constructs wherein parents define themselves as supporters, advocates, and facilitators of their child's learning.

Self-efficacy is another aspect of a parent's motivational beliefs that enable them to become involved in their child's learning. Parents who have well-developed, positive perceptions of their own efficacy tend to demonstrate higher levels of involvement (Grolnick, Benjet, Kuroswki, & Apostoleris, 1997; Hoover-Dempsey et al., 1992; Swick, 1988). That is, parents who believe that they are important and efficacious in their children's learning tend to demonstrate higher levels of engagement (Ames, 1993). Parents' sense of efficacy, or belief that they can help their child succeed in school, enables them to assume that their participation may influence their child's learning and performance in a positive way (Hoover-Dempsey & Sandler, 1997). Parents must see that their efforts are directly related to improvement or the possibility of improvement in their children's education. Experiencing self-efficacy (confidence) enables parents to assume that their involvement activities will positively influence children's learning and school performance and predisposes a parent to choose an active involvement role in education. This aspect has been identified as the "linchpin" for parents to sustain their engagement (Comer, 1995). When parents judge that they are unlikely to be successful, their low efficacy might keep them from becoming engaged (Lareau, 1987).

Parental perceptions of invitations for involvement from their child, their child's teacher, and their child's school appear related to their involvement behaviors. This component concerns the degree to which parents believe their child and their child's school personnel desire their involvement, including whether a climate of opportunities and demands exists. The extent to which schools establish opportunities and communicate expectations for involvement exerts influence on parents' basic decisions to be involved. Thus, there is a responsibility for schools to provide meaningful and relevant opportunities (i.e., roles), which are culturally sensitive and appropriate for the family. It is also desirable to create partnership opportunities and formats that are sustainable over time, setting, and learning contexts to promote a pathway for continued participation and collaboration.

Perceived life context concerns parents' perceptions of resources available for involvement, including time and energy, and skills and knowledge as related to involvement. In survey research, parents have reported that time and energy are often barriers to their involvement (Gettinger & Waters-Guetschow, 1998). Skill and knowledge related to involvement may also affect the level and type of parental involvement (Lareau, 1989; Leitch & Tangri, 1988). Alternatively, there is evidence that parents can be involved in meaningful ways when educators actively help them become involved (Dauber & Epstein, 1993). Partnerships, including home–school consultation-based strategies, provide opportunities to develop parents' skills and competencies for facilitating their child's learning and development.

The psychological variables appear to predict parent involvement behaviors in unique ways. In an early investigation of the model, Walker et al. (2005) found that collectively, these psychological variables explained 33% of the variance in parents' home-based involvement and 19% of the variance in parents' school-based involvement. Perception of specific invitations from the child was the strongest predictor of parents' home-based involvement (explaining 21% of the total variance), and parents' motivational belief was the biggest predictor of school-based involvement (accounting for 12% of the variance). Perceived life context was differentially related to involvement for different groups of parents. Specifically, it was a strong predictor of *home-based involvement* for parents who reported lower time and energy and skills and knowledge. Conversely, it was a strong predictor of *school involvement* for parents who reported higher levels of time and energy and skills and knowledge.

Evidence-Based Models of Family–School Partnerships

Since the mid-1990s, increasing emphasis has been placed on evidence-based interventions and models of service in psychological and educational practice. This emphasis is based in part on developments in psychology, medicine (e.g., psychiatry), education, and prevention science (e.g., Hoagwood, Burns, Kiser, Ringeisen, & Schoenwald, 2001; Kratochwill & Stoiber, 2002; Power, 2003). There seems to be consensus that researchers, trainers, and practitioners move in directions that will yield functional and meaningful scientific information for psychological and educational practice (i.e., evidence-based practice). The Task Force on Evidence-Based Interventions in School Psychology was formed to identify, review, and code studies of psychological and educational interventions for behavioral, emotional, and academic problems and disorders for school-aged children and their families (see Gutkin, 2002; Kratochwill & Stoiber, 2002).

The empirical support for five types of home–school or family-based interventions was reviewed using the Task Force criteria in an investigation coordinated by Carlson and Christenson (2005). Specifically, research support related to the following interventions was explored: family–school interventions with preschool children; parent consultation; parent education; family–school collaboration; and parent involvement. A thorough review of the findings is beyond the scope of this book; interested readers are referred to Carlson and Christenson (2005). A summary of programs that were found to have adequate support to be considered "promising" are in Table 1.3.

Of the many intervention studies reviewed, 15 studies yielded sufficient positive outcome data in the context of appropriately rigorous designs. Of these, and particularly relevant to this text, parent behavioral consultation and CBC

TABLE 1.3. Family-based interventions with evidence supporting their effectiveness.

Type of family-based program	Intervention(s) with preliminary evidence-based support	Representative reference(s)
Family–School Interventions with Preschool Children	Incredible Years Training Series	Webster-Stratton, Reid, and Hammond (2001)
	PARTNERS Parent Education Program	Webster-Stratton (1998)
	Parent Child Interaction Therapy (PCIT)	Funderburk et al. (1998) Hembree-Kigin and McNeil (1995) McNeil, Eyberg, Eisenstadt, Newcomb, and Funderburk (1991)
Parent Consultation	Conjoint Behavioral Consultation	Sheridan, Eagle, Cowan, and Mickelson (2001) Sheridan, Kratochwill, and Bergan (1996) Weiner, Sheridan, and Jenson (1998)
	Parent Behavioral Consultation	Cavell and Hughes (2000) Rhoades and Kratochwill (1998)

(*Continued*)

TABLE 1.3. Family-based interventions with evidence supporting their effectiveness—Cont'd.

Type of family-based program	Intervention(s) with preliminary evidence-based support	Representative reference(s)
Parent Education	Aware Parenting	Bronstein et al. (1998)
	Reading Made Easy	Mehran and White (1988)
Family–School Collaboration	School-Based and Family Literacy Program	Morrow and Young (1996)
	Parent–Teacher Action Research (PTAR) Teams plus Social Skills Instruction	McConaughy, Kay, and Fitzgerald (1998)
	School–Home Notes and Family Problem-Solving Game	Blechman, Taylor, and Schrader (1981)
Parent Involvement	Parent Tutoring	Duvall, Delquadri, Elliott, and Hall (1992)
		Hook and DuPaul (1999)
	Parents Encourage Pupils (PEP)	Shuck, Ulsh, and Platt (1983)
	Reciprocal Peer Tutoring with Parent Involvement	Heller and Fantuzzo (1993)
Parent Training and Family Interventions	Problem-Solving Skills Training (PSST) plus Parent Management Training (PMT)	Kazdin, Esveldt-Dawson, French, and Unis (1987)
		Kazdin, Siegel, and Bass (1992)
	Social Learning Family Therapy (SLFT)	Sayger, Horne, Walker, and Passmore (1988)

were found to be the only parent consultation models that appeared to demonstrate adequate and sufficient evidence. Three models in the areas of family–school preschool interventions (Incredible Years, PARTNERS, and Parent Child Interaction Therapy) and parent involvement interventions (parent tutoring, Parents Encourage Pupils [PEP], and reciprocal peer tutoring with parent involvement) were found to have support. Likewise, three models were identified within the family–school collaboration area: Family Literacy Program, Parent–Teacher Action Research [PTAR] teams plus social skills instruction, and school–home notes. The Aware Parenting Program was identified within the parent education area as having effectiveness evidence. Finally, Problem-solving Skills Training plus Parent Management Training were found to be effective within the area of parent training.

Summary

Despite a history in education and mental health systems that recognize families as part of a child's background, little concerted attention has been paid to establishing effective and reliable means for establishing partnerships beneficial to their care and socialization. Recent conceptualizations of family–school partnerships promote meaningful linkages between multiple ecological systems to optimize learning and development. Collaborative relationships, defined by interdependence and shared responsibility in decision-making, characterize our approach to "best practice."

Ecological–behavioral theory provides the framework for consultation-based partnerships (including assessment, intervention, and evaluation). Additionally, descriptions of FCS contribute specific principles for working with families via supportive and strength-enhancing means. The main foci of FCS place emphases on creating conditions wherein families can be empowered; promoting new skills and competencies; expecting families will participate in identifying their own needs and priorities; using family strengths to support goal acquisition; and developing social networks to support families and their growth. These same principles can be applied to models of services that focus on families and schools in partnership with each other, moving the focus from schools *or* families to schools *and* families working collaboratively as a joint support system for a child's optimal development. Such partnerships provide opportunities for continuity and consistency among ecological systems. When implemented with an effective approach, inclusive attitude, and inviting atmosphere, the proliferation of evidence-based actions (i.e., interventions) across home and school contexts is facilitated.

2
Definitional and Procedural Characteristics of Conjoint Behavioral Consultation

Within educational and mental health contexts, consultation practice typically takes one of at least three forms. These approaches are reviewed in detail elsewhere (e.g., Kratochwill & Bergan, 1990; Kratochwill & Pittman, 2002) and will be mentioned briefly here. Among the variety of features of problem-solving consultation, the indirect service delivery aspect of consultation is a major identifying characteristic, wherein the consultant's efforts have an indirect influence on a client. Kratochwill and Pittman (2002) provided an overview of several possible optional consultation services along with detailed definitions and illustrations of the various approaches that could be enacted in school or community-based practice. Table 2.1 provides the alternative consultation relationships that can be developed.

In general, three major domains of possible consultee–mediator consultation relationships are possible: case-centered consultation, technology training consultation, and organizational consultation. Traditional case-centered approaches involve a consultant working through a consultee to serve a client. The focus in case-centered consultation is on individual problem-solving efforts for specific target issues and concerns identified by the consultee(s). The consultee in these cases may be a teacher, parent, administrator, or peer, or a combination thereof as in the case of conjoint behavioral consultation (CBC) (wherein parents and teachers serve as joint consultees).

A second form of indirect service involves consultee skill development and is known as "technology training" (Vernberg & Repucci, 1986). This focus may include efforts to train teachers or parents in various components of the process, such as data collection, intervention implementation, or data-based problem solving. In the case of CBC, an extensive body of literature exists on methods to facilitate and empower parents to participate in intervention services for their child. The reader is referred to the miniseries on family intervention strategies in *School Psychology Quarterly* (see Carlson & Christenson, 2005) for a review.

The third domain, organizational (system-based) consultation, involves a variety of practices aimed at addressing needs at an organizational level and may include issues such as group dynamics, organizational structure, and

TABLE 2.1. Alternative consultation relationships.

Consultee–mediator definition	
Case-centered consultation	
Teacher-based consultation	Teacher serves in the role of mediator in service delivery
Parent-based consultation	Parent serves in the role of mediator in service delivery
Conjoint consultation: Teacher–parent	Teacher and parent(s) share a joint responsibility in the role of mediator in service delivery
Child-based consultation	Child serves in the role of mediator in service delivery with adults
Peer-mediated consultation	Child serves in the role of mediator in service delivery with peers
Technology training/consultation	
Teacher training	Teacher serves in the role of mediator and is trained in the intervention and/or service delivery
Parent training	Parent serves in the role of mediator and is trained in the intervention and/or service delivery
Organizational consultation	
System-level consultation	System-change agents serve in the roles of mediator in service delivery

Source: From Kratochwill, T.R., & Pittman, P. (2002). Defining constructs in consultation: An important training agenda. *Journal of Educational and Psychological Consultation, 13*, 69–95. Copyright 2002 by Erlbaum. Reprinted with permission.

group problem solving (Kratochwill & Pittman, 2002). Organizational consultation is typically focused on system change and various agents of system change. This focus of consultation can facilitate other models of case-centered and technology training consultation in applied settings.

Regardless of the form that consultation services take, certain core assumptions define the practice of consultation. Gutkin and Curtis (1999) reviewed some of the primary characteristics that have traditionally served as a framework for consultation practice. These include the indirect nature of consultation services, coordinated relationships among participants (consultant and consultees), the voluntary role of consultees, and confidentiality of the process. With advances in consultation research, training, and practice over several decades, the manner in which these core defining constructs have been conceptualized has evolved. For example, whereas collaborative relationships have traditionally characterized consultant–consultee interactions, it is now recognized that exchanges within consultation are commonly considered cooperative and mutual and at times directive and guiding (Gutkin, 1999; Sheridan, Meegan, & Eagle, 2002). Similarly, whereas consultant and consultee roles were defined, respectively, by their indirect and direct involvement with the client, it is now commonplace for consultants to share in some aspects of intervention delivery, particularly when training consultees in effective strategies. These and other traditional and revised assumptions of consultation constructs are presented in Table 2.2.

TABLE 2.2. Traditional and revised core characteristics of consultation services.

Characteristic	Traditional assumption	Revised assumption
Service delivery format	Treatment is delivered through a consultee (e.g., parent or teacher) rather than directly through the psychologist	Treatment is delivered through direct and indirect contact with the client
Consultation focus	Provision of services to clients	Provision of services to client and/or consultee
Goals of consultation	Remediation and/or prevention process goals: skill development	Remediation and/or prevention process goals: skill development
Consultant–consultee relationship	Meaningful collaborative relationship characterized by openness and trust	Collaboration ranges from maximum to minimum depending on the knowledge and skills of the consultee
Coordinate power status	A coordinate power status is vital; a hierarchical relationship may militate against good communication and rapport	Power status can range from coordinate to hierarchical depending on the status of the consultee
Right to reject consultant suggestions	The consultee has the right to reject the consultant's suggestions	The consultee may or may not be able to reject the consultant's suggestions depending on the negotiated relationship
Consultee involvement	The consultee should be actively involved in the consultation process	The consultee should be actively involved in the consultation process and may share treatment responsibilities with the consultant
Voluntary participation	The consultation relationship is initiated voluntarily by the consultee	Voluntary participation is ideal but may be impossible with some consultant–consultee relationships
Confidentiality	Confidentiality of consultee–consultant communication is essential in successful consultation	Confidentiality may not be possible with some consultees such as children

Source: Adapted from Kratochwill, T.R., & Pittman, P. (2002). Defining constructs in consultation: An important training agenda. *Journal of Educational and Psychological Consultation, 13*, 69–95. Copyright 2002 by *Journal of Educational and Psychological Consultation*. Adapted with permission.

Conjoint Behavioral Consultation

CBC is an extension of traditional case-centered (teacher or parent) consultation, which focuses on a child's learning and development as they are manifested across multiple ecological contexts and settings. A conceptual schemata of CBC, depicting the overlapping and interactive nature of multiple systems in a client's life and the role of consultation at the intersection, is shown in Figure 2.1. By joining parents, teachers, and other relevant caregivers and supportive adults in the decision-making process, attention to the individual and interacting systems over contextual and temporal bases (i.e., across settings and time) is possible. Whereas teachers and other support staff vary throughout children's developmental transitions, parents are constant – through their active and meaningful involvement in the process of identifying goals, coconstructing interventions, and monitoring their child's progress; continuity over time and across transition periods is possible.

Drawing from behavioral case-centered conceptions of consultation, traditionally CBC has been defined as "a structured, indirect form of service-delivery, in which parents and teachers are joined to work together to address the academic, social, or behavioral needs of an individual for whom both parties bear some responsibility" (Sheridan & Kratochwill, 1992, p. 122). As presented in Chapter 1, it is conceptualized from an

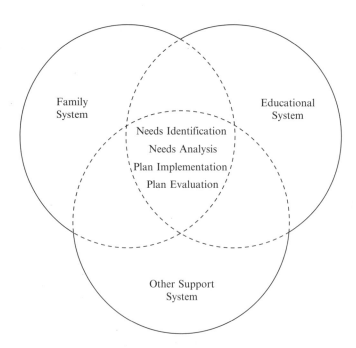

FIGURE 2.1. Conceptual model of CBC.

ecological-behavioral framework, with important conceptual contributions from the family-centered service literature (Dunst, Trivette, & Deal, 1988). Furthermore, goals related to child outcomes are maximized and most readily attainable when operating from a cross-systems partnership. Therefore, recent conceptualizations of CBC define it in terms that encompass the mutual and shared responsibility among family members, educators, and other care providers (e.g., extended family members, medical specialists, school support staff) for supporting a child's learning and development. Thus, for purposes of this book, CBC is defined as: *A strength-based, cross-system problem-solving and decision-making model wherein parents, teachers, and other caregivers or service providers work as partners and share responsibility for promoting positive and consistent outcomes related to a child's academic, behavioral, and social-emotional development.*

In CBC, parents, teachers, and other caregivers engage in a structured problem-solving process with a consultant to address the needs of children collaboratively across settings. Parents, teachers, and other supportive adults work together to share in the identification of needs for children and to develop, implement, and evaluate interventions to address those needs. All stages of consultation are conducted with parents and teachers together, in a simultaneous (rather than parallel) manner (Sheridan, Kratochwill, & Bergan, 1996).

Adopting an ecological-systems perspective (Bronfenbrenner, 1977; Sheridan et al., 1996), CBC acknowledges that children function within and across various systems in their environment. The two primary systems in most children's lives are the home and school. CBC recognizes that children, families, and schools have a bidirectional, reciprocal influence over each other and that the connections between home and school systems are essential for facilitating positive outcomes for children. The CBC process acknowledges the vital role played by families in children's learning and development and includes families as equal participants in the goal-setting and decision-making process. In addition, in some situations there are other caregivers or support staff providing services (e.g., medical specialists) or in other settings (e.g., daycare facilities) that must be incorporated into the assessment and intervention process. CBC secures these connections by bringing together systems and caregivers in a supportive and collaborative manner to address the needs of children.

CBC is a vehicle by which constructive, goal-directed, solution-oriented services are fostered for children. It emphasizes meaningful cross-system supports and family involvement in a child's learning and development and promotes *cross-system partnerships* in the context of cooperative and collegial problem solving. In CBC, service providers and caregivers work jointly and cooperatively with each other in a mutual and respectful relationship. Structured, joint problem solving facilitates clear communication, shared goals, and congruent practices, with an emphasis on consistency in approaches, attitudes, and actions across home, school, and other support systems (Christenson & Sheridan, 2001).

Goals and Objectives of Conjoint Behavioral Consultation

There are three overarching goals and several objectives of CBC, as outlined in Table 2.3. The first goal concerns the reason and purpose for coming together: to promote academic, socioemotional, and behavioral *outcomes for children* through joint, mutual, cross-system planning. The second goal is to promote *parent engagement* within a developmental, culturally sensitive context. Finally, CBC strives to *strengthen relationships* between systems on behalf of children's learning and development by (a) addressing the priorities and concerns of all parties, (b) strengthening social supports and promoting partnerships and collaboration among systems, and (c) developing and enhancing competencies and skills of parents and educators.

Subsumed within these overarching goals of CBC are several outcome and relational objectives. Outcome objectives generally refer to child-oriented results, which occur as a function of conjoint planning and problem solving. Relational objectives are those that address the partnership – they are concerned with the relationships among systems and caregivers to support immediate and ongoing benefits.

TABLE 2.3. Overarching goals and objectives of conjoint behavioral consultation.

Goals
Promote academic, socioemotional, and behavioral *outcomes for children* through joint, mutual, cross-system planning
Promote *parent engagement* wherein parental roles, beliefs, and opportunities for meaningful participation are clear, within a developmental, culturally sensitive context
Establish and strengthen *home–school partnerships* on behalf of children's learning and development, immediately and over time

Outcome objectives
Obtain comprehensive and functional data over extended temporal and contextual bases
Establish consistent intervention programs across settings
Improve the skills, knowledge, and behaviors of all parties (i.e., family members, school personnel, and the child-client)
Monitor behavioral contrast and side effects systematically via cross-setting intervention agents
Enhance generalization and maintenance of intervention effects via consistent programming across sources and settings
Develop skills and competencies to promote further independent conjoint problem solving between the family and school personnel

Process objectives
Improve communication, knowledge, and understanding about family, child, and school
Promote shared ownership and joint responsibility for problem solution
Promote greater conceptualization of needs and concerns and increase perspective taking
Strengthen relationships within and across systems
Maximize opportunities to address needs and concerns across, rather than within, settings
Increase shared (parent and teacher) commitments to educational goals
Increase the diversity of expertise and resources available

The goals of CBC are achieved via structured, supportive interactions among consultants, parents, educators, and other relevant service providers. These interactions occur via a dynamic and ongoing process, not simply a series of steps or meetings that occur devoid of a relationship with mutual goals and shared responsibilities. This process is put into practice via four stages, all conducted in a conjoint fashion: needs (problem) identification, needs (problem) analysis and plan development, plan implementation, and plan evaluation. As a process, it is important to emphasize that CBC stages are dynamic; they are not simply a series of interviews conducted in linear fashion. In a flexible and responsive fashion, much of what is required to meet the objectives of each stage occurs outside of the interview meetings. For example, a wealth of assessment information is collected beyond the formal interviews via direct observations, work samples, behavioral checklists, and other assessment methods; the interviews constitute just one method of data collection. In addition, many of the CBC objectives (such as strengthening home–school relationships, developing parents' skills, and facilitating open communication channels) occur through a series of actions and activities in the natural home and school environments, throughout the entire CBC process.

Characteristics/Assumptions of Conjoint Behavioral Consultation

As presented in Chapter 1, CBC is conceptualized as a partnership-centered model. This approach builds on family-centered principles (Dunst et al., 1988), but recognizes the strengths, values, goals, and priorities of educators as well as families. Thus, the priorities of family *and* school in partnership, rather than those of the family *or* school separately, are at the center. As a partnership-centered model, at least four primary characteristics are apparent. First, CBC is concerned with both outcomes and processes. Second, CBC services are responsive to the needs of consumers (i.e., family members, educators, other caregivers). Third, CBC promotes competency acquisition in all parties. Finally, CBC promotes partnership and collaboration among systems (Dunst, Trivette, Davis, & Cornwell, 1994). In the following sections, these central principles of partnership-centered CBC are presented.

Conjoint Behavioral Consultation Is Concerned with Both Outcomes and Processes

CBC promotes active engagement and skill development and assists partners to actively participate in enhancing their own competencies and those of the children for whom they are jointly responsible. Consultees (e.g., parents and teachers) are engaged proactively in identifying needs, developing strategies, mobilizing resources, and accomplishing goals established for children. These outcomes are achieved most effectively by focusing on strengths (rather than deficits) within and across systems, developing consultees' capacities, structuring opportunities for communication and collaboration, and fostering consistency and continuity across contexts. Through such an approach, attainment of long-term outcomes is maximized, including those pertaining to the child and to the home–school partnership.

Although the attainment of child goals is the primary outcome of interest, it is the process by which professionals assist families and educators (i.e., one that enables consultees to continue developing skills and capacities) that is the cornerstone of CBC service delivery. Through the process, consultees acquire a strategy for both problem solving and plan development and implementation. Specifically, they work with the consultant to jointly identify and prioritize needs, establish reasonable goals, develop appropriate plans, and monitor student progress, thereby maximizing opportunities for positive outcomes. Furthermore, plan strategies that are relevant and feasible across settings result in desired outcomes, enhance continuity and consistency over time and setting, and provide new knowledge and skills that will likely be utilized again in the future when similar needs are present.

Conjoint Behavioral Consultation Is Responsive to Consumers' Needs

CBC provides help that is congruent with family members' and educators' appraisals of a child's needs. A model such as CBC, concerned with exploring and addressing consultee-determined needs, is distinguished from an expert model that is based on professionally determined agendas. In CBC, target behaviors and interventions are defined through a mutual process that incorporates consultees' (parents and teachers) and professionals' assessments of child needs (Sheridan et al., 1996). The consultant facilitates the process of helping consultees select target behaviors and interventions that can lead to desirable outcomes; provides help requested by consultees in relation to problem solving and intervention implementation; assures the voluntary nature of consultation (Gutkin & Curtis, 1999); and supports consultees' abilities to make decisions based on information and skills attained through experience with the CBC process (Dunst et al., 1994). Additionally, the design of data collection and interventions are based on what works best within consultees' home and school environments. These are essential principles of effective helping and empowerment (see Chapter 1; Dunst et al., 1988). Accepting families and teachers "where they are" (i.e., acknowledging parents' and teachers' frames of reference; Sheridan et al., 1996) ensures that consultants do not attempt to focus on the deficits of consultees, but rather also on the strengths and resources they bring to the process (Dunst et al., 1994).

Conjoint Behavioral Consultation Promotes Competency Acquisition

A primary goal of CBC is to increase consultees' skills and knowledge to address future problems. This task is done by (a) using a structured problem-solving approach, (b) implementing strategies founded on data-based decisions, and (c) promoting knowledge of appropriate interventions. Skill acquisition gives consultees the opportunity to be independent in addressing the current and future needs of the clients in their care. In this way, the collaborative problem-solving process is modeled, and in essence, "given away" to consultees (Dunst & Trivette, 1987; Miller, 1969). Promoting consultees' skills and competencies in problem solving also increases their sense of self-efficacy, an essential principle necessary for the empowerment of clients and consultees (Dunst & Trivette, 1987; Dunst et al., 1988).

Conjoint Behavioral Consultation Promotes Partnership and Collaboration

An overarching goal of CBC is the establishment of partnership and collaboration among family and school systems (Christenson & Sheridan, 2001; Sheridan et al., 1996). Throughout consultation, home and school systems are collaboratively involved in a joint problem-solving process to address common goals for children. This process allows schools and families to share in decision making and adopt equal responsibility for both the concerns addressed and the solutions developed in consultation. In CBC, both parents and teachers actively participate in determining meaningful target behaviors and goals for children, and they are mutually involved in systematic data collection and intervention procedures. Consultees work together and remain focused on a common goal – addressing the needs of the child. With this approach, consultees learn methods for collaborating across home and school systems and establishing working partnerships.

Description of the Conjoint Behavioral Consultation Model

The CBC process consists of four stages, implemented in a collaborative manner. These stages are (a) conjoint needs (problem) identification, (b) conjoint needs (problem) analysis, (c) plan implementation, and (d) conjoint plan evaluation (Sheridan et al., 1996). Some descriptions of behavioral consultation offer a preliminary stage of relationship building, which precedes problem identification (e.g., Kratochwill, Elliott, & Carrington Rotto, 1995). In CBC, building rapport, establishing shared expectations, specifying roles, and strengthening partnerships (all considered part of relationship building) occur as a process that begins before formal problem solving, permeates all interactions between consultants and consultees (including those that occur outside of formal interviews), and evolves as the relationship matures. Thus, we choose not to describe relationship building as a "stage" within CBC, but rather as a process that includes several primary goals, as described in Chapter 3.

Conjoint Needs (Problem) Identification

The first stage of CBC is conjoint needs (previously problem) identification. The main objectives of the conjoint needs identification stage are outlined in Table 2.4. They include prioritizing needs, specifying and defining target concerns, and establishing procedures for collecting baseline data. Although some work related to assessment and conceptualization of concerns can begin immediately upon referral, the needs identification stage is often procedurally operationalized during the conjoint needs (problem) identification interview (CNII). Objectives, examples, and interview forms useful for conducting Needs Identification Interviews are given in Appendices A and B.

Prioritizing Needs

During the needs identification stage, consultants work with parents, teachers, and other relevant consultees to identify and prioritize a child's needs across the home, school, and other natural settings. Based on several factors (e.g., severity, relationship with other behaviors, cross-setting manifestation), consultees prioritize a target concern to address in assessment and intervention. The process of prioritizing a behavioral focus begins with a consultant eliciting behavioral descriptions of the child's functioning, with a focus on specific behaviors in terms that can be understood by an independent observer. For example, a consultant may ask about general concerns that interfere with expectations or skill acquisition, and follow up with a request for as many examples of the concern as possible. Careful specification is essential to identify the precise concern, direct the focus of an intervention, and monitor progress. The consultant may assist consultees to focus on a specific target problem by summarizing the primary concerns raised and observations conducted following a referral.

The process of prioritizing a target concern that will become the focus of CBC problem solving is guided by several considerations. Guidelines for selecting or prioritizing target concerns are in given Table 2.5. Importantly,

TABLE 2.4. Objectives of conjoint needs (problem) identification interview.

Identify strengths of the child, family, teacher, and systems

Behaviorally define the concern or need as it is represented across home and school settings

Explore environmental conditions that may be contributing to or motivating problem behaviors (antecedent, consequent, and sequential conditions)

Determine a shared goal for consultation

Clarify specific settings within systems that will be the focus for intervention

Explore within- and across-setting environmental factors that may contribute to or influence behaviors

Identify potential setting events (events or factors that may occur in a time or place that is distal to the target behavior, but still influence its occurrence)

Establish and implement baseline data collection procedures to set the stage for careful, systematic, data-based decision making

TABLE 2.5. Guidelines for target selection.

Focus on building a client's skill repertoire, rather than simply extinguishing behaviors

Prioritize urgent or dangerous behaviors if they pose serious risk or invoke serious consequences

Select a target that leads to the best treatment outcome (e.g., one that will be naturally reinforced)

Identify a response chain and target the first behavior of the chain

Select behaviors that will likely generalize to other behaviors (e.g., work completion with generalization to on-task or accuracy)

Organize behaviors in terms of their topographical or functional properties

Prioritize behaviors that have general utility and that the environment will likely maintain (e.g., social skills)

Change the "easiest" behavior to encourage further treatment efforts

Change behaviors that are most irritating to or preferred by the consultees to ensure their buy in; recycle to additional targets as necessary

Never stop at the resolution of a simple behavior that is part of a larger problem

selection of a behavioral priority should always include consideration of means to build skills into a child's behavioral repertoire, rather than simply extinguish undesirable behaviors. Likewise, selection of a target concern that will lead to the greatest benefit to the child (e.g., will likely generalize to other behaviors, result in meaningful outcomes, or improve the child's quality of life) is also important. In situations in which behaviors pose pending danger to the child or others, those behaviors should become the primary target for intervention. Questions that consultants and consultees can consider when selecting concerns to target in CBC are in given Table 2.6.

Two issues commonly considered in behavioral assessment, and in the selection of target behaviors, are behavioral constellation and behavioral covariation. Behavioral constellation recognizes that behavioral concerns are rarely circumscribed and isolated; rather, they are usually part of a larger constellation (e.g., depression). CBC requires consultants to narrow the target definition, assess objective components, and delineate assessment conditions. As an outcome, complex and multifaceted problems are simplified.

TABLE 2.6. Questions to consider in selecting target concerns.

Is the desired behavior age appropriate?

Does the replacement/desired behavior satisfy the same function (or need) as problem behavior and/or result in the same outcome?

Is the desired behavior in the student's repertoire, even at low rates of occurrence?

Is the desired behavior incompatible with the problem behavior?

Is it more reinforcing for the student to engage in the desired behavior than the problem behavior?

What is the likelihood that the desired behavior will be elicited in regular settings?

What is the likelihood that the desired behavior will be reinforced in regular settings?

Source: Adapted from Quinn, M. (2001b). *Using data to determine intervention: Removing the guesswork*. http://cecp.air.org/present/default.asp Accessed 20.05.06.

However, many different behaviors may in fact cooccur, and focusing on only one narrow behavior (e.g., dysphoric mood) may fail to consider the full gamut of symptoms that account for clinical significance and that together impact client functioning.

In CBC, care must be taken so as not to ignore the larger syndrome of which a target behavior is a part. It is sometimes important to evaluate the breadth of the clinical problem and probability of extending to the behavior constellation. It is possible that focusing on one or two "core" target behaviors in a constellation will impact others in a desirable manner.

Response covariation refers to the correlations among several different responses, none of which alone may be a "symptom" or problem behavior (e.g., loss of interest, loss of appetite). Behaviors may be organized into "clusters" that systematically covary. Alteration of one target behavior may have consequences for other behaviors; therefore, it is recommended that consultants concurrently assess multiple behaviors and evaluate their relationship and pattern of change over time. A considerable literature exists on methods and criteria to select target behaviors (e.g., Kratochwill, 1985b). More recent work on various issues related to selection of target behaviors has been published in a number of books on behavioral assessment (see Brown-Chidsey, 2005; Shapiro & Kratochwill, 2000).

In summary, the CBC process allows a consultant to manage the consultation process by focusing on one problem at a time; assessing the effects of altering one behavior on other behaviors that may or may not covary; and recycling through the problem-solving process to address other behaviors of concern.

Specifying and Operationalizing Target Concerns

Once priorities are established and agreed upon by the consultant, parents and teachers, the primary concern or need as it is represented across home and school settings is defined operationally in terms that are clear, measurable, and manageable. Seminal research has demonstrated the importance of clear, operational definitions in behavioral consultation and its positive relationship to effective outcomes (Bergan & Tombari, 1976). Careful specification and operational definitions of the concern are essential for several reasons. First, they ensure shared understanding of the concern. Second, they provide a clear focus for assessment and intervention. Finally, operational clarity allows consultees to monitor progress in objective and systematic ways. Specific settings within home and school systems that will be the focus for intervention are also clarified in this stage to focus on and clarify procedures.

An important part of prioritizing a target for intervention is operationalizing the concern in terms that are manageable and concrete. An *operational definition* is a precise description of the behavior of concern. In general, an effective operational definition meets three important criteria. First, an operational definition should be objective. It should include only observable and measurable characteristics of behavior. Second, it is clear; operational clarity refers to the need for behaviors to be defined in terms that are unambiguous, specific, and reliable. A rule of thumb is that the behavior should be explainable to others and should not require interpretation on the part of an observer who was not part of the discussion. Third, an operational definition must be complete. That is, it should describe what is included and excluded in the behavior, leaving little to the judgment of an independent observer. Examples of common target behaviors and operational definitions are given in Table 2.7.

Determining Data Collection Procedures

During the CNII and the needs identification stage, baseline data collection procedures are established and implemented to set the stage for careful, systematic, data-based decision making. In CBC, consultants work with parents and teachers who assist in determining the most feasible and meaningful way to collect data that can be used in decision making and outcome monitoring. The involvement of parents and teachers in identifying feasible and reasonable procedures may serve to increase buy-in and follow through in the collection of data. Indeed, practical and meaningful strategies are important.

Several methods of data collection are available in consultation. Generally speaking, multisource, multimethod, multisetting assessment strategies are useful to provide a comprehensive account of a child's functioning across settings and contexts. *Multisource* procedures allow consultants to collect information from a variety of individuals including teachers, parents, peers, the child himself or herself, and others who have knowledge of the child and his or her environments. *Multimethod* procedures capitalize on the strengths of different approaches to collecting information, such as rating scales, interviews, and observations. From a *multisetting* assessment perspective, data are collected across the broad settings of home and school and other relevant settings as appropriate (e.g., classroom, playground, lunchroom, library, community settings, and others).

The multisource, multimethod, multisetting approach to assessment includes measurement that takes place through both direct and indirect means. *Direct measures* involve direct measurement of a behavior through live observation or skills assessments. At times, permanent products also provide a direct measure of a child's performance. *Indirect measures* include informant reports by parents, teachers, peers, or others who have first-hand knowledge of the child. Such reports can be gleaned through rating scales, checklists, or interviews. Oftentimes, self-reports are useful sources of information, especially when the child is the only person with certain information that is relevant to a situation (e.g., cognitions, feelings, and other subjective experiences).

TABLE 2.7. Examples of operational definitions for common classroom behaviors.

Positive behaviors

Compliance:[1] The child exhibits within 10 sec or the time specified by the adult a behavior that has been specified in a command issued by a staff member, or ceases to exhibit for at least 10 sec a behavior, the cessation of which has been specified in a command issued by an adult.

Appropriate social behavior:[2] All positive social interactions (verbal and nonverbal communication) with peer or adult such as participating in cooperative play, conversing, helping another child, affectionate touches, or cooperative play initiated by the child.

Ignoring a negative stimulus:[1] The child shows no observable negative response to any verbal or nonverbal behavior from another child that would typically illicit annoyance or distress from the recipient.

Engaged time:[3] The child is actively attending to the assigned work (can include staying in the area/with the group).

On-task behavior:[4] Appropriately writing, reading, talking about the assignment, or waiting to ask the teacher a question regarding the assignment.

Hand raising:[4] Student places one hand over head, makes eye contact with teacher, and refrains from making sounds or extraneous movements.

Relevant comment/question:[4] Student emits a comment or question that has direct relationship with what is being discussed at the time. It is delivered in an appropriate manner (e.g., appropriate tone of voice, appropriate volume).

Homework completion:[4] Student turns homework in on time with all questions attempted.

Negative behaviors

Noncompliance:[2] The child is given an instruction or direction by an aide or teacher and makes no effort to comply with the request by the end of the next observation interval, or the teacher reprimands the child or reminds him/her to follow earlier instructions.

Off-task:[2] Child fails to attend to assigned lessons for 3 consecutive seconds after having begun to do so; not listening when the teacher is presenting a lesson (e.g., staring blankly; this can include leaving an assigned area and/or leaving the group).

Nonphysical aggression:[2] Child emits verbalizations and physical gestures that are abusive or threatening and directed toward other people; all negative, noncontact communication; and inflicting physical damage on an object by hitting, throwing, etc.

Physical aggression:[5] Child makes a forceful movement directed at another person, either directly or by utilizing a material object as an extension of the hand.

Verbal aggression:[2] Child attempts to hurt another person by nonphysical means such as verbally threatening, tattling, teasing, or name-calling. Verbal aggression includes only words; not animal noises, grunts, etc.

Interference:[2] Behavior that disrupts classroom functioning and/or makes it difficult for others to perform their work (e.g., initiating conversations during quiet work periods, calling out in class, moving around the room, making noises that distract others). Interference refers only to behaviors that are intentional.

Talking out:[4] Student emits any noise without first raising hand in appropriate manner and waiting for permission to speak.

Motor movement:[2] The child is either out of his or her seat or has one buttock off the chair.

Tantrum:[4] Student shows inappropriate signs of anger (e.g., clenched fists, yelling, cursing, kicking, refusal to follow directions, punching, or using obscene gestures).

Sources: (1) Pelham, W.E., Greiner, A.R., & Gnagy, E.M. (1998). *Children's summer treatment program manual.* Buffalo, NY: Author; (2) Gadow, K.D., Sprafkin, J., & Nolan, E.E. (1996). *ADHD school observation code.* Stony Brook, NY: Checkmate Plus; (3) Shapiro, E.S. (2004). *Academic skills problems workbook* (rev. ed.). New York: Guilford Press; (4) Quinn, M. (2001a). *Collecting data while teaching, and other circus acts.* http://cecp.air.org/present/default.asp Accessed 20.05.06; (5) Abikoff, H., & Gittelman, R. (1985). Classroom observation code: A modification of the Stony Brook code. *Psychopharmacology Bulletin, 21,* 901–909.

There are several purposes of direct assessment in consultation practice. First, by directly assessing target concerns, consultants and consultees are able to elucidate aspects of behavior and aid in their understanding, thereby increasing the treatment utility of the assessment, which leads to meaningful intervention outcomes. A second purpose for direct assessment is to allow the consultation team to assess overt and explicit behaviors as they are occurring in real time, rather than relying on memory or second-hand accounts of behavior. Third, direct assessments provide more reliable and objective information on a child's functioning. Fourth, when used in a continuous manner, they allow for direct monitoring of treatment effects and help determine the need for modifications to the treatment plan, behavioral goals, or other aspects of problem solving.

On-going and repeated measurement, rather than pre-/postassessment only, is most useful in CBC. Procedures that are commonly used by parents, teachers, consultants, or others on the CBC problem-solving team are given in Table 2.8 and include permanent products, direct observation, performance-based assessment, curriculum-based measurement, and self-monitoring. Reviews of procedures for conducting comprehensive behavioral assessments are available in Shapiro and Kratochwill (2000).

Consultants can increase the ease of data collection by providing forms and/or using permanent or tangible evidence of the child's performance. An example of a simple and useful form, *The Behavioral Record*, used in clinical work and research (Sheridan, Eagle, Cowan, & Mickelson, 2001), is given in Figure 2.2 and in Appendix C. Others are available in Rhode, Jenson, and Reavis (1996) and at www.interventioncentral.com. Tips CBC consultants may consider related to data collection are given in Table 2.9.

From Child Assessment to Ecological Assessment

Despite discussions encouraging broad-based environmental assessments in consultation, in practice the emphasis is often on child-related variables (e.g., skill or performance deficits) that affect learning and performance. An ecological emphasis in assessment emphasizes environmental factors that influence learning and the "fit" between child and environment. The *Functional Assessment of Academic Behavior* (FAAB; Ysseldyke & Christenson, 2002) is a thorough environmental assessment package, which provides tools and strategies for a comprehensive assessment of home and school factors that influence a child's academic performance. The FAAB, previously *The Instructional Environment Scale* (TIES-II; Ysseldyke & Christenson, 1993), incorporates multiassessment measures such as interviews, observations of classroom environments, and instructional environment checklists to complete an ecological assessment of home and school variables related to academic performance. Specifically, the FAAB evaluates the supports, such as instructional supports, home supports, and home–school supports, that

TABLE **2.8.** Definitions and examples of uses of direct assessment methods.

Method	Definition	Examples of uses
Permanent product	Concrete evidence of a student's behavior taken from an existing source	Percent of homework assignments completed Number of worksheets completed in a subject area Number of pages read Number of problems attempted/completed/ accurate Organization of work on a page
Direct observation	Measurement of discrete behaviors when they are occurring	On task/off task
	Can be completed using event (frequency), interval (partial or whole), and momentary time sampling procedures	Disruptive behavior Out of seat Talking out Initiating conversations Compliance with commands
Performance-based assessment	Use of rating scales to record behaviors over time periods, based on a Likert scale	Aggression Oppositional behavior Active participation in activities
Curriculum-based measurement	The practice of obtaining direct and frequent measures of a student's performance on a series of sequentially arranged objectives derived from the curriculum used in the classroom	Reading fluency and accuracy Math digits correct Spelling words correctly Number or letter recognition
	Standardized short-duration measures taken from a student's curriculum used to monitor progress and as the basis for decision making	
Self-monitoring	An observation technique wherein students are responsible for recording their own behaviors	On-task behaviors Following instructions Beginning work on time Completing chores/tasks Cognitive events (e.g., using self-control, problem solving, affective symptoms)

impact a child's academic behavior and performance. The steps of the FAAB are consistent with the stages of CBC, with an emphasis on understanding the student's instructional needs and collecting data on the student's instructional environment. Among the assessment forms are the *Instructional*

Environment Checklist, the *Instructional Environment Checklist: Annotated Version*, the *Instructional Needs Checklist*, *Parental Experience with Their Child's Learning and Schoolwork*, and the *Intervention Documentation Record*.

Consultation Behavior Record

Child's Name: _____
Person Recording: _____
Dates of Recording: _____

"Target" behavior -- <u>what</u> we are focusing on:

"Target" setting -- <u>where</u> we will focus:

"Target" time -- <u>when</u> information will be collected:

Pointers -- <u>how</u> information will be recorded:

Day/Date Time, Etc.	Behavior Occurrence	What Happened Before?	What Happened After?	What Else Was Going On?

More data collection on reverse side…

FIGURE 2.2. Behavioral record.

(*Continued*)

Day/Date Time, Etc.	Behavior Occurrence	What Happened Before?	What Happened After?	What Else Was Going On?

FIGURE 2.2. cont'd.

TABLE 2.9. Tips for data collection.

Keep it simple
Clearly define what is to be recorded
Match the data collection procedure to the target behavior
Consider retrospective baseline data when applicable
Graph the data to monitor progress
Record data that have a range (i.e., not simply yes/no)

Conjoint Needs (Problem) Analysis

The second stage of CBC is conjoint needs (previously problem) analysis. In the conjoint needs analysis stage of CBC, parents and teachers evaluate the baseline data, decide upon behavioral goals for the child, and discuss various factors that may influence the child's behavior (e.g., events functionally related to the target concerns). Hypotheses are generated regarding the environmental or functional conditions that may contribute to the occurrence of the target behaviors, and a plan is developed collaboratively to address the needs of the child. Specific objectives of this stage are presented in Table 2.10. The main objectives are to conduct a functional assessment and develop intervention plans to be used across home and school. This stage involves a structured interview (*Conjoint Needs Analysis Interview*, CNAI). Objectives, examples, and interview forms useful for conducting Needs Analysis Interviews are given in Appendices D and E.

Conducting Functional/Skills Assessments

Virtually all behaviors occur within a particular context and serve a purpose. Children behave and perform in certain ways based on what is attained as an

TABLE 2.10. Content objectives of needs (problem) analysis interview.

Explore baseline data collected across settings
Evaluate and obtain agreement on the sufficiency and adequacy of baseline data across
   settings
Identify setting events, ecological conditions, and cross-setting variables that may be impacting
   the target concerns
Investigate trends across settings (e.g., home and school) and highlight when appropriate
Elicit and provide information about the function or motivating features of the behavior that
   are based on environmental (rather than internal) explanations
Collaboratively design an effective intervention plan that is sensitive to setting-specific
   variables across environments
Link assessment to intervention through the interpretation of concerns in terms of
   environmental conditions and not internal causes
Discuss general strategies and plans to be included in an intervention package across home
   and school settings
Summarize the plan, being clear about what is to be done, when, how, and by whom

outcome of the behavior or because they lack the prerequisite skills to perform a more appropriate response. Identifying the function of a behavior, and determining whether the child has the necessary skills to demonstrate alternative, more desirable responses (either behavioral, social, or academic), is an important objective of the needs analysis stage. With this information, strategies to address the concern (including instructional, ecological, or operant techniques) can be identified, clarified, and implemented to address the concerns.

The steps of a basic functional assessment are easily remembered with the acronym "VAIL" (Validate, Assess, Interpret–Link to intervention; Witt, Daly, & Noell, 2000). In the validation step, consultants gather and interpret data to determine whether a problem exists to an extent that warrants further evaluation. The second step is assessment, which involves gathering information about the student and his or her behaviors or performance. The interpret–link step entails interpretation of the data and linking the results of the assessment to an appropriate intervention. The first steps of VAIL occur throughout the needs identification stage; the interpret–link step is a main goal of needs analysis.

Interpretation of the behavioral data involves identifying antecedents, consequences, and setting events that contribute to (or control) the occurrence of target behaviors. *Antecedents* are events that occur before a behavior that may predict or "set off" its occurrence. Examples are types of instructions given by teachers, interactions with certain peers, and bus rides to school. To obtain information about antecedents, a consultant might ask "What do you notice happening before Maria tears up her worksheet?" and "Sometimes we notice certain things that happen before a behavior that might prompt the behavior to occur. What do you notice happening in the classroom or at home before Martin pulls his hair?" *Consequences* are events that occur following the presence of the target concern and may maintain its occurrence. Examples are attention from a parent, removal of expectations, and avoidance of tasks. Questions that elicit information about consequences include "What happens after Kaerli refuses to cooperate with her partner?" and "Describe what occurs next, after Stefan yells an obscenity."

Behavioral observation data collected across settings, permanent products, and responses to questionnaires all provide unique information, which the consultant integrates and interprets during the needs analysis stage. Given the cross-setting nature of data collected in CBC (including data collected across home and school over several hours and days), it is possible to identify *setting events*. Setting events are environmental conditions that are removed in time or place from the primary concern, but that influence its occurrence. They may also be ecological conditions (e.g., physical arrangement of a classroom, availability of playground equipment, number of siblings sharing a bedroom) and cross-setting variables that may be impacting the target concerns. For example, problems between peers on the playground might set the occasion for a child to demonstrate anger and irritation when he or she returns to the classroom, despite the fact that the antecedent (problem with peer) did not occur in that setting. In CBC, trends and patterns *across home and school settings* can be investigated and highlighted by exploring whether events that occur in one setting trigger or contribute to a behavior's occurrence in another setting. This assessment might involve exploring how a child's morning routines affect his or her classroom behavior, whether the child receives sufficient sleep and nutrition, or how alterations in schedules (e.g., living arrangements, routines on weekends) influence school performance. Likewise, events occurring in school often affect behaviors exhibited by the child at home or other out-of-school settings. For example, poor performance on an exam, being teased by a classmate, or altercations on the school bus may occasion angry reactions at home. The process of identifying setting events is strengthened by the fact that parents and teachers together explore the behaviors and identify setting-specific observations that can elucidate important information. This information helps identify the presence of common events that occur across settings that trigger or maintain a behavior and other temporally and contextually distal events.

There are multiple ways that the CBC participants can conceptualize the function of a behavior. For example, it is possible to consider whether the child's behavior is communicating a desire to "get something" that is positively reinforcing to him or her, such as attention or approval. In the same vein, the behavior may be demonstrated in an attempt to escape or avoid an unpleasurable or aversive circumstance, such as a math assignment or interactions with a particular peer. Likewise, it is often important to consider whether the child has the prerequisite skills to perform in an appropriate or desirable fashion. "Skill deficits" are apparent when a child is unable to perform the appropriate behavior, such as when a child lacks the skills necessary to solve problems calmly or perform basic multiplication. "Performance deficits" are hypothesized when the child has demonstrated an ability to engage in desirable behaviors in some situations (e.g., highly controlled settings such as analog assessments or one-on-one interactions), but fails to engage in that same behavior in other situations (e.g., when challenging task or environmental demands are present or cues are unavailable).

In some cases in CBC, target concerns require skills to be mastered (e.g., blending letter sounds, multiplication of double digit problems, starting a conversation). In these cases, functional assessments involve identifying variables that may be addressed in support of the child's mastery of these skills. For example, a match between the academic curricula used in the classroom and the child's skill level, or the complexity of instructions provided to students, may influence a child's learning of material. The analysis that occurs with skills analyses addresses the skills that the student has or does not have, rather than the function that a behavior serves. Conducting skills assessments involves (a) identifying the target skill that should be present in the child's repertoire to complete a task; (b) breaking the skill down into component steps; (c) assessing the child's ability to perform each step; (d) determining the uppermost level at which the child can perform the skill; and (e) developing an intervention starting at that point, with an emphasis on building the skill repertoire.

TABLE 2.11. Common functions of behavioral excesses and deficits.

Behavioral excesses
Often Maintained by:
Attention
Escape
Obtain preferred objects or activities
Sensory stimulation

Academic skill or behavioral deficits
Often Maintained by:
Lack of motivation
Insufficient practice
Insufficient guidance or assistance
Lack of exposure
Difficulty level

In the open and collaborative spirit of CBC, it is helpful to ask parents and teachers their opinions of the function of a behavior, or their "hypotheses" about why a child may be performing as he or she is. Common functions of behavioral excesses and deficits are presented in Table 2.11, with a chart for parents and teachers in Appendix F. When eliciting parents' and teachers' perceptions about the purpose or function of the behavior, environmental (rather than internal) explanations should be emphasized. This assessment can be accomplished by summarizing the discussion about antecedents, consequences, and sequential (situational) events surrounding the behavior; repeating some of the functions already mentioned; and noting the presence of skill deficits when apparent. This summary, as with other summary statements made in CBC, can strategically educate consultees about important information that contributes to systematic and data-based decision making, while at the same time serve to invite them to contribute meaningful interpretations. Interpreting the problem in terms of environmental conditions, rather than internal causes or conditions, provides an important link between assessment and intervention.

Developing Intervention Plans

Upon completion of a functional assessment, data-based, ecological hypotheses about what may be motivating a target concern (e.g., attention, escape from an undesired event or task, lack of information or skill) are used to begin determining an appropriate intervention. Ideally, the participants in CBC (consultant, parent, teacher) share ideas and offer resources in the design of an effective intervention plan across settings. This task often requires that the consultant provide information on evidence-based strategies that address functional features of the target concern (e.g., escape, attention), which are then shaped by consultees to fit existing structures, settings, routines, and other considerations in the natural home and school environments. General intervention options commonly included in intervention programs are presented in Table 2.12.

TABLE 2.12. Behavioral intervention options.

Modify aspects of the setting. For example:
  Alter physical arrangements of the classroom
  Improve general classroom management strategies
  Use home–school communication tools, such as home-notes, to maximize cross-setting
    consistency and integrity of behavioral plans
Teach the student acceptable behavior that serves the same function as the inappropriate
  behavior. For example:
  Provide teacher attention for student corrects
  Allow peer attention through tutorial instruction
Manipulate the antecedents precipitating the behavior. For example:
  Alter the schedule of activities
  Adapt the curriculum or task-specific aspects of instruction
  Vary the size of instructional groupings
  Provide special directions regarding instruction
  Introduce precorrective strategies before problems occur
  Teach students rules
Manipulate the consequences that maintain the target concern. For example:
  Provide precise positive praise or attention following desired behavior
  Alter the length of the reinforcement interval (shorten the length of time between a behavior
  and positive consequence initially, when teaching a new behavior)
  Ensure that the reinforcers are considered reinforcing to the child
  Vary the amount, delivery, or nature of the reinforcers when maintaining a desired behavior
Implement changes in classroom curriculum and/or instructional strategies. For example:
  Offer individualized instruction
  Use small groups of equal ability levels
  Use peer tutoring programs
  Involve parents by requesting that tutoring or academic strategies be used at home

Source: Quinn, M. (2001b). *Using data to determine intervention: Removing the guesswork.*
http://cecp.air.org/present/default.asp Accessed 20.05.06.

The determination of specific plan strategies is based on at least three considerations. First, as described earlier, identification of the function or purpose of a behavior often suggests intervention strategies for implementation. Intervention descriptions and options tied to two commonly identified functions of behavior (i.e., attention, escape) are listed in Table 2.13. Second, procedures selected for implementation at home and school should be empirically supported. Indeed, it is the responsibility of the consultant to ensure that evidence-based interventions are offered to address the target concern. Although it is beyond the scope of this text to review the entire variety of evidence-based interventions, Table 2.14 provides an overview of a number of web-based organizational task forces and agencies that provide lists of evidence-based interventions and procedures. Likewise, the US Department of Education's "What Works Clearinghouse" website (http://w-w-c.org) provides an additional source for information on evidence-based educational interventions. The reader is encouraged to consult this list for a variety of programs that focus on prevention and intervention initiatives in psychology and education.

Third, to ensure that the procedures will be implemented by consultees in their natural environments, the manner in which the components are organized,

TABLE 2.13. Intervention options based on functions of behavior.

Function	Description	Examples	Intervention options	Ineffective strategies
Attention-seeking behavior	Unmet student need for attention, coupled with perception that attention is unlikely to occur	Call outs Swearing Yelling at classmate or teacher Tantrum Noncompliance with adult request	Noncontingent attention Contingent attention following appropriate behavior Withdrawal of attention following misbehavior Instruction in appropriate attention-seeking strategies	Verbal reprimands or student put downs
Escape-motivated behavior	Student need to escape from an aversive situation	Difficult, irrelevant lengthy or ambiguous assignment Undesirable group placement Negative peer or adult interaction	Contingent escape following prosocial or appropriate request Task completion demand Curricular accommodations Instructional modifications	Time-out

structured, and delivered should be acceptable. That is, they should be consistent with teacher and parent beliefs and values, require relatively little time and effort beyond what is reasonable, be consistent with the skill level of the teacher and parent (which may suggest the need for training), and interfere minimally with the natural environments at home and in the classroom. Thus, the consultant, parent, and teacher together should discuss general strategies and plans to be included in an intervention package that is acceptable to them as treatment agents and that can be implemented reasonably across home and school settings. Joint determination of the plan tactics (i.e., the specific components that will be incorporated into the plan and the manner in which they will be implemented) maximizes the chances for implementation success. Examples of plan details include who will be responsible for aspects of the intervention, the timing of intervention features, and other important variables that are specific to unique features of classrooms, homes, and families. For example, some families may express discomfort providing monetary or material reinforcers (e.g., stickers, tokens) for the display of desired behaviors. In such situations, other social or natural reinforcers (e.g., selecting an activity for a family outing) may be discussed. The plan details should be recorded on a form such as the *Intervention Plan Worksheet* shown in Figure 2.3 (and in Appendix G) to maximize adherence to the plan (i.e., maximize treatment integrity).

TABLE 2.14. Sources for intervention ideas.

Author and year	Title	Publisher
Rhode, Jenson, & Reavis (1996)	*The Tough Kid Book*	Sopris West, Inc.
Jenson, Rhode, & Neville (2002)	*The Tough Kid Parent Book: Why Me?*	Sopris West, Inc.
Rathvon (2003)	*Effective School Interventions: Strategies for Enhancing Academic Achievement and Social Competence*	Guilford Press
Shinn, Walker, & Stoner (2002)	*Interventions for Academic and Behavior Problems II: Preventive and Remedial Approaches*	National Association of School Psychologists
U.S. Department of Education (2001)	What Works Clearinghouse	Available at http://w-w-c.org/

In efforts to increase continuity across settings, it is useful to plan procedures that are complementary and consistent at home and school. However, it will not always be required that identical procedures are used across home and school. Differences in specific target concerns, perspectives, routines, and resources may in part determine the degree to which plan strategies are implemented across settings. It is generally the case, however, that joint problem solving and decision making allows for the establishment of procedures and tactics that retain high degrees of coordination and congruity, which facilitates a child's response to programs.

Plan Implementation

The third stage of CBC consists of plan implementation. During this stage, parents and teachers implement the intervention procedures in the home and school, supporting implementation across settings. This stage does not involve a structured interview; however, the consultant remains in close contact with parents and teachers (e.g., phone calls and personal visits) throughout implementation of the intervention to provide support, ensure understanding of the plan, offer assistance, reinforce parents' and teachers' intervention efforts, and determine the need for any immediate plan modifications.

Although there is no formal interview associated with the third stage of CBC, there are several important consultant roles necessary for effective intervention delivery. These include monitoring intervention implementation for integrity of delivery and assessing a child's response to the delivered intervention.

Intervention Integrity

In the intervention implementation stage of CBC, consultants have the important responsibility of monitoring implementation of the intervention across

Week of: _____

Consultation Plan

Behavioral Goal:

_____

_____

Plan Summary:

_____

_____

_____

Please list the primary steps of the plan on the lines below. Then, each day, please check in the appropriate box in the matrix to the left whether each step was completed.

Plan Steps:

Sun	Mon	Tue	Wed	Thu	Fri	Sat

1. _____

2. _____

3. _____

4. _____

5. _____

Goal Rating

At the end of the week, please use the following scale to rate how closely the above goal was met. The consultant will collect this form each week. Thank you!

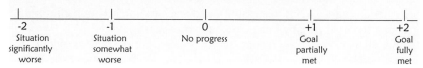

-2	-1	0	+1	+2
Situation significantly worse	Situation somewhat worse	No progress	Goal partially met	Goal fully met

FIGURE 2.3. Intervention plan worksheet.

settings. Intervention integrity, or the degree to which consultees implement plans as developed and intended (Gresham, 1989; Noell, 2008; Sanetti & Kratochwill, 2005), is an issue in consultation research and practice. Although no clear research findings have identified necessary or optimal levels of integrity and their relationship to child outcomes, it is generally considered important to the overall benefits associated with interventions. Intervention plans that are not implemented, or are not implemented as developed, are not likely to have an effect on a child's performance. Strategies that have been suggested to facilitate intervention integrity include manualizing the intervention or using a previously developed intervention, providing training or feedback to the consultees related to intervention implementation, providing scripts or checklists of the plan, and requesting that consultees self-monitor implementation of intervention steps. An example of a manualized intervention for increasing compliance at home (including intervention components of daily rules, effective commands, positive reinforcement, and a home–school note) is given in Appendix H. An *Intervention Plan Worksheet* (see example given in Figure 2.3 and in Appendix G) can be used to summarize the concerns being targeted, list the steps of the plan, and encourage consultee self-recording of plan implementation. If it is determined that consultees require additional information or skills to implement the plan effectively, consultants can provide training to the parents and teacher. Performance feedback on observations of plan implementation has been shown to be effective in increasing integrity (Noell, 2008) and provides a useful strategy for remaining involved in implementation of interventions in natural settings.

Assessing a Child's Immediate Response to the Intervention

Another useful role for consultants during this stage is that of assessment of immediate intervention effects. By observing a child's initial response to an intervention, immediate alterations to a plan can be made in an effort to be more responsive to his or her needs. Behavioral side effects and contrast effects can be monitored to determine whether the intervention may be causing any unforeseen problems or unplanned effects.

Conjoint Plan Evaluation

The final stage of CBC is conjoint plan evaluation. Objectives of this stage are presented in Table 2.15. During this stage, consultants, parents, and teachers examine the behavioral data collected to evaluate the effects of the intervention and determine if the goals of consultation have been met across the home and school settings. Additional assessments are also warranted, such as assessment of goals and social validity. Objectives, examples, and interview forms useful for conducting the Conjoint Plan Evaluation Interview (CPEI) are given in Appendices I and J.

TABLE 2.15. Content objectives of the plan evaluation interview.

Analyze intervention data in relation to baseline data

Determine if the shared goals of consultation have been attained

Evaluate the effectiveness of the plan across settings

Discuss strategies and tactics regarding the continuation, modification, or termination of the
   intervention plan across settings

Schedule additional interviews if necessary

Discuss ways to continue conjoint problem solving or shared decision making

Assessing Intervention Effects

In the CPEI, discussion centers around whether the plan was effective across
settings and the need for continuation, modification, or termination of the
intervention based on the child's progress toward his or her goal. Additional
interviews are scheduled if necessary.

Determining effects of an intervention is a main objective of the plan
evaluation stage of CBC. In CBC, data are collected repeatedly during a
baseline period and continue to be collected during a subsequent treatment
period. This process allows practitioners to be accountable and begins to
allow statements about the likelihood that improvement in behavior is due to
treatment. However, it may be difficult to conclude that the effects seen in a
child's performance are due to the intervention designed and delivered as a
function of CBC unless procedures are put into place to strengthen the
consultation case studies.

There are many ways to improve consultation evaluation and case studies
(Galloway & Sheridan, 1994; Kratochwill, 1985a). First, to determine that
the effects seen in a child are a function of the specific consultation and
intervention procedures, it is important that data collection procedures be
established and implemented at the earliest point in a case (i.e., at baseline).
Objective (e.g., frequency counts) rather than subjective data should be
collected. The data should be collected and graphed continuously throughout all phases of a case (baseline, treatment, follow-up). The assessment and
treatment procedures should be standardized, including the specific consultation procedures utilized. For example, by using structured interview forms
and standard intervention programs, the details of *what* was done and *how*
become clear. By graphing data throughout the process, consultants and
consultees can see progress made as a function of the intervention plan.

The strength of intervention effects is greatest when they are repeated or
replicated. This component is among the cornerstones of single case analysis
(Hayes, Barlow, & Nelson-Gray, 1999). For example, simple case study designs
are strengthened when they incorporate a repetition of the baseline and treatment conditions after an initial effect is seen. This structure represents an
improvement of a simple A/B design to a withdrawal design or an ABAB
design. If the same effects are seen after implementing a return-to-baseline

phase and a reintroduction of the intervention, consultants can be more confident that the intervention was in fact successful.

Another form of replication occurs when the intervention is delivered to address a different concern in the same child, when it is used to address a similar target concern in a new setting, or when it is used to combat a similar concern with another child. Collection of objective behavioral data in each of these situations can represent replicated A/B designs. On the other hand, simultaneous collection of baseline data and planned, staggered introduction of the intervention in each of the unique circumstances (i.e., with a different behavior, across a new setting, with a different child) can help control many variables that may interfere with the ability to draw conclusions about treatment effects. Multiple baseline designs are particularly desirable when interventionists want to impose experimental control into their casework (Hayes et al., 1999; Kazdin, 1982; Kratochwill, 1985a). Other suggestions for improving case studies are given in Table 2.16.

Social Validity

Kazdin (1977) and Wolf (1978) described social validity as the social significance of the target behavior chosen for treatment, the social appropriateness or acceptability of the treatment procedures, and the resulting behavior change. Specifically, the aims of social validity are to determine the degree to which: (a) treatment goals are socially significant, (b) treatment procedures are considered socially appropriate, and (c) treatment effects are

TABLE 2.16. Tips for improving case studies.

Assess treatment integrity to ensure that the intervention was implemented correctly
This allows for immediate revisions or attention
Only when interventions are implemented appropriately can effects of the intervention be determined
Assess clinical meaningfulness of outcomes through social validation procedures
Treatment acceptability
Perceptions of effectiveness of interventions
Subjective measures of outcomes
Degree to which consultation goals were met
Formalize procedures for analyzing case data
Level changes from baseline to treatment
Immediacy effects
Overlap in data points across phases
Within-phase variability
Trend in baseline and treatment
Use formal design structure when possible
ABAB (reversal design)
A/B/B + C/A (multielement design with reversal)
Multiple baseline designs
Assess generalization and follow-up

clinically meaningful. Common methods for assessing social validity are through subjective evaluations of treatment effects and social comparison.

Assessment of Goals

Early in CBC, consultants, parents, and teachers jointly identify goals for performance in relation to target behaviors exhibited by a child. A relatively straightforward procedure for assessing progress toward the established goal is *Goal Attainment Scaling* (GAS; Kiresuk, Smith, & Cardillo, 1994). GAS is a form of criterion-referenced social validity measurement that provides an indirect account of the degree to which consultation goals have been achieved. The scale requests individuals knowledgeable about the child and his or her behaviors to rate his or her performance using descriptive behavioral criteria on a scale of −2 (least favorable) to +2 (most favorable). The basic method requires the consultant, parent, and teacher to (a) identify and define the target concern, (b) describe the desired behavior or outcome in objective terms, (c) construct the Goal Attainment Scale by generating five sequential descriptions of probable outcomes from "least favorable" to "most favorable," (d) implement an intervention designed to address the concern, and (e) request that consultees or treatment agents complete the GAS at a certain frequency (e.g., daily) to evaluate progress toward the goal (Elliott, Sladeczek, & Kratochwill, 1995; Roach & Elliott, 2005).

As an example, homework completion is a common concern discussed in CBC meetings. Consultees concerned about a child who is demonstrating difficulties completing assignments may establish a goal such as "Natasha will complete 80% of her assigned homework each day." A rating of −2 might be defined as "Natasha completes none of her homework"; a rating of zero can be used to specify baseline levels of performance ("Natasha completes 40% of her homework"); and a rating of +2 can be defined as "Natasha completes 80% of her homework." Using GAS as a repeated measure of performance allows the consultation team to asses both over- and underattainment of behavioral or academic goals (Kratochwill, Elliott, & Carrington Rotto, 1995).

Several single-case researchers have used GAS to report perceptions of goal attainment (Santa-Barbara et al., 1977; Sladeczek et al., 2001; Woodward et al., 1981), demonstrating its clinical utility. Its benefits include efficiency in use, individualized approach, nonintrusive nature, flexibility of use across settings and behaviors, no skill or specialized training needed for data collection and interpretation, and ability to track performance continuously. However, there are drawbacks, including its subjectivity, lack of empirical research on its psychometric characteristics, limited guidelines for use, and global nature. Nevertheless, GAS can prove to be a very versatile clinical tool with particular benefits for use in consultation contexts. A framework and suggestions for constructing and using GAS are given in Table 2.17.

TABLE 2.17. A framework for developing and utilizing GAS ratings.

Step 1: Identify concerns. Teacher(s) identify academic or social behavior strengths, performance problems, and acquisition problems by considering data on performance gathered via standardized assessments, observations, and/or work samples.

Step 2: Analyze concerns. Teacher(s) identify a target behavior and define it in objective terms so that it can be read and accurately paraphrased.

Step 3: Plan instruction or intervention. First, teacher(s) establish the instructional or intervention goal, defining the desired outcome in concrete terms. In many cases, the target behavior and desired outcome will be the same. After identifying the desired outcome, teacher(s) describe the general instruction or intervention strategy that will be used to achieve this goal.

Step 4: Construct the goal attainment scale. The basic elements of GAS are a 5-point scale ranging from +2 to −2 and descriptions of the target behavior and instructional support that correspond with the following conditions: best possible outcome (+2), no change in behavior/performance (0), and worst possible outcome (−2). The following characteristics or dimensions may be helpful in developing descriptions for the different GAS rating points:

    Frequency (never–sometimes–very often–almost always–always)

    Quality (poor–fair–good–excellent)

    Development (not present–emerging–developing–accomplished–exceeding)

    Usage (unused–inappropriate use–appropriate use–exceptional use)

    Timeliness (late–on time–early)

    Percent complete (0%–25%–50%–75%–100%)

    Accuracy (totally incorrect–partially correct–totally correct)

    Effort (not attempted–minimal effort–acceptable effort–outstanding effort)

    Amount of support needed (totally dependent–extensive assistance–some assistance–limited assistance–independent)

    Engagement (none–limited–acceptable–exceptional)

Step 5: Implement instruction or intervention.

Step 6: Evaluate instruction or intervention. Graph the GAS ratings (collected daily or weekly) of student progress.

Source: From Roach, A.T., & Elliott, S.N. (2005). Goal attainment scaling: An efficient and effective approach to monitoring student progress. *Teaching Exceptional Children, 37*, 9. Reprinted with permission.

Planning for Maintenance of Child and Partnership

Maintenance interviews are often desirable several weeks following the final plan evaluation interview to assure continued performance in a positive direction. These interviews are important to evaluate the ongoing progress and determine whether recycling through any problem-solving steps is warranted. Importantly, methods and procedures for continuing conjoint problem solving or shared decision making among parents and teachers can also be discussed to encourage continued collaboration and partnering across home and school contexts.

Conjoint Behavioral Consultation in the Context of Response to Intervention

Recently, there has been growing interest in the development of a system using evidence-based instruction/intervention to address student needs and define students who need additional services in regular and special education. This process, referred to as Response to Intervention (RtI), involves using evidence-based interventions while monitoring student progress over time in both academic and behavioral domains (Batsche, Elliott, Schrag, & Tilly, 2005; Brown-Chidsey & Steege, 2006). RtI fits in nicely with problem-solving consultation and especially conjoint consultation models, because data are used to make decisions about the effectiveness of an intervention that is typically structured within a multitiered system (see Kratochwill, Clements, Kalymon, 2007, for further information). In this section of the chapter, we provide a brief overview of RtI and depict the manner in which conjoint problem-solving consultation fits into the multitiered framework of RtI services (see also Kratochwill, in press, for a general discussion of the multitiered model and problem-solving consultation).

Brief Overview of Response to Intervention

Response to intervention involves two specific components that can be conceptualized as dependent and independent variables (Kratochwill et al., in press). The "R" in RtI involves selecting students who are at risk for a variety of academic and/or social-emotional concerns and is prominent as a technology at the universal or primary level of prevention. In this situation, the numbers of children who are identified as at risk serve as an important measure of base rates of concerns within a particular school population (e.g., the number of students who are below benchmark performance on reading measures and/or the number of office disciplinary referrals from teachers). Another dimension of the "R" involves "progress monitoring," or ongoing measurement of student performance at various intervals across the phases of an intervention program (essentially the same process that has been affiliated with behavior consultation for many years; Bergan & Kratochwill, 1990). Note that in some cases initial progress-monitoring measures can serve as a screening technology for determining at-risk status. Usually, progress monitoring is an ongoing process similar to the ongoing assessment that occurs prior to and during the implementation phase of an intervention in conjoint problem solving.

The independent variable in RtI refers to one or more interventions that are implemented to meet student needs. However, in recent federal legislation the interventions must be evidence-based or have strong scientific support for their efficacy. The other unique feature of the RtI framework is that interventions are structured within a multitiered system of intervention (Kratochwill, Albers, & Shernoff, 2004). That is, commonly interventions are developed within the context of universal, selected, and indicated interventions (otherwise known as primary, secondary, and tertiary). Interventions at the universal level are targeted at all students within the system and are designed to reduce the base rates of problems. Interventions at the secondary level are designed to meet or address the needs of students who are not making adequate progress in regular education and require some type of customized intervention. Usually, these interventions are implemented with small groups of students. At the tertiary level, interventions are much more focused on individuals or small groups of individuals who share common problems. Such interventions are often highly customized and may even be based on functional assessment and analysis.

Generally, the purpose of RtI is to implement interventions while ongoing progress monitoring allows school-based professionals to make decisions about how a student is progressing. Such information can be used to make further decisions about the need for special education. Generally, RtI occurs prior to special education consideration. We next turn our attention to how conjoint consultation can fit into the RtI framework.

Conjoint Problem Solving and Response to Intervention

Conjoint consultation offers special advantages for implementation of RtI and decision making in educational settings. In fact, RtI has as one of its foundations problem solving or behavioral consultation, and so the application of conjoint problem-solving consultation is uniquely suited to implementation of RtI (NASDSE, 2005). Nevertheless, some important conceptual issues are noteworthy.

First, much of the literature on RtI has not integrated parents into the problem-solving process (see Kratochwill et al., in press). Nevertheless, as we have argued throughout this text, involving parents in the problem-solving process is highly desirable and can improve student outcomes. Conjoint consultation linked to the various levels of intervention can be very helpful in ensuring student success and sustaining positive educational outcomes.

A second issue that is important is the specific linkage of conjoint consultation to the various levels of intervention. Bear in mind that earlier in the text we outlined different models of how consultation might be implemented. Building on some of the earlier work of Kratochwill and his associates, we noted that consultation problem solving can occur at the client or consultee level (individual or group), or could involve system-level intervention such as technology training to facilitate intervention implementation and integrity (see Kratochwill & Pittman, 2002). In the latter case, conjoint problem-solving consultation can occur with the consultant training various stakeholders (including parents) in intervention systems that are targeted at the universal or selected levels – especially when groups are involved. The unique role of the conjoint problem-solving consultant is that he/she would help in the selection of evidence-based prevention/intervention programs and provide ongoing consultation and technology training in the implementation of these strategies.

At the indicated level of services, the more common form of conjoint problem-solving individual consultation is with one or a few students. In this regard, most of the applications of conjoint problem solving discussed within this text are suitable proxies for use of interventions within an RtI system at the tertiary level.

Conjoint problem solving offers special advantages to individuals implementing an RtI system. Extensive knowledge of prevention science and prevention technology programs as well as services provides the best option for individuals hoping to blend the unique aspects of conjoint problem solving with the recent mandate for RtI in educational settings to serve student needs (Kratochwill et al., in press; Kratochwill & Shernoff, 2004).

Planning and Conducting Conjoint Behavioral Consultation Meetings

Along with the problem-solving goals and objectives of the CBC meetings, several years of research and practice have led us to identify strategies that support success in CBC service delivery. Consultants' efforts in planning and conducting meetings should be thoughtful and planned to maximize efficient and effective delivery. Some efforts are required prior to meetings, and these should not be minimized as they provide a framework for establishing rapport, building relationships, and setting the stage for collaborative work.

Initial contacts with family members should be done with care. It is important to identify the technique that is most effective in connecting with families, whether it is a phone call at home or work, an e-mail, a note home with a child, or a conversation when the child is being dropped off or picked up from school. When a meeting is being scheduled, it is useful to have optional times that include early morning, mid-day, and late afternoon. Once a mutual time is established, it is important that simple strategies be used to remind family members and teachers of the upcoming meeting. A reminder note, phone call, or e-mail can increase attendance at meetings (Shivack & Sullivan, 1989). Other tips to encourage attendance at meetings are given in Table 2.18.

Initial contacts with family members should be viewed as the beginning stages of service provision (McKay & Bannon, 2004). The goal of these contacts is to maximize the chance that the parent will agree to participate as a partner in joint problem solving, including agreeing to attend meetings to engage in collaborative decision making. Thus, professional skills that include

TABLE 2.18. Tips for encouraging meeting attendance.

Extend a verbal reminder the day of or night before the scheduled meeting
Send a reminder flier home in student's folder
Provide child care
Provide dinner or refreshments at the meeting
Offer tangible incentives such as a raffle or door prize
Provide transportation

building trust and rapport should be part of every interaction with parents. Initial contacts are the first step in establishing a working alliance with parents, increasing chances that they will attend meetings and come ready to participate actively with a belief in their own abilities to be collaborative partners in problem solving. To maximize their utility for these purposes, communications should be clear (i.e., establishing the purpose and objectives of the contact), positive and constructive (i.e., focusing on strengths and needs, rather than deficits and problems), and two-way (i.e., inviting questions and ideas from the other party).

In face-to-face meetings with parents and teachers, consultants not only desire to have parents engage in the problem-solving process, but want to facilitate mutual ownership in problem resolution and encourage ongoing collaboration. That is, they want parents to "come back." Thus, the manner in which the meeting is conducted, including efficiency and the degree to which family members feel needed and validated, is important. Objectives of initial meetings, including those that orient parents to the consultation process, include clarifying roles and responsibilities, setting the foundation for a collaborative working relationship, identifying concrete and practical issues that can be addressed, and developing a plan to overcome barriers to ongoing involvement (McKay, Nudelman, & McCadam, 1996). If potential barriers (e.g., language, meeting times, transportation, child care) can be identified and discussed proactively, means for addressing them will be improved, thereby increasing chances for participation.

A common issue related to CBC service delivery concerns length of time spent in face-to-face meetings. Indeed, consultants and consultees often have a finite amount of time to spend in meetings, with a wealth of information to get through. Effective planning prior to meetings should be a priority of the consultant. Specifically, consultants should engage in efforts to collect, summarize, and organize known information in a way that facilitates communication while at the meeting. For example, collating behavioral concerns discussed in initial contacts, scoring baseline assessment measures, and summarizing ecological observations prior to a meeting allows for an efficient method of narrowing in on behavioral priorities. Likewise, collecting the data from parents and teachers before a meeting and graphing those data for consultees are helpful in visualizing levels of performance without the need for lengthy discussion. Finally, an agenda for the meeting is often useful, particularly when it is organized so that parents and teachers can anticipate the types of questions and topics of conversation that will be covered. Examples of agendas for CBC are given in Appendix K.

Summary

Since the earliest writings on the topic, CBC has evolved from a model concerned with problem resolution to one that encompasses three mutually important goals: (a) promoting positive outcomes for children, (b) encouraging parent engagement, and (c) strengthening relationships at several levels (including the home–school relationship and relationships among many support systems). Consistent with family-centered and ecological principles, the focus is on the identification and resolution of needs by building supports within and across multiple interacting systems, thereby strengthening networks on behalf of children.

The four stages of CBC are common to many structured problem-solving models. Each stage has a series of specific goals and objectives, and three of the four stages are accompanied by a formal CBC interview, with parents, teachers, and other caregivers engaged in a structured discussion with the help of a consultant. In addition, a great deal of work is completed outside of formal meetings through informal, ongoing contacts with consultees to demonstrate support and offer assistance. Recommendations for achieving the problem-solving goals of CBC stages are presented in this chapter, with expanded discussions of relationship building, consulting with diverse families, and working in unique contexts presented in other chapters in this book.

3
Conjoint Behavioral Consultation in Practice: Promoting Positive Family–School Relationships

Chapter 2 addressed the behavioral (outcome) objectives of CBC, including the specific child-related issues addressed and the degree to which joint problem solving results in desirable outcomes for the child. Certain prerequisites are also necessary to maximize the outcomes of home–school actions. Specifically, the "4 A's" – approach, atmosphere, attitudes, and actions – constitute what are among the important conditions that need to be in place for the formation of effective partnerships (see Chapter 1). Within the specific framework of CBC, additional prerequisite conditions for effective outcomes are embodied in relational, or relationship-building, objectives. Relational objectives concern aspects of the CBC model that support the development of relationships and partnerships on behalf of the child. Decades of clinical work with CBC have suggested that it is not only *what* is done in the context of problem solving, but also *how* parents and teachers are brought together and relate to one another and the manner in which their relationship is supported that determines the broader benefits of CBC. It is to these relationship-building objectives that we turn in the present chapter.

Relational (Relationship-Building) Objectives in Conjoint Behavioral Consultation

Whereas outcome objectives in CBC tend to be child focused and concerned with structural features of problem solving, relational objectives focus on the partnership or relationship between adults. The relational objectives of CBC are listed in Table 3.1 and explored briefly below. Example strategies to achieve the relational objectives are also presented alongside the objectives in Table 3.1. It should be noted that there is some degree of overlap between objectives and between the examples presented therein. The examples should be used in a manner that is flexible, dynamic, and responsive to the situations presented.

TABLE 3.1. Relational objectives and examples.

Objectives	Examples
Improve communication, knowledge, and understanding of child, family, and school	Identify strengths in child, family members, and teacher Support parents "where they are at" Elicit ideas, information, and perspectives from all parties using open-ended questions Paraphrase and validate messages from parents and teachers to check for understanding
Promote shared ownership and joint responsibility for problem solution	Provide rationales and expectations for families and schools to work together (i.e., "make process overt") Engage in shared eye contact Verbally encourage and reinforce future independent conjoint problem solving among parents and teachers Draw distinct similarities across settings Structure interventions that require cooperation and communication, such as home–school notes
Promote greater conceptualization of needs and concerns, and increase perspective taking	Increase responsibility for successful outcomes by including all participants, including the child when appropriate Describe rationale and expectations for joint home–school problem-solving efforts Use nonverbal listening skills that convey understanding and acceptance of various perspectives Verbally acknowledge different perspectives with statements such as "I see your point" or "I hadn't thought of it that way before"
Strengthen relationships within and across systems	Reframe problems into opportunities for skill development Emphasize positive efforts of all parties Reframe negative comments into areas of care and concern Point out unique strengths of parents, teachers, and students Use physical arrangement of meeting room to encourage eye contact and dialogue between parents and teachers (e.g., remove physical barriers such as large tables, encourage parents and teachers to sit next to each other) Use gestures to communicate joining of home and school parties (e.g., arm and hand movements that suggest coming together)
Maximize opportunities to address needs and concerns across, rather than within, settings	Point out the importance of out-of-school opportunities for a student to experience success Comment on the benefits of congruence and continuity of experiences for students, families, and educators Highlight similarities across settings

(*Continued*)

TABLE 3.1. Relational objectives and examples—Cont'd.

Objectives	Examples
Increase shared (parent and teacher) commitments to educational goals	Ask for help
	Develop plans that are consistent across settings and that support achievement in and out of school
	Emphasize a team concept with inclusive language such as "we," "us," and "together"
Increase the diversity of expertise and resources available	Involve students when possible
	Invite family members beyond parents to be involved
	Allow parents to bring additional support persons to meetings
	Ask parents for ideas for interventions and incorporate them into plans

Source: Adapted from Christenson, S.L., & Sheridan, S.M. (2001). *Schools and families: Creating essential connections for learning.* New York: Guilford Press.

Improve Communication, Knowledge, and Understanding of the Child, Family, and School

Perhaps one of the most significant features of effective relationships is the ability to communicate openly, frequently, and constructively. Thus, improving the communication among all parties is a main priority in CBC. Opportunities to communicate are structured in the process through a series of interviews wherein information, observations, and ideas are gathered and shared. The purpose of the communication should always be child focused and related to efforts to support the child in achieving his or her developmental goals. When approached in this way, open and frequent communication can serve the purpose of increasing understanding of the child and his or her supporting systems (i.e., home and school). Communication in CBC can serve to improve a parent's understanding of a teacher's expectations, classroom rules, and school norms. Likewise, through effective communication, a teacher's knowledge about a family's situational demands, cultural beliefs, and potential to assist in the child's learning may be increased.

CBC meetings set the stage for frequent and meaningful (child- and solution-focused) communication to occur. However, multiple additional opportunities for communication are present before, after, and between meetings and in contexts other than the structured interview. Tips for effective communication are presented in Table 3.2, and consultants are encouraged to adopt and model these strategies in all interactions between families and school personnel.

Promote Shared Ownership and Joint Responsibility for Addressing Needs

A second relational objective of CBC is the promotion of shared ownership and responsibility for all aspects of decision making. From this perspective, the entire CBC process (from identifying primary needs to determining

TABLE 3.2. Tips for communicating with families.

Always start with a positive message
Communicate regularly and often to increase parents' understanding and trust
Express concerns early and genuinely – think, what would I want if this were my child?
Never hesitate to ask the parent for help
Convey the desire to work together to help the child. Emphasize that you both have the same
    goal: helping the child be successful
Use good communication skills to promote cohesion. For example:
    Use common and clear language; ensure that parents understand clearly what you are
        trying to communicate
    Use the parents' own words when possible
    Listen quietly to what the parent says, verbalizing initially only to convey understanding
        (such as through mmm-hmm, ok, or other similar minimal encouragers) – really listen!
    Use words to unify, such as we, our, and together, rather then I and you
Express the fact that the parent's input and perspective are very important
Respect that the family members are experts, that they are doing the best they can, and
    that they want what is best for their child
Clearly describe expectations for school behavior and ask the parents if they agree and
    can support the expectations
Keep in mind responsibilities of each person – yourself, parents, and students
Avoid giving advice as much as possible
Thank the parent for listening, caring, and helping

Source: Adapted from Christenson, S.L., & Sheridan, S.M. (2001). *Schools and families: Creating essential connections for learning.* New York: Guilford Press.

whether goals have been met and planning for generalization) is considered from a mutual, collaborative stance. Although each party in the relationship (i.e., parent, teacher, child, consultant, and others as appropriate) has unique roles and tasks, the responsibility for addressing needs and establishing conditions for goal attainment are shared across systems. Statements or questions such as "our goal for the child" (vs. "your goal at home or at school"), or "what can we do?" (vs. "what can you do?") present subtle opportunities to emphasize a shared orientation to decision making.

Promote Greater Conceptualization of Needs and Promote Perspective Taking

By design, CBC allows for more information about a child to be shared among parties. Beyond sharing knowledge and content information, CBC provides a unique context within which teachers, family members, and other participants can broaden their views, thoughts, and perspectives about a given situation. Asking about family members' and teachers' perspectives presents a unique opportunity for each participant to consider a situation from the other's vantage point. Ensuring that this outcome happens requires the consultant to point out examples of each view and model the strength of considering alternate perspectives. Statements such as "from your perspective" or "the way you see it" convey that the consultant understands the importance of unique views.

Considering a child's situation or needs from alternative perspectives adds breadth to decision making. Although pointing out different perspectives may be perceived as highlighting differences across systems (in a process that attempts to form bridges between home and school), it should be conducted in a manner that demonstrates the richness that such perspectives add to decision making. Furthermore, it provides an opportunity to understand the unique interpersonal contexts within which children must function.

Strengthen Relationships Within and Across Systems

At times, a positive connection exists between family and school. Other times, family members and educators are strangers or worse, adversaries. Regardless of the quality of the interactions between home and school, it is the case that there is always a relationship between family members and their child's educators (Pianta & Walsh, 1996). The goal of CBC is to promote a positive, constructive relationship among these key systems in a child's life to serve as both a protective factor and an asset for their learning and development (Christenson & Sheridan, 2001). Unfortunately, although both systems are considered critical microsystems for children's development, they are often accustomed to operating independently and autonomously from each other. Active, constructive home–school partnerships, in which parents and teachers truly operate as partners and allies, are considered a relatively new phenomenon in many areas.

Decades of research has demonstrated that family–school partnerships are essential for students' learning and development. For example, family–school relationships have been shown to be essential in developing educational and behavioral programs for children with Attention-Deficit/Hyperactivity Disorder (ADHD) (August, Anderson, & Bloomquist, 1992), conduct disorders (Reid & Patterson, 1992; Webster-Stratton, 2003), social skills deficits (Colton & Sheridan, 1998; Sheridan, Kratochwill, & Elliott, 1990), academic gains (Hansen, 1986; Heller & Fantuzzo, 1993), and homework completion difficulties (Jayanthi, Sawyer, Nelson, Bursuck, & Epstein, 1995; Weiner, Sheridan, & Jenson, 1998). Many features of CBC allow for the opportunity to strengthen relationships within and between systems and create the situational context for problem solving around these and other issues to be addressed. Positive relationships are characterized by communication, cooperation, coordination, and collaboration (Marx & Wooley, 1998), all of which are central features of the CBC process.

Maximize Opportunities to Address Needs and Concerns Across, Rather than Within, Settings

Efforts to address a child's needs across important settings and contexts promote consistency among systems in support of a child's development. CBC practice is thus concerned with enhancing continuity between home and school by establishing congruent educational practices, messages, and supports. In short, the more in sync schools and families are regarding learning and development, the better the outcomes for children (Christenson & Sheridan, 2001). Pianta and Walsh (1996) highlighted the importance of continuity across systems and stressed the importance of interactions that promote shared meaning between home and school. Accordingly, a significant risk factor for youth exists when interactions do not produce shared meaning and there is a mismatch between systems with regard to education, communication, and support. Children who experience discontinuity among contexts have difficulty making transitions and are at risk for academic underachievement and mental health concerns (Phelan, Davidson, & Yu, 1998).

Early behavioral research identified an interesting phenomenon coined "behavioral contrast." Behavioral contrast occurs in situations wherein effective attempts to exert control over behaviors in one environment may serve to cause a contrast in the effects in other settings (Johnson, Bolstad, & Lobitz, 1976). Similarly, behavioral "side effects" occur when the positive effects of behavioral programming in one condition cause undesired effects under other conditions. Because CBC brings family members and teachers together to codevelop and implement complementary interventions, the chances for the identification of contrast and side effects are increased and the chances that these effects will develop are greatly minimized.

Increase Shared Commitment to Educational Goals

Parents and teachers generally desire similar things – for children to perform to the best of their ability and succeed in their educational efforts. This shared commitment to help a child achieve can occur when both parties are committed to adopting complementary roles, as long as the focus remains on the shared goal. Thus, a collaborative relationship is imperative in CBC. Working collaboratively in a context in which input is sought, roles are defined, and expectations are specified provides opportunities to increase commitment.

Collaboration is defined as a student-centered, dynamic framework that endorses collegial, interdependent, and co-equal styles of interaction between families and educators who work jointly together to achieve common goals (Welch & Sheridan, 1995). It is considered an evolving process that enables parents and educators to develop and have access to new, creative alternatives. The collaborative ethic (Phillips & McCullough, 1990) represents a philosophy or set of values about the importance and essential nature of family participation. It serves as a framework for the overall operation of a school. Thus, collaboration is not a concrete activity or event, but rather a guiding belief or process. The emphasis is on relationships between family members and educational personnel, rather than distinct roles that each may play. As such, the responsibility for educating and socializing children is within the shared domains of home and school in relationship with each other. Both families and schools are essential for the growth and success of children. In practice, collaboration can be modeled by consultants, thereby creating opportunities for parents and teachers to also engage in collaborative interactions. Some of the ways in which collaboration is demonstrated are listed in Table 3.3.

Increase the Diversity of Expertise and Resources Available

In CBC, several individuals come together to identify goals and develop strategies to maximize a child's functioning. The benefits of shared planning and decision making are best realized when all individuals recognize the value and importance of the contributions of all parties. Indeed, parents and teachers have unique expertise regarding a child. Parents are knowledgeable about a range of information that is otherwise unavailable to school personnel. This knowledge includes information on a child's prenatal and early life experiences; developmental history; family values, practices, and traditions; home-based rules, routines, expectations, and norms for behavior; child response to discipline, nurturance, and other parenting activities; family constellation and a child's fit within the family unit; and a host of other important facts to which school-based personnel are not privy. Teachers are knowledgeable of instruction and pedagogy, curricular issues, content areas, classroom discipline, and the child's response to formalized educational efforts and activities. Consultants must be knowledgeable about all aspects of data-based decision making, including defining target concerns, conducting functional assessments, assisting in the generation of hypotheses regarding behaviors, effective interventions and their design, and evaluation. In addition, consultants have particular expertise in guiding the collaborative process so that all participants are meaningfully involved, ensuring that relevant information is shared and used in ways best suited to support the child's goal attainment.

TABLE 3.3. Various ways in which consultants demonstrate collaboration.

Invite and listen to all perspectives
View differences as strengths
Focus on mutual interests across home and school
Share information across systems to coconstruct understandings and interventions
Respect the skills and knowledge of each other by asking for ideas and opinions
Plan together and make decisions that address parents', teachers', and students' needs
Share in decision making about a child's educational program
Share resources across settings to work toward goal attainment
Develop a common message about schoolwork and behavior
Demonstrate a willingness to address conflict
Refrain from finding fault
Attribute successes to mutual efforts of families and schools

As noted, CBC is based on a concept in which collaboration among parties is seen as desirable and beneficial. In addition to the unique expertise that each party can "bring to the table," various resources representing strengths within systems can be identified and combined. This process presents opportunities to maximize resources available to address concerns and to address concerns in a coordinated, comprehensive manner. Thus, CBC provides a unique means to coordinate services and thereby ensure that individuals from diverse and relevant areas of expertise (e.g., parents, teachers, physicians, other specialists) work together to optimize the outcomes for children and families.

Interpersonal and Relational Skill Domains

Early consultation authors noted that "At its most basic level, consultation is an interpersonal exchange. As such, the consultant's success is going to hinge largely on his or her communication and relationship skills" (Gutkin & Curtis, 1982, p. 822). Effective communication has always been considered important to behavioral consultation practice. In like fashion, CBC consultants must be skilled at interacting with parents and teachers and at negotiating the relationships with and between these parties. The interpersonal and relationship-building skills highlighted in this chapter are organized into four skill domains: communication, perspective taking, building partnerships, and managing conflict. Various strategies will be discussed and illustrated in each of these areas.

Communication Strategies and Skills

Although the CBC interviews do not independently define CBC, they are perhaps the primary concrete mechanism by which CBC services are delivered. These interviews, and many other consultant–consultee interactions, require that participants communicate on an interpersonal level. General guidelines for communicating effectively with families are presented in Table 3.4. The nature, quality, and influence of the interpersonal exchange among participants are therefore essential features of the consultation process.

Interpersonal communication is defined as "a complex, reciprocal process through which participants create shared meanings as messages are transmitted continuously from one sender-receiver to another via multiple communication channels" (Friend & Cook, 1992, p. 72). This critical aspect of the consultation process has received little attention in research literature. In early behavioral consultation research, Bergan & Tombari (1975) developed the *Consultation Analysis Record* (CAR) to evaluate the effectiveness of consultant communication behaviors within the consultation dyad. The CAR contains operational definitions to code a message's source (who spoke), content (topic of conversation), process (the function of what was stated), and control (whether information was elicited or emitted). The CAR is the only system

TABLE 3.4. Guidelines and practices for effective communication with families.

Guideline	Possible practices
Strive for a positive orientation rather than a deficit-based or crisis orientation	Good news phone calls Invite and incorporate parent reactions to policies and practices Contact parents at the first sign of a concern Communicate an "optimistic" message about the child
Consider tone as well as content of your communications	Reframe language from problems to goals for child Focus on a parent's ability to help
Develop and publicize regular, reliable, varied two-way communication systems	System-wide family–school communication/assignment notebooks Shared parent–educator responsibility for contacts Handbooks Newsletters "Thursday folders" including relevant home and school information Telephone tree Electronic communication technology
Use effective conflict management strategies	Discuss and focus on mutual goals and interests Use words such as we, us, and our, vs. you, I, yours, and mine
Keep the focus of communication on the child's performance	Bidirectional communications regarding classroom activities, progress, suggested activities for parents Home–school notebooks/notes Family–school meetings with children present Shared parent–educator monitoring system (e.g., educational file, contract)
Ensure that parents have needed information to support children's educational progress	Several orientation nights with follow-up contact for nonattendees Parent support groups to disseminate information on school performance Home visits Home–school contracts with follow-up Curriculum nights Monthly meetings on topics of mutual interest
Create formal and informal opportunities to communicate and build trust between home and school	Multicultural potlucks Grade-level bagel breakfasts Family fun nights Committees designed to address home–school issues Workshops where parents and school personnel learn together Principal's hour
Underscore all communication with a shared responsibility between families and schools	Communicate the essential nature of family involvement Share information about the curriculum of the home Discuss coroles (e.g., cocommunicators) and implement shared practices (e.g., contracts, common language about conditions for children's success) Back to School Night

Sources: Christenson, S.L., & Hirsch, J. (1998). Facilitating partnerships and conflict resolution between families and schools. In K.C. Stoiber & T. Kratochwill (Eds.), *Handbook of group interventions for children and families* (pp. 307–344). Boston: Allyn & Bacon; Christenson, S.L., & Sheridan, S.M. (2001). *Schools and families: Creating essential connections for learning.* New York: Guilford Press.

designed specifically for quantifying verbal exchanges within consultation (Martens & DiGennaro, 2008). Erchul and colleagues (Erchul et al., 1999; Grissom, Erchul, & Sheridan, 2003) conducted a series of studies concerning relational communication within behavioral consultation and CBC, with a focus on functions of statements (e.g., domineeringness, dominance). Neither the early work by Bergan and Tombari, nor the work of Erchul addressed specific skills necessary for effective consultation and communication practices. It is to these skills that we now turn.

Communication skills are discrete verbal and nonverbal proficiencies that consultants use to obtain and share information and to establish and maintain positive relationships with consultees. Some important communication skills that consultants use to create and maintain meaningful and positive relationships with consultees include (a) nonverbal cues, (b) open questions, (c) minimal encouragers, (d) paraphrases/summarizations, and (e) reflection. These are reviewed next, followed by general suggestions for effective communication.

Nonverbal Cues

Individuals in consultation, as in other interpersonal exchanges, communicate nonverbally in several ways. The power of these communications cannot be overstated, as it has been suggested that the source of 93% of the impact of spoken messages comes from components other than their verbal content (what is said). This format includes facial expression (55%) and vocal components (volume, pitch, rhythm; 38%). The remaining 7% of the impact of a verbal message is conveyed by its verbal component (Mehrabian & Ferris, 1967).

The primary classes of nonverbal cues are body movements, vocal cues, and spatial relations. Body movements include nonverbal actions such as posture, eye contact, and facial expressions. Vocal cues (i.e., the "paralanguage" aspect of language) include voice tone, pacing of speech, and voice quality. Spatial relations refer to the physical distance between participants and can also include the verbal space given between statements (Friend & Cook, 1992). There is no correct nonverbal behavior within consultation; however, consultants need to be aware of the messages they are conveying to parents and teachers, both verbally and nonverbally, in all interpersonal interactions.

Silence is a special case of nonverbal communication. Although silence sometimes creates feelings of discomfort and anxiety, it can be a very powerful communication tool. Silence and pauses in communication related to speech flow and pace are important for several reasons. First, they can communicate interest, concern, empathy, and respect toward others (Friend & Cook, 1992). As a form of minimal encouragers (to be described more fully later), they allow others to think about questions or situations, which often results in more effective responses. The alternatives to silence include interruptions (the disruption of one speaker's message by another speaker who delivers his or her own message), overtalks (the result of more than one speaker talking simultaneously until the communication is relinquished to one speaker), and reduced verbal spacing (disruption in the pace of a verbal exchange when one speaker interrupts a brief pause of another speaker). These can be deleterious to interpersonal communication; they communicate that the individual committing the intrusion desires to control the interaction, has more perceived knowledge than the other person, or is disinterested in what the other person has to contribute.

Open Questions

Open questions are those for which an infinite number of responses are possible. Open questions typically request more than a single word or yes/no response. They can be used effectively for several important purposes such as opening up a conversation or line of questioning; encouraging others to begin speaking, continue speaking, or embellish what they have already said; obtaining consultees' perceptions about an event, situation, or option; and otherwise putting the *conversational ball* in the consultee's court. Examples may include "What are your thoughts on this?" "Tell me more about what happened" and "How do you think we can help him be more successful?" These types of questions encourage consultees to share their thoughts and elaborate on their responses. They also convey openness to consultees' ideas and perspectives.

In contrast, closed questions are those whose response options are limited. These questions are structured in such a way that they can be answered in very brief (e.g., one or two word or yes/no) responses and are very focused in their intent. Examples are "How many math problems did Juan complete correctly yesterday?" "Is it possible to collect information on this form?" and "Would you prefer to start the plan on Friday or Monday?" Closed questions tend to keep the control of the conversation with the consultant, thereby limiting the information flow and exchange. Consultants who often think ahead to the next question they will ask are likely using closed or otherwise ineffective questions.

The selection of the type of question to ask depends on the purpose for asking it. If the consultant's goal is to open a conversation, learn as much as possible about relevant events or situations, or explore various possible perspectives, open-ended questions will generally yield the best results. If, however, consultees need redirection, such as when an open-ended question is misunderstood by the consultee or he/she begins deviating from the main topic, a consultant is advised to follow with a more focused question. It is not always the case that an open-ended question will result in a wealth of information being provided by the consultee or that a focused question will restrict how a consultee replies. However, the nature of the question provides parameters for the type of response a consultant hopes to achieve (Friend & Cook, 1992).

Minimal Encouragers

Much like open questions, minimal encouragers communicate openness to consultees' thoughts and ideas. Minimal encouragers are statements or gestures that encourage the consultees to communicate their thoughts or ideas. They can also facilitate further elaboration by consultees. Minimal encouragers can take both verbal and nonverbal forms. Examples of verbal encouragers might include phrases such as "um hum" and "ok." Nonverbal encouragers might include simple gestures such as head nods and smiles or may include a general open body posture such as having one's arms and legs uncrossed and their body facing consultees. When used together, both verbal and nonverbal minimal encouragers provide an open and encouraging atmosphere for consultees. They indicate that you are listening and understand what is being expressed, and they encourage the speaker to continue communicating.

Paraphrase/Summarize

A paraphrase is defined as a statement that rephrases the content of the consultee's message using one's own language. Consultants use paraphrases by restating in their own words what they think the consultee has said, with little or no inference. Paraphrases are used to communicate to consultees that they listened to what was said and to clarify that they heard the information correctly. Paraphrasing allows consultees to feel heard by consultants, thus strengthening the consultation relationship.

Like paraphrases, summaries are also used to ensure clarity in communications and build relationships within the consultation team. A summary is defined as two or more paraphrases that condense the essential elements of consultees' messages. It differs from paraphrasing in important ways. Whereas paraphrases are immediate and brief responses to discrete pieces of information, summarizations respond to several pieces of information provided over the course of multiple verbal exchanges, possibly including statements made by several individuals. Thus, they are strategic and purposeful, made in an effort to encapsulate key points of a discussion.

Consultants use summaries to identify major themes in consultees' communication, highlight information that is directly relevant to the problem-solving process, and transition the discussion to new objectives. In other words, summarizations can be used to draw out the most relevant information to support problem solving, thereby providing due attention to the content that will contribute most directly to successful interview outcomes. In this way, summaries can serve an instructive function. In addition, summarizations provide the necessary structure to recap relevant information and move to new objectives in the problem-solving process. By using summaries, consultants demonstrate their attention and consideration to consultees' messages, while at the same time keeping the consultation process focused on discussion that is pertinent to problem solving.

Reflection

It is important that consultants convey an understanding of the consultees with whom they are working. Expressions of understanding often come in the form of reflection of feelings. A reflection is a technique in which the consultant restates key information sent by the consultee for purposes of gaining greater clarity and often responds to the emotional tone of the consultee's message. Consultants may reflect consultees' stated or implied feelings to communicate understanding and support. Consultants may use phrases such as "It sounds like you may be feeling . . . ." or "This must make you feel. . . ." By acknowledging and reflecting consultees' feelings, consultants provide a caring foundation for consultees to share their feelings about the consultation process and its outcomes.

Perspective Taking

Perspective taking is another important domain in the area of interpersonal and relationship-building skills. For effective problem solving to occur it is important that consultants, parents, and teachers understand each others' perspectives. There are several skills that consultants can use to convey that they understand and appreciate consultees' perspectives. Such skills can also encourage consultees to consider each other's points of view. Important perspective-taking skills include listening to and acknowledging different perspectives, adopting a nondeficit approach, and being responsive.

Listen To and Acknowledge Different Perspectives

It is important that consultants truly listen to and acknowledge the different perspectives of consultees. To actively solicit different ideas and thereby keep the process inclusive, consultants can use open questions to invite the opinions and perspectives of parents and teachers, recognizing the unique contextual circumstances that may contribute to a child's current situation. Consultants can demonstrate their understanding of consultees' points of view by making overt the various ideas that parents and teachers mention or imply in their conversation. By acknowledging or restating consultees' perspectives, consultants model perspective taking for parents and teachers, helping them appreciate that situations can be viewed from a number of vantage points.

Adopt a Nondeficit Approach

By adopting a nondeficit approach to working with consultees, consultants place attention on the relative and shared strengths of the home, school, and child, rather than on efforts to "fix" the child, family, or school problems. Each parent and teacher has a unique set of strengths and life experiences that influence their perspectives and expectations for their children. Accepting consultees for who they are and for where they are in life can eliminate unnecessary expectations that consultants may have for consultees. It is important that consultants understand unique differences and not view differences as deficits. Rather, consultants should adopt an open and nonjudgmental attitude when working with parents and teachers. They can identify and build on the strengths of consultees, and help them in ways that meet their unique needs.

Related to adopting a nondeficit approach is the need to model a non-blaming attitude. When parents and teachers (and perhaps consultants) perceive fault and place blame on each other, the home–school relationship is at risk. This practice often results in a me versus you conflict paradigm (rather than one that emphasizes us vs. the problem), sets up conflictual patterns, and leads to ineffective communications. There are a number of techniques that can be used to block blame in parent–educator interactions (see Christenson & Sheridan, 2001; Weiss & Edwards, 1992). Consultants can assist parents and teachers in refraining from this practice by proactively promoting an orientation toward solutions, rather than blame.

Building Partnerships

Building partnerships between home and school is an important component of the consultation process. There are a number of strategies that consultants can use to facilitate cooperative partnerships within the consultation team. Some strategies that consultants can use to build partnerships within CBC include (a) modeling positive communication, (b) pointing out similar experiences, (c) pointing out consultee contributions, (d) using language to unify, and (e) creating opportunities for meaningful roles.

Model Positive Communication

One way that consultants can help build strong partnerships between teachers and parents is to develop opportunities for positive communication. In consultation, problems are often a central focus of discussion, hence parents and teachers may become accustomed to talking about negative issues. To break this negative pattern, it is helpful for parents and teachers to share in positive interactions whenever possible. Consultants can play a central role in facilitating opportunities for parents and teachers to communicate in positive ways. For example, home–school notes or phone calls that include communication of strengths and positive messages about a child can be particularly helpful (Christenson & Sheridan, 2001). Persistent efforts such as frequent letters home and good news phone calls convey the message that the school personnel wish to work with the family and share the successes of the child. School personnel may need to visit families in a comfortable or neutral environment (e.g., the family's home, a fast-food restaurant) before families feel welcome at school.

Point Out Similar Experiences

Earlier we described the importance of acknowledging and using the unique perspectives and expertise of individuals in consultation to maximize information sharing and resource utilization. At the same time, it is beneficial to point out similar experiences between consultees to promote joining and build partnerships. Within the consultation relationship, parents and teachers may have different experiences with the same child and may have different perceptions about the problem focus or treatment. By acknowledging similarities between parents and teachers, consultants provide opportunities for consultees to come together, recognize their shared goals related to benefits for the child, and develop those shared goals.

In some cases, diversity among consultees may present challenges, such as situations where cultural, ethnic, or language differences exist. Chapter 4 discusses these unique consultation issues and offers strategies for addressing such differences. When attempting to build partnerships in these situations, it may be desirable to both acknowledge and respect the uniqueness of each party (e.g., ask about perceptions of an intervention plan and its fit within the culture of the home or classroom), while also identifying areas where similarities are present (e.g., mutual concerns about a child's understanding of social cues or information, similar approaches to encouraging social interactions with family members and classmates). Pointing out like experiences and perspectives allows parents and teachers to acknowledge the similarities between them, build understanding and trust, and strengthen the relationship.

Point Out Consultee Contributions

It is important that consultants acknowledge the contributions that consultees bring to the table. Consultants have expertise in interventions and the problem-solving process, and parents and teachers are experts in their own domains. Parents know what it is like to live with their child and provide support for their child in the home. Similarly, teachers have expert knowledge in education and the types of strategies that work with children in the classroom. For effective partnerships to be built, parents and teachers must feel valued. It is important that consultants actively point out the contributions of parents and teachers and acknowledge that each person brings something essential and unique to the process.

Use Language to Unify

Another way that consultants can strengthen the home–school relationship within CBC is by using unifying language. Specifically, words such as we, us, and our signify a shared responsibility among the consultation team. Unifying language coveys a sense of equality and shared purpose among consultees. In contrast, words such as you, I, and me relay a very different message to consultees – one that separates people into different camps. These terms can be interpreted as placing distance and separation between parents and teachers. In some cases, they can also imply blame on one or more individuals.

Create Opportunities for Meaningful Roles

In Chapter 1, the work of Hoover-Dempsey and colleagues was summarized. This work demonstrates a clear relationship between parental involvement in education and the degree to which parents believe that their specific efforts result in positive results for their children; that is, that the parenting practices in which they engage produce positive learning outcomes. Thus, it is important that parents and teachers believe that positive outcomes for children occur partly or largely as a result of their own efforts. Actively involving parents in making decisions and choices related to their children's lives provides opportunities for meaningful roles related to important educational objectives. Additionally, continued involvement in decision making, planning, and strategy use (e.g., delivering aspects of an intervention at home, such as reading with a child, structuring the home environment, and reviewing homework completion) can result in increased parental self-efficacy, which also has a positive relationship with involvement (Walker, Wilkins, Dallaire, Sandler, & Hoover-Dempsey, 2005).

Roles for family members should be individualized and responsive to current familial realities and demands. This emphasizes the importance of establishing positive rapport and using effective communication skills to assess these idiosyncratic situations. It is important to keep in mind that there are many ways that parents support educational goals. Harry (1992) argued that in the special education process, professionals must provide opportunities for parents to be involved, and articulated several meaningful roles. Those most relevant to the CBC process are parents as assessors (e.g., sharing information about child strengths, providing observational information) and report givers (e.g., reporting on the status of a child's progress in relation to IEP or CBC goals).

An extension of creating meaningful roles for parents is the notion of establishing shared (i.e., co-) roles for parents and educators. The U.S. Department of Education (Moles, 1993) has described five roles that can be shared by families and school personnel: cocommunicators, cosupporters, colearners, coteachers, and codecision makers. These roles are organized as a pyramid (see Figure 3.1), with each subsequent level (from co-communicators at the base to co-decision makers at the apex) requiring a greater degree of active participation, commitment, and skill. This framework respects the various roles that parents can play and takes into account individual needs and circumstances (Christenson & Sheridan, 2001).

Managing Conflict

Many times parents, teachers, and consultants have different views about behaviors, interventions, or the consultation process. Conflicts in consultation are inevitable. Although conflict is not necessarily bad, it is important that it be managed to allow for constructive dialogue and problem solving. Tips for managing challenging situations are given in Table 3.5. Some specific interpersonal skills that consultants use to manage conflicts within the consultation relationship include: focus on mutual goals, reframe, provide structure, and read nonverbal language.

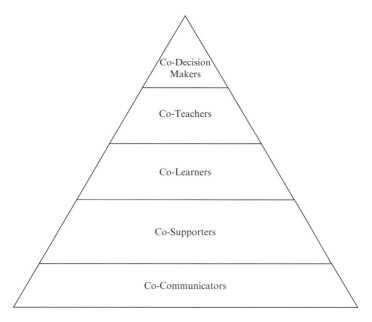

FIGURE 3.1. Co-roles shared by families and educators.

Focus on Mutual Goals

Although consultees may have different views on issues such as the behaviors of a child or an intervention, they share in some common goals. Specifically, parents and teachers generally want to help a child have successful experiences and function effectively at school and home. Consultants can help prevent and manage conflicts between parents and teachers by discussing and focusing on the mutual goals of consultees. This focus centers the consultation team on a common theme and helps prevent differences from evolving into conflicts.

A win–win orientation helps to circumvent blame when students face learning and behavioral difficulties in school. Educators portray a win–win attitude when they state a desire to work toward resolution, avoid making attributions for problems (e.g., student is unmotivated or lacks home support), and discuss what can be done at home and school to achieve goals for the student.

Reframe

Consultants can also use reframing to manage conflicts in consultation. Reframing is defined as the renaming or relabeling of a consultee's thoughts, feelings, or beliefs about a particular individual, situation, or process to provide an alternate positive frame of reference. Consultants can use reframing to transform consultees' negative or destructive comments

TABLE 3.5. Tips for managing challenging situations.

Separate the person from the issue by using a cooperative rather than competitive approach
    Cooperative approach: we versus the problem – promotes win–win result
    Competitive approach: me versus you – results in win–lose situation
Focus on mutual interests
    Positive educational outcomes for students are at the center of the relationship and should
      remain the focus of communications
Explore several options prior to making decisions
    Ensures that a reasonable amount of information is brought to the table
Base decisions on objective information
    Minimizes potential for emotionally laden decisions on both parts
Engage in effective problem solving
    Identify the desired outcome or goal
    Explore values and perspectives around the goal
    Discuss factors that enhance or impede goal attainment
    Explore alternatives or options for achieving goal
    Develop a plan
    Evaluate movement toward goal

into a more positive and constructive way of approaching the same issue. By using reframing, consultants help keep the conversational tone positive.

Provide Structure

Using structure to keep the consultation team focused on a common solution-oriented theme can help prevent and manage conflicts. Because consultation meetings can become forums for consultees to express frustrations and concerns, it is important that consultants not let the team digress from a problem-solving focus. Using structure by verbalizing or making overt the steps of the problem-solving process throughout consultation can help keep consultees focused on the constructive resolution of concerns. This consultant behavior is critical for guiding the consultation process and should be done within a collaborative context, being sensitive and flexible to the needs of consultees.

Read Nonverbal Language

Earlier, we discussed the importance of consultants using their own nonverbal language in ways that allow them to remain focused and communicate clearly. It is also important to learn to read consultees' nonverbal language effectively and be prepared to address what is being conveyed. A significant portion of consultees' messages are conveyed through nonverbal communication rather than words. A trained consultant can often identify parent's and teacher's feelings by reading their nonverbal cues. For example, a parent may feel irritated when learning that her child's misbehaviors resulted in extra classroom chores to be completed in place of daily recess. These feelings may be communicated by sighs, a furrowed brow, and folding of the arms.

By attending to consultees' nonverbal messages, consultants are in touch with the feelings of consultees and can be sensitive to these feelings in their communication. Reading the nonverbal language of consultees and reflecting on feelings can help prevent conflict by attending to negative feelings before they evolve into conflict situations.

Empowerment

Parents are experts on their children, and teachers and support personnel are experts on learning and instruction. Inviting parents to be partners and asking for their assistance in resolving an educational issue (e.g., information sharing about the child) recognizes the unique expertise they bring to problem solving. Furthermore, parents are typically a constant connection for children. Unlike most school personnel, they know and see their children in various settings across school years.

Implicit in beliefs that espouse a partnership orientation is the notion of empowerment. Empowerment is defined as a process by which individuals begin to see themselves as responsible for evoking positive changes in their own lives (Dempsey & Dunst, 2004). It implies that many competencies are already present or possible to develop and involves proactively promoting an individual's sense of control through their ability to use existing strengths. The ability to provide opportunities for empowerment and strengthen families in a way that makes them more competent and capable requires a breakdown of the typical role of relationships between professionals and families (Rappaport, 1981). When consultants approach their role as one that includes providing a context for consultees to feel empowered (rather than one that relies on providing solutions and direction to consultees), they provide a mechanism by which consultees gain mastery over their affairs. From an empowerment perspective, a failure to display competence is not due to the deficiencies of families and/or children, but rather to a failure of social systems, including schools, to create opportunities for competencies to be displayed.

Summary

In addition to behavioral objectives and outcomes in CBC, there is a concern for promoting partnerships and supporting relationships at all levels. To achieve these objectives, consultants are advised to use communication strategies that convey belief, trust, respect, and high expectations for family involvement. Using open-ended questions that invite information, perspectives, and opinions sends a message that parents' expertise is necessary. Similarly, extending parents' ideas, validating their comments, and paraphrasing their statements using their own language sets the tone that they are meaningful investors in the process. Opportunities to convey the message that consultants hear and understand parents' observations and perspectives are frequent in CBC and should be used in a manner that reinforces their role and importance vis-a-vis their child's learning. Efforts to create and model meaningful roles such that each partner is essential in supporting a child's learning are necessary for long-term, constructive relationships. Finally, a thoughtful approach to addressing and managing conflict between families, educators, and other caregivers is essential to ensure that the focus remains on goals for the child and not on personal issues between adults.

4
Conjoint Behavioral Consultation in Practice: Working with Diverse Families

Diane C. Marti, Jennifer D. Burt, and Susan M. Sheridan

Conjoint behavioral consultation (CBC) is concerned with achieving important child-related goals by establishing and strengthening partnerships among primary systems that support development. Given its joint foci on content (the tangible implementation of evidence-based interventions for socially valid targets) and process (the intangible mechanisms used in practice to achieve optimal outcomes), no two consultation interactions or relationships are identical. Rather, within the structure of the CBC model, delivery of services can be responsive to individual needs, circumstances, and priorities. The flexibility to adapt to situations that are inherently idiosyncratic is particularly important when working with families and children from diverse backgrounds and cultures, which is the focus of this chapter.

American educators are faced with challenges to meet the unique needs of increasingly diverse classrooms. In 2002, the U.S. Department of Education reported that 60.3% of students were White, non-Hispanic; 17.2% Black, non-Hispanic; 17.1% Hispanic; 4.2% Asian/Pacific Islander; and 1.2% American Indian/Alaska Native. In addition, the number of children in immigrant families has grown rapidly in nearly every state across the country. According to the 2000 Census, one of every five children in the U.S. is an immigrant or a child of immigrant parents (Hernandez, 2004). Educators and mental health service providers are challenged more than ever before to be knowledgeable and responsive to the diverse needs of their students while remaining sensitive to individual needs.

CBC has the potential for practitioners to implement culturally sensitive services in which important individual differences are recognized, including family strengths and individual needs (Marti, Bevins, & Sheridan, 2005; Marti, Burt, Sheridan, Clarke, & Rohlk, 2004; Sheridan, 2000; Sheridan, Eagle, & Doll, 2006). As described in Chapter 3, CBC embodies a complementary relationship between families and educators that facilitates communication, fosters trust and mutual awareness, and allows the strengths of the diverse families to be utilized effectively in plan development. These and other elements inherent within CBC are consistent with those suggested for culturally relevant services.

The purposes of this chapter are to describe how CBC provides a useful framework for working with diverse families and to describe strategies for working effectively with these families within a consultation context. In addition, recommended approaches and practices will be highlighted that have been demonstrated to be effective for working with diverse families. Finally, a case study will be presented that demonstrates the use of a strength-based, partnership orientation within cross-cultural CBC. A comprehensive review of consultation with diverse families is beyond the scope of this book. For a review of the literature, see Ingraham (2000; 2008). We begin by defining some key constructs and raising conceptual issues within the literature.

Conceptualizing Culture and Diversity

Diversity is defined as demonstrating characteristics that are unique or different from the mainstream society, including those of ethnicity, socioeconomic status, parental educational level, language, and family stability (Sue, Bingham, Porche-Burke, & Vasquez, 1999). With increasing diversity in American schools, there is a need for school consultants to be aware of the complexities brought forth within these diverse contexts, including unique considerations necessary for working with consultees who are culturally different from the mainstream (Brown, 1997; Lynch & Hanson, 1998).

Culture is a term used to describe shared customs, values, and beliefs. It is defined as "an organized set of thoughts, beliefs, and norms for interaction and communication, all of which may influence cognitions, behaviors, and perceptions" (Ingraham, 2000, p. 325). These cultural norms may be influenced by a variety of factors (e.g., ethnicity, language, sociometric status, geographic location), as well as each individual's interpretation of or value placed on these factors (Ingraham, 2008; Lynch & Hanson, 1998). Consultants need to be aware of unique cultural norms present when working with diverse consultees.

Cross-cultural competence is "the ability to think, feel, and act in ways that acknowledge, respect, and build upon ethnic, (socio)cultural, and linguistic diversity" (Lynch & Hanson, 1993, p. 50). Importantly, this definition assumes that all individuals and groups are diverse and does not imply one group as the norm. It acknowledges that an individual's personal experiences often play a role equal in importance to ethnicity, language, or culture.

To date, the majority of the literature relating to cultural diversity and consultation has focused on two main topics: (a) cultural modifications for working with parent consultees who are different from the mainstream culture (Brown, 1997; Edens, 1997; Lynch & Hanson, 1998; Miranda, 1993; Tarver Behring & Gelinas, 1996), and (b) consultation with educators about culturally and linguistically diverse (CLD) students with special needs (Harris, 1991). Although the importance of involving parents in the consultation process has been identified as essential to improve outcomes for diverse children (Ramirez, Lepage, Kratochwill, & Duffy, 1998; Sheridan, 2000; Tarver Behring & Ingraham, 1998), there has been a lack of consultation research with diverse populations.

Conjoint Behavioral Consultation and Diversity

CBC can provide a context for culturally sensitive services in which important individual differences are recognized including family strengths and individual needs (Sheridan, 2000). Elements inherent within CBC are consistent with those suggested for culturally relevant services and include (a) helping teachers develop an awareness of students' differences, (b) taking time to establish and foster effective home–school relationships, (c) assisting parents to understand differences and similarities among themselves and the larger school culture, (d) building trust among parties, and (e) developing shared commitments to student success (Sheridan, 2000; Tarver Behring, Cabello, & Kushida, 2000). CBC embodies a complementary relationship between families and educators that facilitates communication, fosters trust and mutual awareness, and allows the strengths of the diverse families to be utilized effectively in plan development. By utilizing each partner's knowledge and observations, parents and teachers support the child's learning and development more effectively than either can independently. Shared responsibility in treatment planning and implementation is achieved through a "mutual effort toward a shared goal" (Christenson & Sheridan, 2001, p. 37).

CBC is responsive to the needs of the family, child, and teacher. The ability for cross-systemic consultation to improve communication, facilitate problem-solving needs on a consistent basis, and address the changing needs across both home and school systems is inherent within the CBC model. CBC provides a structure for families to identify their most important needs, and to communicate and prioritize their values, beliefs, and cultural heritage. Similarly, CBC provides the teacher with a structured and meaningful approach to communicate important classroom roles and expectations, curriculum information, and individual child needs to position the family in a strength-oriented role to assist their child to be successful in school. Consultants utilizing CBC are in a position to assist the family and teacher(s) to select the needs that are most essential to attain short- and long-term goals, and can use collaborative consultation strategies to help the consultees develop effective interventions to improve child outcomes.

Sheridan et al. (2006b) investigated the efficacy of CBC with diverse clients by examining client case outcomes. The authors defined diversity in terms of ethnicity, socioeconomic status, language spoken in the home, number of adults in the home, and maternal education level. Sheridan et al. argued that *risk* was not a single demographic variable, but the cumulative effect of these diversity factors on outcome variables. Outcomes were assessed by investigating behavioral change and academic performance in child participants.

In addition, consultees' (parents and teachers) subjective perceptions of case outcomes were assessed, as were their perceptions of their acceptance of and satisfaction with CBC. Results demonstrated that in general, positive behavioral outcomes were found for students regardless of the presence and number of diversity indicators. Thus, variability of case outcomes was presumed to be related to factors other than demographic features of families, such as the strategies used by consultants to meet the general CBC objectives and the supports provided to enhance outcomes with diverse clients in consultation (Sheridan et al., 2006b). In the next section, specific strategies are presented to elucidate key approaches consultants may use to improve their work with diverse families.

Effective Consultant Practices for Culturally Sensitive Conjoint Behavioral Consultation Services

Although empirical support is lacking regarding the application and effectiveness of intervention strategies that address specific behaviors of culturally diverse students within the classroom and home settings (Nastasi, Bernstein Moore, & Varjas, 2004), general recommendations are offered to enhance working with diverse families within a CBC framework. Specifically, the following approaches and strategies are recommended to augment CBC work with diverse children and families: (a) practice cultural sensitivity, (b) build trust and establish a relationship with the family, (c) address diversity issues, (d) enhance communication, and (e) implement a family-centered approach. These approaches are presented in Table 4.1 and discussed briefly later.

Practice Cultural Sensitivity

As described in Chapter 3, the goal of CBC is to promote a positive, constructive relationship among the key systems in a child's life (Christenson & Sheridan, 2001). Although these key systems are typically accustomed to operating independently and autonomously from each other, this independent functioning can create disconnects that are pronounced when working with diverse families. Resulting discontinuities that may be experienced across home and school highlight the importance of building strong relationships with diverse families. Consultants must approach these relationships in a sensitive and responsive manner to enhance opportunities for effective and positive relationships.

It is recommended that consultants first examine and understand their own cultural assumptions before considering issues of diversity with consultees. To be most effective in working with diverse families, it is important for consultants to develop a sense of cultural self-awareness, including an awareness of how cultural beliefs, values, and traditions may influence perspectives

TABLE 4.1. Strategies for effective CBC practices with diverse families.

Practice cultural sensitivity
    Examine one's own cultural beliefs
    Engage in cross-cultural learning
    Use clear communication strategies
    Focus on family-identified needs
Build trusting relationships
    Spend time getting to know families
    Learn about unique cultures
    Follow-up with family after consultation services have ended
Address diversity issues directly
    Demonstrate respect for different cultural styles
    Learn about the family's beliefs and values from family members themselves
    Use a *cultural guide* to learn about culture
Enhance communication
    Use descriptive and concrete terms
    Refrain from using jargon
    Help parents prepare for upcoming meetings
    Ask family members to share observations and information
    Use frequent summary statements
    Reframe potentially stereotypical statements
    Train interpreters in the importance of translating content and relational aspects
        of communications
Implement a family-centered approach
    Listen and respond to family's needs
    Use open-ended questions to elicit family members' perspectives
    Refrain from making assumptions about family

and actions (Henning-Stout, 1994; Locke, 1992; Lynch & Hanson, 1998). The influence of one's own culture on their actions, approaches, values, and beliefs is significant. However, culture has a pervasive presence in virtually all aspects of one's life to the extent that it may become indiscernible or obscure. Readers are referred to several helpful reflective tools to assess and enhance this personal cultural exploration (Christenson & Sheridan, 2001; Lynch & Hanson, 1998).

The importance of approaching work with diverse families in a culturally sensitive manner is demonstrated through the concept of "culture specificity" (Nastasi et al., 2004). A consultant who is attentive to this concept seeks to individualize intervention processes to ensure that they are culturally relevant for participants. The consultant may be sensitive to the language, values, and beliefs of the participants and address the role culture plays in sustaining newly identified behavioral goals. For example, the consultant can use clear and concrete terms that are free of jargon to ensure consultee understanding or schedule meetings that do not intrude on important family rituals.

A key component in CBC is the inherent sensitivity and responsiveness of the model to the unique and individual needs of all families receiving services. CBC provides an opportunity for consultants to work individually with a family's belief system to provide culturally sensitive services tailored to the family's unique needs. The relational features inherent within CBC provide an excellent context within which consultants can demonstrate cultural sensitivity. For example, the phases of CBC consistently emphasize the individual needs and goals of the family and teachers. This sensitive approach has been identified as the cornerstone of effective cross-cultural consultation (Lynch & Hanson, 1998).

Build Trusting Relationships with the Family

Ideally, consultation occurs in the context of an ongoing relationship (Christenson & Sheridan, 2001), not a one-time interview that may feel unfamiliar and formal to families. Too often, parental contacts with schools occur in response to a problem that has occurred (Thorp, 1997), and decisions regarding students are often made without input from parents. These experiences can lead to feelings of distrust. Although building trusting relationships between families and schools is an important approach for all consultants, it is believed to be especially important when working with diverse families.

Trust is built in the context of a relationship wherein individuals learn about each other. The cultural learning process is ongoing and reciprocal, one in which family members feel that they can share their stories and communicate their experiences, and wherein they perceive that they have opportunities to learn from and with professional(s). It is within this developing relationship that effective communication can occur, and where discussions take on a shared problem-solving focus. The relationship also becomes the mechanism that facilitates the establishment of trust between the consultant and consultees, as well as between the parent and teacher(s).

Specific practices utilized by the CBC consultant to build trusting relationships include devoting time to get to know the family and learn about their culture and unique needs, and providing follow-up after the initial phases of consultation has ended. The multiple phases of the CBC process enhance the opportunity for ongoing support as the structured nature of on-going contact is developed into the model.

Address Diversity Issues

The importance of using a culture-specific approach that actively recognizes and addresses diversity issues when working with diverse families cannot be overstated. In a study on consultant practices in cross-cultural consultation, Rogers (1998) found that the attentiveness and responsiveness of the consultant to racial issues brought up during consultation was the most important determinant for ratings of consultant effectiveness and multicultural sensitivity. Specifically, consultants that directly addressed culture and diversity issues demonstrated more positive outcomes when compared with consultants that approached consultation with a culture-free (e.g., race-sensitive issues were not addressed) approach.

Strategies directed to diversity issues include making home visits; speaking in the family's language or ensuring that an interpreter is present to aid communication; and demonstrating respect for the parents' cultural style, gender roles, and values (Tarver Behring et al., 2000). Additionally, the consultant can also analyze learning tasks to find competencies that overlap across cultures and remain alert to atypical developmental vulnerabilities that may be unrelated to culture (Sheridan, 2000).

As CBC allows for increased communication and opportunities to build meaningful relationships with diverse families, it is important for the consultant to make every effort to learn directly from the families themselves, rather than relying on other resources that may provide information about a certain cultural group. However, sometimes language and other factors present real or perceived barriers. In these instances, it may be useful to use a *cultural guide* (Lynch & Hanson, 1998; Thorp, 1997). A cultural guide is someone from the culture who can act as a mediator and translator and can help the consultant to better understand families from a particular culture. It must be recognized that no individual can completely interpret the cultural experience of another; thus, caution should be exercised not to overemphasize the role a cultural guide can play in understanding a family's needs, values, and goals.

Enhance Communication

The structure of the CBC process provides multiple opportunities for two-way communication between parents and teachers. CBC can serve to improve a parent's understanding of a teacher's expectations, classroom rules, and school norms. In addition, through effective communication, a teacher's knowledge about a family's situational demands, cultural beliefs, and potential to assist in the child's learning may be increased. These opportunities for enhanced communication are especially critical when working with diverse families. Effective cross-cultural communication includes the ability to show respect for diversity issues and to continuously use a shared perspective-taking approach; to remain open, flexible, and maintain a sense of humor; and approach interactions with a desire to learn (Lynch & Hanson, 1998).

Frame of reference is a communication approach that can be applied to consultation in multicultural contexts. Frame of reference refers to the "ways in which a person views the problem at hand; it does not focus on every aspect of the individual's background or characteristics" (Soo-Hoo, 1998, p. 329). For example, a consultant may work with a teacher and Latino/a family to address school refusal concerns with a child. A teacher may interpret certain behaviors, such as canceling scheduled meetings, as the family being uninvolved in their child's education. However, the consultant may learn that meetings have been missed due to work and child-care conflicts. Using this frame of reference, the consultant may help the teacher to understand the priorities of the family culture (e.g., work and family needs vs. single child needs) and help the teacher to reframe the belief that the family is uninvolved to one that acknowledges the efforts the family makes to address basic needs (e.g., food, clothing, housing).

Additional communication strategies include using descriptive and concrete terms to describe the consultation procedures. It is important to avoid the use of technical language that may potentially alienate a family through jargon and hard-to-understand assessment and intervention terminology (e.g., antecedent conditions or data collection techniques). Consultants may consider meeting with family members before consultation meetings to help prepare them for the goals of upcoming meetings. For example, the consultant may bring an outline of what will be covered in the meeting, ask parents to describe what they would like to have accomplished at the meeting, and explore other possible areas of confusion or information sharing. They may spend time explaining terminology such as "identifying strengths within their child," "prioritizing the most important needs they may have for their child," and other commonly used language to assure the family that participating in the consultation process does not imply that there is something wrong with their child.

Additional effective communication strategies that a consultant can use during consultation meetings include using frequent summary statements to check for understanding as well as continuously clarifying questions or issues throughout consultation meetings. The technique of reframing was described in Chapter 3 as an effective way to manage conflicts in the consultation process. Reframing was defined as the re-naming or re-labeling of a consultee's thoughts, feelings, or beliefs about a particular individual, situation, or process to provide an alternate positive frame of reference. The practice of reframing with diverse consultees can help teachers avoid stereotypical bias in interpreting what may be perceived as distancing behaviors of families (e.g., nonparticipation, little communication in meetings, lack of homework support at home). Reframing can also be helpful when describing a child's difficult behaviors by describing how they can be normal within the perspective of the child's culture of origin (Ingraham, 2008).

Significant communication barriers can be present in working with non-English-speaking consultees and it may be necessary to use interpreters to facilitate the communication during consultation. There are several advantages in using interpreters in consultation. Interpreters are generally effective at increasing the clarity of communication between consultation participants and improving access to information by establishing lines of communication between the consultees both during and after meetings. They can be helpful in assisting with establishing rapport and trust among the consultation participants. However, there are inherent challenges that consultants must be aware of when using interpreters to aid communication. First, the use of interpreters may influence the pace of the consultation meetings by increasing the time needed for meetings, as well as the overall process of scheduling meetings with both consultees and interpreters (Lopez, 2000). In addition, difficulties may occur due to lost eye contact, difficulty maintaining open body positions between consultees and interpreters, and disjointed or incomplete information communicated between parties. Training of and frequent dialogue with interpreters often helps ensure that clear and complete information is shared in ways that capture both content and relational aspects of communication (Lopez, 2000).

Implement a "Family-Centered" Approach

Relationship-building strategies that address the needs of the family, as well as provide supportive services and information in family-requested areas of need, are key elements in culturally sensitive CBC. Many of these strategies are related to principles and practices of family-centered services that operate on the goals "to promote positive child, parent, and family functioning and increase the likelihood that family members will become self-sustaining in addressing their needs over time" (Sheridan, Eagle, & Dowd, 2005, p. 171). For example, FCS assumes that families are in the best position to identify their most important needs, and prioritizes existing family strengths and capabilities to mobilize family resources. This issue is especially important when working with diverse families, as the process can also promote engagement, self-determination, and skill development (Sheridan, Warnes, et al., 2004).

Consultants can use approaches that facilitate parent's interest, involvement, and ownership in the consultation process. The interpersonal strategy of listening to and responding to the parent's identified needs will aid the consultant in assisting the family to determine those needs that are most essential for attaining short- and long-term goals. The consultant can also use open-ended questioning strategies that allow parents' ideas to be brought into the process readily. In addition, asking parents about their goals, desires, and concerns is a way to incorporate their ideas into the process. Consultants can be responsive to the priorities of the family and base interventions on these family-identified needs. As such, CBC provides an on-going process that provides multiple opportunities to assess progress, identifies need for change, and remains focused on consultee goals for the child.

Summary

CBC is a model of consultation that can be implemented to provide culturally sensitive services for diverse children and families. Elements inherent within the CBC model, including recognizing family strengths and individual needs and developing a shared commitment to the child's success across settings, are consistent with those strategies recommended for culturally sensitive services. Specifically, CBC is a model of service delivery that facilitates communication across settings, fosters trust and mutual awareness, and provides the opportunity for family strengths to be acknowledged and integrated into the intervention plan. Although structural components inherent within the CBC model are poised to address the needs of diverse children and families, the consultant can enhance culturally sensitive services by using the strategies mentioned here to build relationships across culturally distinct systems. A case study is presented later to illustrate how the CBC process and relationship-building strategies can be used with a diverse child and family.

Case Study: Donny

Donny was a 4-year-old, Chinese male attending Head Start at a Midwestern public elementary school. He lived with his biological father and mother, Mr. Hong and Ms. Hong, and did not have any siblings. Donny and his family had lived in the USA for 2 years. Mandarin Chinese was the family's first language and English was their second language. Mr. and Ms. Hong attended graduate school at the University of Nebraska-Lincoln. Head Start was Donny's first school experience; however, he previously attended daycare at a University Lab School.

Donny's Head Start teacher, Ms. Hopkins, was a Caucasian female and this was her first teaching experience. She had worked previously as a school counselor for 3 years in a rural Midwestern public elementary school. As a school counselor, Ms. Hopkins participated in about ten consultation cases.

The consultant in this case, Ms. Johnson, was a Caucasian female. The consultant was a first-year doctoral student in school psychology, who had received advanced training in behavioral interventions and completed a structured training program in CBC. The consultant conducted services under the supervision of an advanced doctoral student in school psychology and a university faculty supervisor. This was the consultant's third consultation case. Previously, the consultant worked as an elementary school teacher and an early childhood after-school care teacher for 3 years in a diverse Southern community.

Donny was referred for consultation services by Ms. Hopkins due to concerns with noncompliance and impulsive behavior at school. Mr. and Ms. Hong were initially reluctant to participate in consultation services for fear that Donny would receive a special education label. However, the consultant and Ms. Hopkins both spoke individually with the parents to describe the consultation process in more detail and to address any question and concerns they had regarding consultation services. After Mr. and Ms. Hong understood that consultation services were focused on mutual decision making to address needs across the home and school settings, they agreed participation in CBC would be beneficial for Donny and their family.

In addition to addressing concerns regarding noncompliance and impulsive behavior, the consultant also addressed the partnership between home and school. Although Ms. Hopkins conducted the required Head Start home visits, there were not any consistent strategies to promote meaningful dialogue between the home and school settings. This lack of communication between settings may have contributed to the inconsistent expectations for Donny's behavior between home and school. Before the initial consultation meeting, little had been done to promote shared ownership and joint responsibility for Donny's academic, social, and behavioral outcomes across settings. As a result, goals for this case included strengthening the relationship between home and school, enhancing communication between and across settings, maximizing the opportunities to address needs across settings, enhancing knowledge of child development across settings, and increasing knowledge of salient cultural expectations in the home setting and expectations in the American school system.

Conjoint Needs Identification

Problem-Solving/Content Issues

During the conjoint needs identification interview (CNII), the target behavior was identified, the setting was prioritized, and procedures for valid data collection were discussed. Ms. Hong and Ms. Hopkins attended the meeting in the family's home. The team decided to meet at the family's home as transportation was difficult for Donny's family. A discussion of Donny's likes and strengths demonstrated that he was a very "bright" student who excelled in the areas of counting and sorting. Ms. Hopkins also reported that he learned new tasks very easily. The team reported that Donny enjoyed playing with blocks and cars and that he seemed to enjoy working with peers. Both Ms. Hong and Ms. Hopkins stated that their goal for Donny would be for him to listen and follow their directions. Ms. Hong also stated that she would like him to learn more Chinese words.

The team also discussed several areas that were impeding Donny's ability to perform to his full potential. At home, Ms. Hong noted that when a direction is given, Donny acts like he does not hear the request and continues to do what he is currently doing. For example, she reported that when it is time for Chinese lessons, Donny will frequently find another activity to do (e.g., getting into the cupboards, playing with toys). Ms. Hong also shared concerns about Donny learning Chinese words. She reported that they have nightly lessons and that she wanted Donny to learn more words and be able to focus on the activity for at least 10 minutes every night. Ms. Hong and Ms. Hopkins shared concerns regarding Donny's refusal to follow directions and complete tasks. Ms. Hopkins reported that when a direction is given, Donny does not acknowledge the request and frequently "goes the opposite direction or looks the other way." Ms. Hong reported that she usually needs to ask him several times before he completes a task or she needs to help him do it and that this can be "embarrassing" for her and Donny's father. Ms. Hong reported that it is important to her family that Donny "minds her" and "shows respect."

The team determined that their priority for Donny at both home and school was to comply with their requests, as it was a behavior that was valued by both the home and school cultures. Compliance was defined as: "a verbal direction is given and Donny will complete the given task within two requests." Ms. Hopkins targeted the last hour of the morning (11:00 AM to 12:00 PM), whereas Ms. Hong prioritized the time after dinner until bedtime (7:30 PM to 9:00 PM). Ms. Hong selected this time because it was when Chinese language lessons were given and the bedtime routine was completed, two activities she identified as challenging for Donny. Event recording was used to collect information on Donny's rate of compliance across settings. Donny's teacher and parents recorded a tally mark each time he complied with a request and a separate tally mark each time he did not comply with a request during the observational period, thus computing the rate of compliance. Observations were recorded for approximately 1 week, during which the consultant remained in close contact with Ms. Hong and Ms. Hopkins to address any questions or concerns about gathering information on Donny's rate of compliance.

Process Goals and Issues

At the beginning of the consultation process, it was evident that there were different expectations for behavior at home and at school. This was Donny's first school experience and his parent's first experience with the American school system. Additionally, this was his teacher's first teaching experience and opportunity to work with diverse families. The consultant made an effort to talk with other Chinese families in the area to gather more information about the Chinese culture to be sensitive to the family's needs. For example, before the first consultation meeting Ms. Hopkins expressed initial concerns with the fact that Donny slept with his parents. The consultant learned that this was typical for Chinese families with young children and shared this information with Ms. Hopkins.

The consultant also encouraged dialogue between home and school about child development and behavioral expectations across settings. For example, Ms. Hong expressed concern about Donny's abilities to speak English with peers and to learn the Chinese letters at home. Ms. Hopkins shared information about Donny's peer relationships and the team agreed to target the time period when Donny had Chinese lessons to enhance compliance and language outcomes. The consultant also explicitly pointed out similarities between home and school in regard to shared observations and goals. Efforts were also made to emphasize the unique expertise of each team member and the important contributions that they make to Donny's success across environments. Consultation meetings occurred within the family's home to provide a convenient and safe environment for the family to engage in consultation services. Additionally, the consultant used specific strategies to decrease any misunderstandings that could have arisen from the language barrier and differing expectations about consultation procedures. For example, the consultant avoided jargon, used descriptive and concrete terms to describe consultation procedures, provided frequent summary statements to check for understanding, and clarified questions or problems that arose.

Conjoint Needs Analysis

Problem-Solving/Content Issues

The conjoint needs analysis interview (CNAI) meeting was conducted 1 week after the CNII to review observations of Donny's behavior regarding compliance, discuss the various factors related to Donny's compliance, establish a behavioral goal, and collaboratively develop an intervention plan. At home, Ms. Hong reported that Donny complied with an average of 30% of requests. She stated that Donny usually continued to do whatever activity he was currently participating in and that she often felt embarrassed that her son would not listen to her. At school, Ms. Hopkins reported that Donny complied with an average of 40% of requests. Based on these baseline observations, the team decided a behavioral goal for Donny would be to comply with 70% of adult verbal requests during the prioritized time period.

Through a functional assessment of Donny's behaviors at home and school, attention seeking was identified as the primary function of his noncompliance. For example, when Donny refused to clean up toys, the teacher walked around the classroom with Donny finding toys for him to clean up. Additionally, at home when Donny refused to wash his hands his parents helped him to complete this task. Observations indicated that Donny eagerly complied with requests when he was provided with additional support and attention. Based on this analysis, intervention procedures were developed to increase the frequency of Donny's compliance across settings.

The intervention included four components to address noncompliant behavior including: (a) precision commands, (b) positive reinforcement, (c) preplanned consequence, and (d) home–school communication. The *Sure I Will Program* (Rhode, Jenson, & Reavis, 1992) was used to deliver the precision request sequence and increase the frequency of Donny's compliance. Precision requests involved the use of commands in a sequenced order and included consistent positive praise and consequences. The precision request sequence provided a consistent environment for Donny, wherein it was expected that he would learn the expectation to complete the original request. Based on the information gleaned through direct observations and behavioral interviews, it was hypothesized that the function of Donny's noncompliance was attention. Therefore, a high frequency of positive reinforcement would be effective in increasing Donny's compliance. Donny's intervention plan included both specific praise and tangible rewards. Specific praise was provided when Donny complied with a request, such as "Donny, you did a great job at putting all of the blocks away!" Positive reinforcement was also provided in the form of positive attention at home (e.g., baking, playing games, and reading stories) and tangibles at school (e.g., stickers, small cars, and pencils), which were both identified by Donny's teacher and parents as reinforcers that motivated him. The use of the precision request sequence requires the use of a preplanned consequence. Time out from attention was selected as a preplanned consequence by Donny's parents and teacher. It was used consistently when Donny failed to comply with the adult directive within two requests. A home–school note was used as a method to strengthen the home–school partnership and provided a system to monitor compliance at school for delivery of reinforcers at home. Ms. Hopkins sent home a "great job" note each day that Donny successfully met the established goal at school and his parents rewarded him with praise for his positive behavior.

Process Goals and Issues

The goals during the CNAI stage of this process were to build the partnership between the consultees and to enhance knowledge of expectations across home and school. The consultant used language to promote the partnership, such as we, our, and together. Equal participation among consultees was also encouraged throughout the process by communicating that everyone's input and perspectives were vital to increasing compliance across settings. For example, the consultant checked in with Ms. Hong to see if she agreed or supported the expectations at school. When there was a difference of perspectives, the team worked together to share more information and make mutual decisions. This was a critical component of building the partnership since the family often did not understand the expectations of American schools and the school was not always knowledgeable of the family's cultural expectations. For example, there were differences in perspectives about the type of reinforcement across the home and school settings. Ms. Hong reported that she preferred to do activities with Donny when he earned the reward and Ms. Hopkins reported that it would be difficult to do this consistently at school. The team agreed to consistently use praise across settings and to use different reinforcers (e.g., tangibles at school and positive attention at home) across settings. Providing opportunities for information sharing enhanced communication and knowledge among individuals in the home and school environments. The consultant also looked for opportunities to build on the strengths of the family, child, and school. For example, the reinforcement component of the plan was tailored to the family's strengths by increasing family time (e.g., baking, games, and reading) and using community resources for larger reward (e.g., visiting the library or the University recreation center).

Plan Implementation

Problem-Solving/Content Issues

The consultant continued on-going contact with Donny's teacher and mother throughout the 4 weeks of implementation to address treatment fidelity and any issues regarding the intervention plan. Mr. and Ms. Hong and Ms. Hopkins also communicated regularly about progress through the home–school communication folder. In addition, the consultant met individually with Donny's teacher and mother to provide training and review the steps of the intervention procedures. Donny's mother and teacher continued to collect behavioral observations of Donny's compliance with adult verbal requests. Ms. Hong and Ms. Hopkins also recorded their fidelity with the intervention procedures by completing a daily checklist of intervention procedures. They also completed a goal attainment scale at the end of each week to report their perceptions of Donny's progress toward the team's consultation goal. The consultant collected the observations and treatment integrity forms on a regular basis to monitor Donny's progress and to do problem solving as necessary with Ms. Hong and Ms. Hopkins. During the implementation stage, alterations to the plan were made as needed. For example, at school Donny met his goal after the first week of treatment implementation during the targeted time period (i.e., 11:00 AM to 12:00 PM); thus, Ms. Hopkins generalized the intervention procedures to the time period between 10:00 AM and 11:00 AM. At home, Ms. Hong expressed that it was difficult for her to play with Donny. The consultant worked with Ms. Hong through modeling and coaching of play strategies to help her feel more confident about her ability to play with Donny.

Process Goals and Issues

One of the process goals during this stage was to reinforce the consultees' strengths and collaboration between home and school. The consultant encouraged home and school communication about progress through a home–school folder that moved between environments daily. It provided an opportunity for Ms. Hong and Ms. Hopkins to share observations about Donny's progress and to celebrate Donny's success. The consultant also made an effort to reinforce the partnership between home and school by emphasizing how their efforts are helping Donny by creating consistent behavioral expectations across settings.

Conjoint Plan Evaluation

Problem-Solving/Content Issues

The final stage of CBC was conducted through the conjoint plan evaluation interview (CPEI). During these interviews, the consultation team examined the behavioral observations, discussed plans for modification of the intervention procedures, and determined whether the goals of consultation had been met. A total of two conjoint treatment plan interviews were conducted with the consultation team to evaluate Donny's progress. During the first CPEI, Ms. Hong and Ms. Hopkins reported that Donny struggled to comply with requests when it was time to clean up toys. The team agreed to modify the intervention procedures to include breaking up requests into small steps and providing Donny with choices (e.g., "Donny you can clean up the blocks or the cars"). Donny's teacher and parents continued with each type of toy (or area) until all of the toys were cleaned up. Additionally, group contingencies were implemented to promote compliance and to provide more structure during clean up at school. The "mystery motivator" system (Rhode et al., 1992) was used to deliver group reinforcers for compliance during clean up time. The "freeze game" was implemented to increase motivation for cleaning up and to provide more structure in the classroom environment. The students "froze" (i.e., stopped moving) when the lights were shut off and instructions to begin cleaning up were provided. When all of the students were finished cleaning, they reconvened on the large carpet to unveil the mystery motivator (e.g., a song, quick game, five extra minutes of recess, or a sticker). The modified plan was continued for an additional 3 weeks (phase 2 of intervention).

During the second CPEI, Ms. Hopkins reported that she had changed the reward system at school. Many students expressed interest in the program, so the activities were generalized to the entire class via a class-wide behavioral chart. She reported that Donny had earned a sticker on the behavioral chart every day with the exception of one. Ms. Hong noted that Donny had several exceptional days when he complied with 75–80% of requests at home. She reported "doing special activities with Donny" on these days (e.g., going for a walk, visiting his father at work) and that as a result he was more willing to comply with requests.

Donny's behavioral data are presented in Figures 4.1 and 4.2. Review of the behavioral observations indicated that the percentage of compliance increased from treatment phase 1 at home and remained stable at school (average percentage for phase 1 at home = 57.8 and phase 2 = 68.4 and at school phase 1 = 89.7 and phase 2 = 89.6). Behavioral observations revealed an overall effect size of 7.38 at school and 2.44 at home, based on a "no assumptions approach" for determining effect sizes (Busk & Serlin, 1992). The team agreed that Donny had been successful with the current treatment plan and had "fully" met the goal. The team decided to keep the current plan in place for Donny, as it was determined that the structure and positive reinforcement assisted Donny to be successful at increasing the number of tasks he completed. Ms. Hong reported that she felt like her relationship was better with Donny because he listened to her better and there was less conflict. Ms. Hopkins stated that she felt that all of the children in the classroom benefited from this because she developed a more consistent system of communicating expectations to the class. Continued communication regarding Donny's progress occurred via home visits,

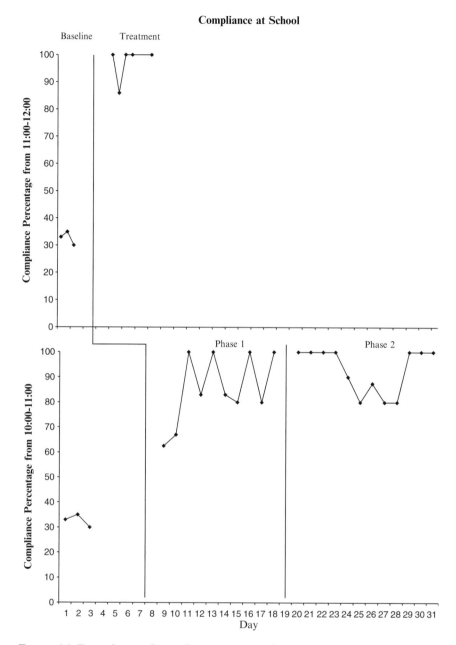

FIGURE 4.1. Donny's rate of compliance across two time periods at school across baseline and treatment conditions.

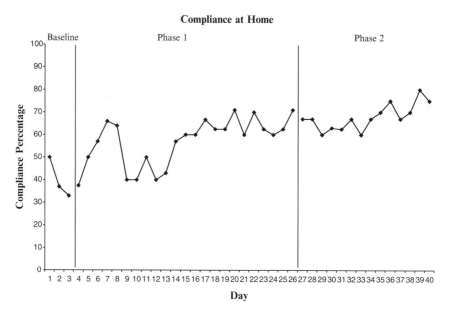

FIGURE 4.2. Donny's rate of compliance at home across baseline and treatment conditions.

classroom visits, and daily home–school notes. The consultant continued to remain in contact with the family and school through classroom visits and telephone calls.

Teacher and parent acceptability of CBC was assessed with the *BIRS* and the *CEF*. In general, Donny's teacher and parents reported that the procedures were very acceptable. Mean item ratings of 6.0 and 4.67 were achieved on the *BIRS* Acceptability factor for teacher and parent scales, respectively (possible score = 1–6, with 6 denoting high acceptability), indicating positive acceptability with the consultation process. Additionally, respective teacher and parent ratings of 7.00 and 6.06 on the *CEF* satisfaction scale (possible score = 1–7, with 7 denoting high satisfaction) indicate positive levels of satisfaction with the CBC consultant. Donny's teacher and parents also reported positive perceptions of goal attainment.

Perceptions of efficacy of CBC were rated with the *BIRS* Effectiveness factor and goal attainment scaling (*GAS*). The *BIRS* Effectiveness factor indicates positive perceptions of treatment outcomes. On the *BIRS* Effectiveness factor, Donny's teacher rated the CBC process as 5.71, and his parents rated the process as 5.14 (possible score 1–6, with 6 denoting high effectiveness). These suggest high levels of perceived effectiveness. On the *GAS*, the parent rating of 4.0 and teacher rating of 5.0 (on a scale of 1–5, with 5 denoting goal fully met) indicate a perception that the consultation goal was mostly or completely met.

Process Goals and Issues

The results of the present case study demonstrate positive effects of CBC with a culturally diverse student and family. This partnership was facilitated through the process goals inherent within the CBC process. The consultant strove to identify and build upon the strengths of Donny, his family, and teacher, as well as encouraging all participants to share information and ideas that were critical to successful child outcomes. The consultant acknowledged differences in perspectives and looked for opportunities to encourage meaningful dialogue around differences to promote greater awareness of home and school environments. Problems were also reframed as new opportunities to improve skills across environments. For example, the target behavior of compliance was selected to improve consistency between environments and to promote Donny's active engagement in learning at both home and school.

CBC was also thought to strengthen relationships among the key systems in Donny's education (home and school). After termination of consultation services, efforts were made to encourage communication and continued collaboration via the home–school communication note, parent visits to the classroom to volunteer and observe, and teacher home visits. Donny's parents and teacher developed a successful partnership as they worked conjointly to develop an intervention plan and communication system to address Donny's compliance across both home and school. Ms. Hong reported that she appreciated Ms. Hopkins taking the time to get to know her family and asking about her goals for Donny. Ms. Hopkins stated that she noticed changes in Donny's behavior and peer relationships because they were able to set similar expectations at home and school. Donny's parents continued to be involved and to support his learning at both home and school after consultation services terminated and Donny's teacher continued to be a source of support and resources to Donny's family.

Summary

This chapter provided a context for how structural components inherent within the CBC model provide a framework for working with children and families from diverse backgrounds. Schools are prominent systems in the lives of diverse families. They provide the setting, context, and experiences that can enable children to develop the skills necessary to function within society. However, differences between mainstream school values and expectations and those of families of diverse cultural backgrounds have been identified as challenges to positive child outcomes. The case study presented illustrates that a strength-based partnership-centered approach to service delivery facilitates positive outcomes for a child and family of a diverse cultural background. Specifically, CBC facilitates communication across settings, fosters trust and mutual awareness, and provides the opportunity for family strengths to be acknowledged and integrated into the intervention plan. Furthermore, preliminary research suggests that positive behavioral outcomes are obtained through CBC services regardless of the number and presence of diversity factors (Sheridan et al., 2006b). These results suggest that the CBC process can provide meaningful outcomes for families from diverse backgrounds to enhance positive school outcomes for children.

5
Conjoint Behavioral Consultation in Unique Practice Contexts

Jennifer D. Burt, Brandy L. Clarke, Shannon Dowd-Eagle, and Susan M. Sheridan

Traditional descriptions of conjoint behavioral consultation (CBC) have presented the model as one that is particularly relevant and effective in school settings, primarily with teacher and parent consultees and student clients. Whereas historical writings have not necessarily constricted the practice of CBC in this way, school settings (most typically elementary schools) and individualized services (focusing on one classroom teacher and parent working with one child client) have been the typical settings for CBC service delivery. Recently, the model has been expanded to novel settings, with demonstrations of its utility in various implementation contexts. In the later sections, we describe the unique circumstances surrounding CBC service delivery in the context of school-based teams (including pre-referral teams), Head Start, and pediatric medical settings. These settings are not exhaustive; that is, many other unique contexts and delivery mechanisms may be possible for CBC implementation. However, they represent a sample of settings where evidence on the usefulness and effectiveness of CBC has been demonstrated. Issues in each of these contexts and recommendations for practice are presented. Additionally, actual case studies are described to illustrate the manner in which CBC goals and objectives were met (including those related to case-related content and relational aspects of CBC) in each setting.

Conjoint Behavioral Consultation in a Teaming Context

Federal and state laws such as No Child Left Behind (NCLB) and the Individuals with Disabilities Education Act (IDEA; 1997) mandate that schools must be accountable for meeting the needs of all students, including those who are considered difficult to teach. Furthermore, those needs must be met within the least restrictive environment. Recent policy reforms such as the IDEA (U.S. Congress, 1999), and the NCLB (2002) highlight the importance of providing opportunities for parents to become meaningful partners in their children's education. Taking responsibility for student success has become increasingly difficult as the number of students that need educational support continues to rise.

The number of students aged 6–21 served under Part B of IDEA for severe emotional disturbance increased by 21.4% between 1989 and 1990 and 1998 and 1999. Likewise, the percentage of those students served within regular education classrooms has also continually increased (U.S. Department of Education 23rd Annual Report to Congress, 2001). Team-based service models have been implemented in many schools to support general education teachers in efforts to meet the growing and changing needs of students. Although in practice CBC has welcomed additional family members and school personnel beyond the parent–teacher–consultant triad, the model has not traditionally been implemented within a problem-solving teaming context. Thus, expanding CBC principles to a team-based format used for educational programming is a timely and innovative application of the model.

The application of CBC principles within a teaming framework provides numerous benefits. First, the emphasis on bidirectional communication within a larger team configuration allows for multiple diverse perspectives to be discussed. By encouraging active dialogue among all members, the team will have a greater understanding of the child's strengths and areas of need. Second, this approach to consultation and teaming allows for a more comprehensive understanding of the child's environment. Third, the inclusion of additional key stakeholders possessing different areas of expertise increases the likelihood of developing an effective treatment plan. Finally, CBC provides a framework for joining schools and families together and fostering partnerships that will maximize the child's success at home and school.

Team Format

Implementing CBC as a school-based teaming approach involves broadening the scope of the model in terms of goals and structure. Consistent with the general objectives associated with CBC, a strong emphasis is placed on both behavioral and relational goals (i.e., bridging the gap between schools and families through the formation of meaningful partnerships, and maximizing positive treatment gains across multiple systems). An additional consideration when working within the context of problem-solving teams centers on referral and placement rates. Thus, when working in this milieu, objectives may be expanded to include reducing inappropriate referrals for special education assessment and placement.

Moving beyond the traditional triad to involve additional key stakeholders is another unique variation of the model. When applying CBC in this manner, the selection of appropriate team members is critical. It is important to ensure that a welcoming environment for the family is not compromised by the larger team format. Consultants should strive to find a balance between including additional school personnel with expertise and knowledge about the child, yet at the same time not overwhelming the family. Although there is no magic number to reach when inviting other professionals to partner with the family, limiting the team to members who can share a unique perspective on the child is encouraged. Some examples include a school social worker, reading specialist, after-school day-care supervisor, or nurse.

Team-Based Relationship Building

Throughout this book, an emphasis has been placed on fostering partnerships between schools and families. Building relationships can be both challenging and time-intensive. These efforts are even more apparent when using a team-based approach. The inclusion of additional stakeholders results in greater diversity in belief systems, perspectives of the concern, and expectations for the child. The degree to which diverse opinions can strengthen the problem-solving process is linked to the environment in which they are shared. Therefore, it is critical to create a positive and nonjudgmental atmosphere.

The first step in team-based relationship building is setting the stage for effective collaboration. All too often, initial communications between schools and families have a negative connotation or problem–crisis orientation. To overcome initial resistance, teams must encourage positive interactions before the first meeting. Good news phone calls and discussions detailing the child's strengths go a long way toward laying the foundation for future partnering. Likewise, flexibility is another key element when working with families in team-based problem solving and decision making. Work obligations and hectic schedules can pose difficulties in finding times for groups of school personnel and parents to come together. To the greatest extent possible, school personnel should try to provide families with multiple dates and times that would be conducive for meetings. In addition, it is helpful to provide advanced notice when scheduling the meetings. Another consideration pertains to the room arrangement. Entering a room with multiple staff members can be a daunting task for parents. Positioning team members with familiar staff seated close to the family may make the room more inviting.

Once the stage has been set, strategies for continued partnership may be used. One important strategy is conveying a commitment to meaningful family involvement. This commitment is communicated through words and actions. For example, families are not just invited to attend meetings, but are encouraged to actively participate in the problem-solving process. A distinctive feature of CBC in this context is that educators and parents engage in joint information gathering and intervention planning. Families help identify the function of the concern by identifying common triggers and consequences of the behavior as they experience them in the home setting. Likewise, parents may take on the role of treatment agent by implementing plan components at home. Importantly, active involvement will be unique to each family depending upon their circumstances and family situations. Some families may have the capacity and resources (e.g., personal, material, time) to implement interventions in their entirety; others may adopt much less active roles related to plan implementation. The application of CBC principles and these partnership-building strategies within a teaming context is best illustrated through a case study.

Case Study: John

This case study took place in an elementary school serving approximately 300 students ranging from kindergarten to fifth grade. The socioeconomic status of families in the school community was considered low to middle class. Before the start of the case, school staff received training in the team-based CBC model through a series of in-services. To establish an infrastructure for continued teamwork and to build capacity of team members, a university graduate student provided on-site support and feedback regarding CBC content and process objectives.

The child in this case was "John," a 7-year-old boy referred to the team by his second-grade teacher, Ms. Evans, for temper tantrums and underachievement in the area of reading. John was an only child who lived with his mother, Ms. Sherman. John's mother had worked closely with her son's first-grade teacher the previous year due to similar academic and behavioral concerns. To support John in improving his performance at home and school, a CBC pre-referral team consisting of John's mother, his first and second-grade teachers, the special education coordinator–team leader, the school psychologist, and the school psychology graduate student was assembled.

Ms. Sherman was a single parent who reported feeling overwhelmed by her son's challenging behavior. In addition, she had received special education services as a child and reported being hesitant about having her son involved in the process. Considering Ms. Sherman's perspective, the school identified several partnership goals which included (a) providing a welcoming environment so John's mother would be comfortable attending the meeting, (b) offering additional information about the pre-referral and special education evaluation processes, and (c) continuing to build a relationship between Ms. Sherman and school personnel.

Needs Identification Phase

The needs identification phase was initiated to (a) prioritize and define the area of need in behavioral terms, (b) explore and identify factors influencing John's behavior, (c) determine a straightforward method for gathering baseline information, (d) establish a welcoming environment for problem solving, and (e) provide an avenue for give-and-take communication between home and school. The first opportunities for teaming occurred during the "invitation" phone call and the conjoint needs identification interview (CNII), which lasted approximately 1 hour.

The special education coordinator contacted John's mother and invited her to attend a team meeting. At the time of the initial call, the coordinator indicated that John had made a great deal of progress during the previous academic year, highlighting the efforts of both John's mother and first-grade teacher. She further indicated that the school wanted to ensure that the positive changes continued during the second-grade year. John's mother shared that she had been having some difficulty at home with her son and was willing to attend the meeting. However, she also expressed some reservations about the process and did not want her son to be labeled in the special education system. The coordinator provided additional information regarding the purposes of the team-based problem-solving process and emphasized that special education eligibility was not a goal of these meetings. John's mother and the coordinator then jointly identified a convenient time to convene the team.

Content Issues

During the CNII, team members described John as a friendly student, who had several positive relationships with his classmates, had a desire to please adults, and was creative. Ms. Sherman also shared that her son had difficulty managing his anger, especially during homework time. She stated that when he became frustrated he would have brief fits consisting of yelling, screaming, and verbal defiance. Ms. Evans' concerns mirrored those described by Ms. Sherman, so together the team decided to focus on reducing the frequency of tantrums at home and school. John's mother and teacher agreed to record each time a tantrum occurred by placing a tally mark on a data sheet. To help identify patterns, they also agreed to note the time of day the tantrum occurred.

Process Goals and Issues

In addition to addressing some child-focused outcome goals, the team leader also attended to several relational objectives. To create a welcoming environment, the team member who had the strongest relationship with Ms. Sherman, his teacher from the previous year, was the first to greet Ms. Sherman. The first-grade teacher proceeded to escort Ms. Sherman to the meeting location and introduced her to the other team members. The room was arranged in a circular fashion to appear less overwhelming. Due to the concerns Ms. Sherman voiced during the initial phone call, the team leader wanted to provide another explanation of the teaming process. However, she did not want to single out Ms. Sherman during the explanation, so she provided every team member with a district brochure that described the pre-referral process and respective roles of each participant. She reviewed the goals of the team and process in lay language and allowed an opportunity for questions. Finally, to begin on a positive note, the consultant opened the meeting with a discussion of John's strengths and interests.

Needs Analysis Phase

A conjoint needs analysis interview (CNAI) meeting was scheduled to (a) review the information collected by John's mother and teacher, (b) discuss factors affecting John's behavior, (c) collaboratively develop a treatment plan,

(d) develop a shared understanding of the concerns, and (e) promote dual ownership in the problem-solving process. As with the previous meeting, team members jointly determined a convenient time for all parties to come together again.

Content Issues

During the CNAI meeting, John's teacher shared that John engaged in an average of three tantrums per day, with a range of 2–5. At home, he averaged one tantrum per day with a range of 0–2. Team members discussed several factors influencing John's behavior including being tired, not getting his way, or a request to start an undesired task, typically homework or his bedtime routine. Team members also noted that transitions and unstructured times negatively affected John's behavior. When John engaged in a tantrum at school he was usually sent to the principal's office; at home, he was sent to his room. Ms. Evans reported that the instructional level matched John's skill level, but that many academic tasks were still challenging for him to complete. It was hypothesized that John was trying to avoid undesired tasks. When developing the plan, the team wanted to adopt a positive orientation and decided to emphasize skill building so John was better able to cope with difficult situations. The intervention consisted of (a) anger management skill instruction conducted by the school psychologist, (b) teacher–mother prompting use of the skills, (c) controlled choices (i.e., order of assigned tasks), and (d) reward for goal attainment. In addition, Ms. Sherman provided extra structure to the evening routine in the form of a written checklist.

Process Goals and Issues

An important goal during the needs analysis phase was continuing to develop constructive partnerships across home and school. By creating an atmosphere in which all parties could share their perspectives, team members realized that they were witnessing similar behavior in both contexts, which helped to develop a shared understanding of the concern. After the meeting, the consultant validated Ms. Evans' efforts and pointed out that Ms. Sherman's regular attendance and involvement during the process demonstrated her investment. A similar comment was directed toward Ms. Sherman via a follow-up phone call. Emphasizing individual team members' contributions to the process was another strategy used to foster relationship building.

Plan Implementation Phase

Content Issues

Although there was not a formal meeting during this phase, the consultant maintained contact with all team participants to (a) assess treatment integrity, (b) evaluate the integrity of the problem-solving process, and (c) provide guidance and support to the consultees. During this phase, Ms. Sherman and Ms. Evans continued to observe and record the frequency of John's tantrumming behavior at home and school. Self-Report Treatment Plan Worksheets were used to assess integrity. The forms, which provided a detailed summary of the intervention including the specific steps of the plan, were completed by the consultees on a daily basis. John's mother and teacher reported that the plan was working well and fit into the home and school routine.

Process Goals and Issues

During this phase, the consultant continued to cultivate home–school connections by offering on-going support and guidance. Regular check-ins via phone and e-mail presented opportunities to review plan progress, address questions, and provide immediate troubleshooting. In addition, it gave the team leader a chance to highlight John's behavioral improvement and validate the team members' efforts and role in his success.

Conjoint Plan Evaluation

Content Issues

After approximately 4 weeks, a conjoint plan evaluation interview (CPEI) meeting was scheduled to (a) review behavioral observations provided by John's mother and teacher, (b) discuss the effectiveness of the plan, (c) determine the need for plan modifications or generalization procedures, (d) validate team members' joint efforts in supporting John, and (e) identify avenues for continued home–school communication.

Data on John's tantrumming behaviors were reviewed at the CPEI. The frequency across baseline and treatment phases at school and home are depicted in Figures 5.1 and 5.2. At home, Ms. Sherman noticed immediate improvement in her son's tantrumming behavior. She reported that John was using his anger management skills and displayed only 4 outbursts during the last 10-day period, reducing his average from 1 to 0.4 tantrums per day (range = 0–2, effect size = 0.74). She further reported that John was becoming a more independent problem-solver and required fewer prompts to use his coping skills. Due to a hectic schedule at home, Ms. Sherman shared that she had not used the evening checklist during the last few days and subsequently John went to bed later than usual. She attributed his increase in tantrumming behavior at the end of the intervention to the change in evening structure and John's lack of sleep. Recognizing the importance of consistency, John's mother planned to regularly implement the checklist at home.

At school, Ms. Evans reported similar improvements in John's behavior. She stated that the intervention instantly resulted in positive changes and John decreased his tantrums from a baseline average of 3 per day to an average of 0.375 per day (range = 0–2, effect size = 1.86). During the meeting, she also empathized with John's mother regarding hectic home schedules and difficulties

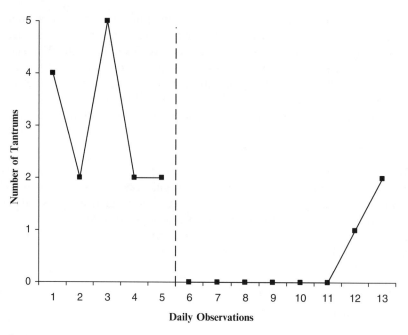

FIGURE 5.1. John's frequency of tantrums at school across baseline and intervention phases.

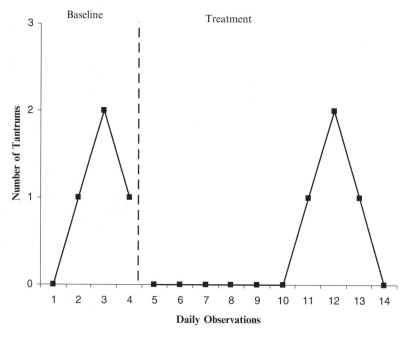

FIGURE 5.2. John's frequency of tantrums at home across baseline and intervention phases.

implementing the intervention in a consistent manner. John's teacher further commented on how helpful it was to know John had gone to bed later than usual, as it was likely affecting his behavior at school as well.

Process Goals and Issues

During the plan evaluation phase, the team leader validated the consultees' contributions by recognizing the time they devoted to implementing the intervention and linking their efforts to John's improved performance. She also hypothesized that John's success was maximized by having the family and school collaborate with one another. The consultant also highlighted some of the benefits associated with regular cross-setting communication, such as knowing in advance the days when John may be tired. At this time, Ms. Evans and Ms. Sherman agreed to use a home–school note to maintain regular contact with one another.

Although Ms. Sherman initially voiced some reservations about the process, she reported being pleased with her son's progress and found working with the team to be very beneficial. Ms. Evans shared similar sentiments and felt confident that John would continue to make progress. In addition to witnessing a reduction in tantrums, she shared that her relationship with John had also improved as a result of the intervention. She felt that she changed the negative interaction cycle consisting of frequent reprimands to a more positive communication pattern filled with skill prompts and verbal praise.

Conjoint Behavioral Consultation in Head Start Settings

A second unique context within which CBC has been implemented in recent years is the Head Start setting. Head Start services are based on the recognition that a child's early educational experiences have a strong influence over the trajectory of their educational career (Alexander & Entwisle, 1988; Entwisle, Alexander, Cadigan, & Pallas, 1986; Husen, 1969; Ladd & Price, 1987; Reynolds, 1991). Parents play an essential role in promoting early academic performance through their valuation of education, enriched home literacy environment, and quality relationships with preschool teachers (Bradley, Caldwell, & Rock, 1988; Hill, 2001). Although early parental involvement is important, it may be even more critical for children who are at risk for school failure because of socioeconomic disadvantage or developmental disabilities.

Head Start is one of several federal programs that recognize the significance of families in providing an important developmental context for young children. Head Start is a comprehensive child development program that serves preschool-aged children who are at risk for school failure because of low income and other risk factors (e.g., developmental disability). The overall goal of the program is to facilitate school readiness for children and families, and it operates within the context of the child's family and his or her community. The Head Start Program Performance Standards (2006) emphasize the need for creating an environment that is receptive to each family throughout its program experience. Specifically, it states goals related to (a) forming relationships with families aimed at improving the quality of family life; (b) helping families identify and use resources; (c) offering families support in carrying out parenting responsibilities; and (d) using strategies for helping families address their concerns, deal with challenges effectively, and achieve their goals. This family partnership agreement process is individualized, strengths-based, family-driven, and staff-supported. Each family determines the direction of its partnership and works with Head Start staff to achieve identified goals. Thus, the family- and partnership-centered philosophy of CBC fits uniquely within the principles of Head Start services.

A variety of mechanisms are available for meaningful parental participation in Head Start, such as classroom volunteering, parent conferences, and home visits. Ideally, approaches that encourage parents to assume a significant role in their young child's learning, and that enhance a parent's competence in actively supporting their child's early developmental goals, are important (Guralnick, 1989). A goal for child-care professionals (including Head Start and Early Head Start teachers, public preschool teachers, and early childhood special educators) is to help parents construct a role that positions them as meaningful, essential partners in their child's learning. Early in a child's formal schooling, the role that parents assume may establish a positive trajectory for ongoing involvement over the course of the child's development. Active, meaningful involvement of parents, in partnership with teachers and early service providers, is critical in the early learning of young children.

Unique challenges associated with risk factors of families participating in Head Start programs (e.g., low income, limited education, changing family constellations) must be taken into account when forming partnerships to ensure a good fit between family needs and services provided. For example, the use of technical jargon sometimes common in consultation and intervention work must be minimized. Several forms of contact (multiple telephone numbers, home and work addresses, phone numbers of extended family members, e-mail addresses) may need to be established as some families change residence, employment, or phone numbers frequently. In addition, several forms of communication (e.g., notes, e-mail, home visits) should be attempted until a consistent and reliable mechanism is identified, and that form should be revisited to ensure that it retains its usefulness. Any written materials must be constructed in a way that family members will understand, attending to language spoken and read by parents, and educational and literacy levels. A good rule of thumb is to present written material at a fifth-grade level or lower.

Relational goals should emphasize the development in parents of a meaningful role and strong self-efficacy to ensure ongoing participation as active partners in their child's learning. Caregiver concerns must be actively solicited and addressed throughout the process and beyond. Specifically, parents must be given an active role to facilitate their child's learning, such as reading at home or reinforcing appropriate school behaviors, and their efforts must be validated as playing an essential (not just desirable; Christenson & Sheridan, 2001) part in their child's success. Future collaboration with the school should be integrated into a generalization plan and parents should receive specific information and training in how to continue to serve as a partner and advocate for their child. For example, parents can initiate contact with their child's teacher at the beginning of each school year to establish a means for communication to share progress or concerns, before problems arise.

In addition, family strengths and resources must be identified and built upon throughout the CBC process in an attempt to provide family-centered services that will maximize the social networks and capabilities of the family. Since Head Start educators are required to conduct home visits, they often have a wealth of knowledge about the family and the resources they have at their disposal. Consultants can directly ask the teachers about positive attributes that they have identified regarding the parent–child relationship, family networks, or available resources (e.g., employment, transportation, federal assistance). Other family service providers, such as family social workers, may also provide information and educate the consultant as to the number of options available to support various families. Additionally, consultants can make direct observations of the family to identify and validate strengths in care-taking capacity, as well as ask families about sources of social support such as extended family or friends. These strengths and resources must then be incorporated into the intervention plans to increase the likelihood of intervention effectiveness and maximize the feasibility of maintaining treatment plans after termination of the consultation process.

The following case study is an illustration of the CBC process with a child and family in a Head Start setting. Important content and process issues are discussed to demonstrate the utility of this approach and specific strategies used to integrate CBC in this unique early childhood context.

Case Study: Allie

Allison, "Allie," was a 4-year-old Caucasian female who attended Head Start in a small Midwestern city. She lived with her biological mother, her adoptive father, and her brothers (ages 3, 7, and 9 years). This was Allie's first school experience. Ms. Granger, Allie's mother, reported that Allie experienced seizures in the past, which may have occurred from neurofibromatosis. Ms. Granger reported that Allie was prescribed Tegratul to decrease the frequency of seizures but that Allie stopped taking the medication approximately 2 months before consultation.

Both Ms. Granger and Ms. Hansen, Allie's teacher, stated that Allie was more alert and active after Tegratul was discontinued. Ms. Granger described Allie's development as normal. She reported that Allie rolled over at approximately 4 months, sat unsupported at 6 months, and walked at 14 months.

Ms. Hansen referred Allie for consultation services because of concerns related to academic progress. Specifically, Ms. Hansen was concerned about Allie's transition to kindergarten because she struggled with school readiness skills, such as recognizing letters, writing her name, and counting. Ms. Hansen approached Ms. Granger about participating in consultation services to enhance school readiness skills during one of the routine Head Start home visits. Ms. Granger reported that she thought Allie "was doing fine in school" but that she would like to support her learning in any way that she could.

Although Ms. Granger and Ms. Hansen communicated easily and appeared to have a respectful relationship, there was limited contact outside of the regularly scheduled home visits and parent–teacher conferences. In this case, it was evident that regular and meaningful bidirectional home–school communication was limited. Ms. Granger expressed an interest in supporting Allie's academic progress but felt unsure about how to help her. The CBC process provided an opportunity for Ms. Granger and Ms. Hansen to share information across settings and to collaborate to develop a shared plan to assist Allie in developing the school readiness skills necessary to improve her transition to elementary school. It also provided a context for the consultant to emphasize the importance of working as a team to help Allie perform to her full potential, as well as to help Ms. Granger understand the positive impact that she could have on Allie's educational success across home and school.

Needs Identification Phase

Content Issues

A CNII was conducted to discuss initial concerns and to identify a target behavior for the consultation process. Ms. Granger and Ms. Hansen both attended the meeting in the family's home. A discussion of Allie's strengths and likes established that Allie enjoyed school, was very willing to learn and try new things, and interacted very positively with her classmates. Ms. Granger and Ms. Hansen also reported that Allie was "very creative" and that she enjoyed dramatic play, art projects, and playing school.

The consultation team shared observations regarding Allie's school readiness skills. Both Ms. Granger and Ms. Hansen reported that Allie could recite the alphabet. Ms. Hansen reported that Allie was able to consistently name the letter "A." She stated that during past assessments Allie was more likely to recognize letters and numbers when provided with choices (e.g., "Is this a B or an H?"). Ms. Granger reported that Allie could count to 20 with assistance and Ms. Hansen reported that Allie was able to count 10 objects unassisted. Based on this information, the team decided to prioritize letter recognition as the target behavior. Ms. Granger and Ms. Hansen assessed Allie's ability to recognize letters with curriculum-based measurement (CBM) lists (Wright, 2006) using a worksheet with all of the uppercase letters in random order (see Figure 5.3). Ms. Granger and Ms. Hansen used a view finder to display one

---

Curriculum-Based Assessment List: Student Copy

Student: _____   Date: _____

Class: _____   Correct Items: _____
                                      Total Items Attempted: _____

S	U	P	M
I	A	Z	N
K	R	D	B
X	H	J	E
T	Y	V	C
W	F	G	O
Q	L	Z	M
W	R	F	S

From: Wright, J. (2006). *Intervention Central.* Available at www.interventioncentral.org
Reprinted with permission.

FIGURE 5.3. Curriculum-based assessment form used for Allie.

letter at a time and provided Allie with 5 sec to name the letter. When the letter was named correctly within 5 sec, it was circled on the evaluation sheet and at the end of the assessment the number of letters correctly identified was totaled. Assessments were conducted twice weekly at home and at school.

Process Goals and Issues

At the beginning of the consultation process, it was evident that Ms. Granger and Ms. Hansen had a friendly and respectful relationship. However, there was an overall lack of consistent and meaningful dialogue between home and school to help Allie achieve positive educational outcomes. Ms. Granger wanted to help Allie become more successful in school but admitted that she struggled in school and that she was quite unsure of how to improve Allie's educational outcomes. Thus, one important relational goal of the consultation process was to enhance Ms. Granger's self-efficacy beliefs regarding helping her daughter to be successful in school. The team agreed to meet at the family's home because it was a convenient and comfortable environment for Allie and her mother. It also helped the team gain more awareness of the natural teaching opportunities available to Allie and her mother within the home environment. The consultant also emphasized the importance of the unique expertise that each participant brought to the process, and reminded the consultees that collaboration and communication across environments were essential for Allie's success. The consultant made sure to explicitly point out the strengths of all team members throughout the process and set up opportunities for Ms. Granger and Ms. Hansen to share information about Allie's strengths across settings.

Needs Analysis Phase

Content Issues

A CNAI was conducted to discuss baseline assessments of letter recognition and to develop an intervention plan to increase the number of letters that Allie recognized. At home, Ms. Granger reported that it was difficult for Allie to complete the assessments. She reported that she conducted one assessment over several short sessions because Allie begged, "No mommy. I don't know them." Ms. Granger stated that during this assessment Allie correctly identified the letters A and P. At school, Ms. Hansen reported that during the first two assessments, Allie correctly identified the letters A and P and that during the third assessment she only identified the letter A. Ms. Granger and Ms. Hansen reported that Allie did not want to do the assessments and became very quiet during and after the assessment. They both reported that she was easily frustrated and often said, "I don't know them." Based on these baseline assessments, Ms. Granger and Ms. Hansen believed a reasonable goal would be for Allie to recognize all of the uppercase letters in her first name (i.e., A L I S O N) by the next consultation meeting in approximately 3 weeks. This goal was selected because the team believed it would be important for Allie to recognize her first name before beginning kindergarten in the fall. Ultimately, they agreed that they would like Allie to be able to write her first name.

Ms. Granger and Ms. Hansen discussed possible reasons why Allie was having difficulty identifying uppercase letters. Both Ms. Granger and Ms. Hansen believed that Allie may be struggling with letter recognition due to side effects from the medication she was prescribed to manage seizures. They described her as "less aware" and "in a haze" on the medication and hypothesized that this may have contributed to her difficulty recognizing letters throughout the school year. Ms. Hansen also hypothesized that Allie struggled to recognize uppercase letters because instructional strategies did not meet Allie's learning needs. For example, Ms. Hansen stated that Allie was a tactile learner and she needed more "hands-on" practice, such as writing letters with sidewalk chalk or gluing beans onto cutouts of uppercase letters. Additionally, both Ms. Granger and Ms. Hansen reported that Allie would benefit from more direct instruction and practice with letter recognition.

Based on the information shared by Ms. Granger and Ms. Hansen, a plan was developed to increase the number of uppercase letters that Allie recognized. The plan included three major components: (a) direct instruction with flashcards, (b) educational games and activities, and (c) a home and school communication folder.

Process Goals and Issues

In addition to goals related to plan development, relational goals for the conjoint needs analysis stage were to continue to build on the strengths of all team members, facilitate meaningful dialogue across settings, and engage in collaborative intervention planning. Ms. Granger and Ms. Hansen reported that Allie was "very creative and artistic" and that she "loved to learn." Additionally, the consultant noted that both Ms. Granger and Ms. Hansen were skilled at setting up creative opportunities to facilitate learning. As a result, intervention planning specifically included one-on-one (parent–child and teacher–child) educational games with direct skill practice. The team generated a list of educational art projects and games that, when implemented, would help Allie to increase the number of letters that she recognized. The consultant explicitly affirmed both Ms. Granger and Ms. Hansen for their knowledge of Allie's learning strengths and for their ability to use natural teaching opportunities to reinforce letter recognition.

Plan Implementation Phase

Content Issues

Ms. Granger and Ms. Hansen were the primary treatment agents. They continued to conduct two CBM assessments per week to monitor Allie's progress in uppercase letter recognition. Ms. Granger and Ms. Hansen also recorded their fidelity with the intervention plan by using treatment integrity checklists and completed a goal attainment scale each week to record their perceptions of Allie's progress toward the consultation goal. The consultant collected the assessments and treatment integrity forms on a regular basis and problem solved with the consultees to address any concerns with the plan. For example, Ms. Hansen reported that she tried to set aside time to practice with Allie during "work time" but that it was often challenging due to distractions within the classroom (e.g., noise level and activities requiring the teacher's attention). The consultant agreed to conduct the flashcard intervention with Allie 1–2 days/week. In addition, Ms. Hansen implemented the intervention with Allie 2 days/week, and the paraeducator worked with Allie the remaining days of the week. Ms. Granger also reported that Allie wanted to practice using all of the flashcards (rather than just the six letters in her name). She agreed to continue practicing all of the flashcards but to focus only on the letters of her name during educational activities (such as alphabet art projects, songs, and games) to ensure maximum exposure to uppercase letters in Allie's full name (i.e., A L I S O N).

Process Goals and Issues

One of the goals during this stage was to reinforce the consultees' strengths and collaboration between home and school. The consultant encouraged home–school communication about progress through a home–school folder that was exchanged daily. It provided an opportunity for Ms. Granger and Ms. Hansen to share observations about Allie's progress and to celebrate Allie's success. Ms. Granger and Ms. Hansen also shared information about additional educational games and art projects to include in the packet. The consultant made an effort to reinforce the partnership between home and school by emphasizing how their efforts were helping Allie gain important school readiness skills that would facilitate a more successful transition to kindergarten.

Plan Evaluation Phase

Content Issues

The team met for a CPEI after approximately 3 weeks of plan implementation. The purpose of this meeting was to discuss Allie's progress toward the consultation goal and to make any necessary modifications to the plan. The number of uppercase letters that Allie recognized had increased from baseline. At home, the number of uppercase letters that Allie recognized increased from 2 letters to 16 letters (see Figure 5.4). At school, she demonstrated an increase from 2 letters to 17 letters known (see Figure 5.5). Ms. Granger reported that Allie was doing "very well" with letter recognition and that her "confidence had increased" since she began working on the letters. Ms. Hansen described Allie as more confident and "willing to take risks and guess" when working on uppercase letter recognition. Both Ms. Granger and Ms. Hansen reported that Allie enjoyed practicing her letters and had begun to approach them when she wanted to practice the letters.

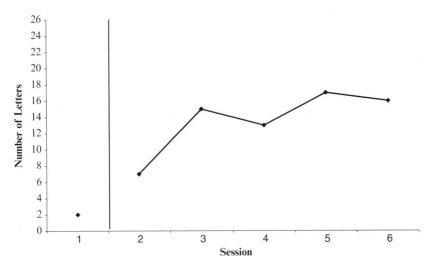

FIGURE 5.4. Allie's letter recognition at home across baseline and intervention phases.

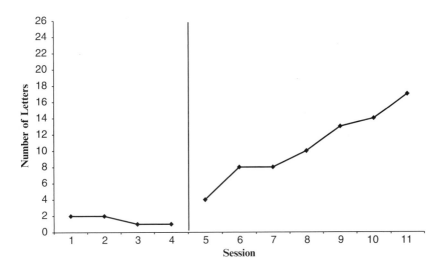

FIGURE 5.5. Allie's letter recognition at school across baseline and intervention phases.

The team agreed that Allie had met and exceeded the goal of learning all six letters in her first name. Both Ms. Granger and Ms. Hansen agreed that the plan was responsible for the changes in Allie's ability to recognize uppercase letters. They believed that the repetition and daily practice were responsible for the increase in the number of uppercase letters that Allie recognized. Additionally, Ms. Granger and Ms. Hansen believed this plan would be effective for other students having difficulty with school readiness skills, such as letter and number recognition. The consultation team agreed that this would be the last formal meeting because it was the last week of school. Ms. Granger agreed to keep the current plan in place for Allie over the summer and continue adding more letters since it was determined that the daily practice was responsible for the improvement in Allie's performance. The team also discussed how Ms. Granger could continue to use the strategies from the plan throughout the summer with other skills such as lowercase letter recognition, number recognition, and letter writing.

Process Goals and Issues

During the CPEI, Ms. Granger reported that she was very happy that she decided to participate in the CBC process. She reported that before the process she believed Allie had the academic skills necessary to start kindergarten; however, at the final meeting she stated that she had learned a lot about how to help all of her children to be more successful in school. Specifically, Ms. Granger reported that she had recently purchased number flashcards and that they were going to work on number recognition throughout the summer. She also stated that she planned to start using multiplication flashcards with her son to help him "get caught up" on his math facts and that Allie had started using the uppercase letter flashcards to teach her younger brother the alphabet. Both Ms. Granger and Ms. Hansen agreed that working together as a team was responsible for Allie's progress in letter recognition. Ms. Hansen stated that she would document the intervention efforts in Allie's cumulative folder so that her kindergarten teacher would be aware of strategies to help Allie be more successful in school. Ms. Granger and Ms. Hansen both believed that Allie was better prepared to start kindergarten as a result of the team effort to help her increase letter recognition. Ms. Granger reported that she felt more confident in helping her daughter at home, and that Allie was more confident and excited about learning.

   This case study illustrates how the CBC model can be integrated successfully into an early childhood (i.e., Head Start) setting. The strategies used by the consultant emphasized building on the strengths of all participants, extending the learning beyond the school setting into everyday situations, and encouraging joint responsibility to foster a collaborative partnership across home and school environments and enhance Allie's educational outcomes as she transitions to kindergarten.

Conjoint Behavioral Consultation in Pediatric Healthcare Systems

A third unique context for implementing CBC is in relation to medical settings. Medical settings are a particularly relevant context given the prevalence of health and academic problems among children with or at risk of health issues; creating a strong need for professionals who can provide an effective interface among the medical, educational, and family systems. Approximately 20% of children and adolescents are afflicted with a mental health disorder (National Institute of Mental Health, 2005); 22% suffer from obesity (Troiano, Flegal, Kuczmarski, Campell, & Johnson, 1995); and another 10% are diagnosed with asthma (Creer & Bender, 1995). The medical and educational needs of these children often require the involvement of a range of professionals spanning many disciplines (e.g., pediatricians, psychologists, nutritionists, school nurses, special educators, general educators, occupational therapists, speech pathologists, audiologists, and/or neurologists). Unfortunately, services for such students are often disjointed, with little interdisciplinary collaboration across educational, medical, and family systems. Reforms in education emphasize the need for schools to address mental and physical challenges that impede the learning process (Adelman & Taylor, 1998). CBC provides an opportunity to develop effective, interdisciplinary partnerships among schools, families, and health-care providers, thereby addressing the multifaceted needs of children cross multiple systems (Power, DuPaul, Shapiro, & Kazak, 2003).

Collaboration and service coordination are necessary to ensure that providers from diverse and relevant areas of expertise (e.g., education, medicine, psychology) work together to optimize the outcomes for children and families. The multisystemic collaborative approach embodied within CBC presents an ideal framework for building partnerships among families, educators, and medical specialists. Recent research and practice has extended the use of the CBC model into pediatric settings using a collaborative team approach (Sheridan, Warnes, Ellis, Schnoes, & Woods, 2006c). Such an approach involves medical, psychological, and educational experts to assess the multiple needs of children with pediatric concerns and the factors that impact their progress in school (Power et al., 2003), allowing management and modification of treatment plans over time (Shellenberger & Couch, 1984). Communication among a team of clinical and educational professionals is critical in planning behavioral, instructional, and pharmacological interventions that are efficacious and sensitive to the medical, psychological, and educational impact of treatments on the child and his or her caregivers. School-linked services (i.e., focusing on interdisciplinary collaboration and services integration across the school and other agencies) are critical for enhancing both the educational and health-care needs of students with special medical needs.

An interdisciplinary approach requires collaboration among caregivers and multiple professionals working on behalf of the child. As an interdisciplinary model, CBC provides a framework for synthesizing information and treatment options across different disciplines. The collective expertise of the treatment team in assessment and plan development is a major advantage of interdisciplinary CBC, as it has potential for enhancing the effectiveness of treatment decisions leading to improved outcomes for students with multifaceted health-care needs. Within an interdisciplinary pediatric model, CBC provides the context for (a) health professionals (e.g., physicians, nurses) to provide pertinent information about a student's health, prognosis, general capacity, and physical abilities, all of which have a direct impact on the child's educational performance; (b) educators to provide helpful information to health-care professionals, thereby making diagnoses possible based in part on the educator's knowledge and observations of a child's functioning in natural school environments; and (c) professionals in the educational community to monitor intervention efficacy, such as medical regimens and how they are influencing cognitive, social, and behavioral skills (Kline & Rubel, 2001).

School-linked consultants have opportunities to educate health-care providers (such as pediatricians) in several important educational realities. Topics around which such education can occur include the ecology of schools, policies affecting educational practices, methods of behavioral assessment, approaches to treating educational and social problems, single-case evaluation strategies, and personnel available in schools to assist with implementing and monitoring interventions (Power, DuPaul, Shapiro, Parrish, 1995, 1998). For example, a consultant may inform a physician of the resources necessary, such as number of personnel required (e.g., paraeducators, nursing staff, general educators, administrators) and supports needed (e.g., staff training, plan materials, emotional support) to feasibly and effectively carry out specific behavioral or medical plans, thereby aiding in treatment planning and decision making. Likewise, health-care providers can educate school personnel in critical areas, including the culture of hospital and clinic settings, medical approaches to evaluating dysfunction, the pediatric providers' roles, constraints of working in a medical setting, and side effects of medications and other prescribed medical treatments (Gadow, Nolan, Paolicelli, & Sprafkin, 1991; Pelham, 1993). Roles of a CBC consultant within this context include (a) channeling information among the school, family, and health-care providers; (b) co-conceptualizing important case issues from multiple perspectives; (c) educating each system about issues, present status, and plans for intervention or placement changes; and (d) co-constructing and coordinating multisystemic intervention plans. Such a professional is responsible for gathering and integrating information gleaned from various assessments, including those related to medical, educational, cognitive, socioemotional, behavioral, and family issues. The consultant can then initiate and coordinate an intervention plan that is carried out in the child's natural environments, using parents and teachers as the primary agents of change (Singh, Parmelee, Sood, & Katz, 1993).

In pediatric CBC, referrals for consultation services are often made by the physician. Physicians may refer families for services to address concerns regarding medication management, behavioral intervention planning, and/or differences in perspective regarding problem identification or treatment across caregivers, educators, or medical staff. When CBC consultants are housed within a medical setting, they may take an active role throughout the intake process by sitting in on family visits to the physician. Once a referral is made, the consultant establishes contact with the family to gain consent for the process and gather background information regarding the concerns to be addressed. This process may be done in person during the medical visit or over the phone. Before the consultation process, the consultant can gather relevant background health, educational, and developmental information regarding the child, as well as pertinent information regarding the home, school, and medical environments (e.g., nature of the relationships and concerns, number of people involved, access to resources, support networks). Health-related assessment and intervention information is integrated by the consultant to broaden the collective knowledge base from which assessments and intervention plans are derived. That is, medical expertise is utilized in the school and family-based decision-making process via the consultant as a conduit of that information. Conversely, the consultant also relays assessment information to the medical professional to assist in diagnosis, intervention planning, and medication management.

The following case study provides an illustration of the use of CBC in a pediatric setting to address the medical, educational, and developmental concerns of a child. Important content and process issues are discussed to demonstrate the utility of the model and specific strategies used to integrate CBC in this unique context.

Case Study: Amanda

Amanda was a 13-year-old Caucasian female who was a patient in a developmental pediatric clinic. She had been previously diagnosed with Tourette syndrome, attention deficit hyperactivity disorder (ADHD)– inattentive type, and a learning disability. She was prescribed Tenex and Clonodine by her physician to help manage her symptoms of ADHD and Tourette syndrome. Amanda was referred for consultation services by her pediatrician to address learning concerns in the area of basic math and organizational skills. Additionally, Amanda's mother, Ms. Reynolds, expressed frustration with the school because she had been unable to schedule meetings to discuss Amanda's unique learning needs. Initially, school personnel were resistant to participating in consultation. Her teachers expressed that they thought Amanda was doing as well as could be expected and that she did not need additional help. They also stated that they had changed the math curriculum to better suit Amanda's needs and that she was making progress; however, the school had not communicated these changes to Ms. Reynolds.

In Amanda's case, it was evident that communication between home and school was limited and that the relationship between Ms. Reynolds and Amanda's teachers was strained due to a difference in perspective regarding Amanda's educational needs. Ms. Reynolds expressed a desire to change Amanda's Individualized Educational Plan (IEP) to address more functional life skills (e.g., basic math, telling time, prosocial interactions); however, her teachers stated that Amanda was meeting their expectations for a child with her disabilities. Her physician expressed concerns regarding Amanda's progress in the area of social relationships with peers. He also requested observations of Amanda's school behavior to determine if her medication was managing her symptoms of inattention and motor tics. The CBC process provided an opportunity to join key individuals (i.e., Amanda's mother, teachers, and IEP manager) to respectfully share concerns and perspectives and collaboratively decide on a plan to help Amanda reach her full potential. It also provided a unique opportunity for the consultant to act as a conduit between the teachers and the physician, allowing the physician to share information regarding her diagnoses and medical treatments and to make observations regarding the effectiveness and side effects of Amanda's medication. To address the initial resistance on the part of the school, the consultant held two meetings with the teachers before beginning consultation to address their concerns and to describe the process and goals of CBC. After these meetings, Amanda's teachers agreed to meet with Amanda's mother to share their perspective on her progress at school.

Needs Identification Phase

Content Issues

The consultant conducted observations of Amanda's school performance and determined that her symptoms of ADHD and Tourette seemed to be well managed with her medication. However, her teachers expressed some concerns regarding immature social behaviors with peers and a lack of help-seeking behavior in the classroom. They reported that these behaviors were inhibiting her academic progress and ability to make and keep friends. Amanda's teachers agreed that these issues were impacting her success in school and that consultation was warranted to address these concerns. Amanda's Resource teacher and IEP manager, Ms. Garret, and Language Arts and Science teacher, Ms. Carter, agreed to participate in CBC.

A CNII was scheduled to discuss initial concerns and determine a target behavior for the consultation process. Ms. Reynolds, Ms. Garret, and Ms. Carter attended, along with Amanda's grandmother and the Special Education Coordinator. A discussion of Amanda's likes and strengths determined that she was a student who did well in the areas of reading, spelling, penmanship, and art. She liked music and did well with routine. The team also reported that Amanda was motivated to do well; however, her "perfectionism" sometimes interfered with her completion of tasks. The team stated that their goals for Amanda were to develop self-advocacy skills and to take advantage of support offered to her. They also stated that they would like to see her initiate more social interactions and establish and maintain friendships.

The team discussed several areas that were interfering with Amanda reaching her full potential. They stated that she had difficulty grasping basic academic skills, especially in math. She often became frustrated, but refused to seek help because she did not like to appear "stupid" in front of her peers. The team also reported that Amanda had difficulty being flexible and displayed perfectionist tendencies. She responded well to strict routines, but had a difficult time adjusting if her routine was disrupted. Additionally, they reported that she seemed immature in social interactions with both peers and adults. Ms. Reynolds also stated that Amanda had a difficult time following directions and she often had to repeat them several times before Amanda complied. Because recent changes had been made to Amanda's math curriculum, the team determined that this concern was being addressed and did not require additional attention. The team decided that their priority was for Amanda to engage in help-seeking behavior because this behavior was most significantly affecting her learning at school. At home, the priority was following directions, since this was the most disruptive behavior in that setting.

Ms. Reynolds, Ms. Garret, and Ms. Carter agreed to record observations of Amanda's behaviors to determine her baseline level of functioning, as well as to record any functional observations that could be used in treatment planning (i.e., antecedents, consequences, and behavioral patterns). At school, three of Amanda's teachers recorded the number of times that Amanda asked for help from an adult across five different class periods. At home, Amanda's mother recorded the number of prompts given to Amanda each time a direction was given, as well as the number of directions that were followed and the number of consequences (e.g., removal of privileges) that Amanda received for not following a direction. A span of 15 sec was allowed between each prompt to allow Amanda a consistent amount of time to respond. Observations were recorded on behavioral observation forms for 1 week. During this time, the consultant continued to conduct school observations and kept in close contact with Ms. Reynolds via phone and e-mail to address any questions or concerns regarding data collection and to continue to assess Amanda's behavior across settings.

Process Goals and Issues

At the beginning of the consultation process, it was apparent that there was tension between Amanda's parents and teachers. Additional members (i.e., the Special Education Coordinator, Amanda's grandmother) were invited to the meeting to help provide extra support and to share their perspectives. The consultant used several relationship-building strategies at this stage of the consultation process, such as pointing out areas of commonality and shared goals, with the goal of developing a sense of mutual respect for the other members of the team. The consultant emphasized the importance of the expertise that each team member brought to the process and how collaboration and consistency across the various systems would benefit Amanda. The consultant also explicitly pointed out areas of shared observations in terms of Amanda's behavior and goals. When differences in opinion or perspective were shared, the consultant made sure to validate each perspective and provide a context for why these differences might occur (e.g., differences in demands across home and school, different levels of comfort across settings). After this initial meeting, Ms. Reynolds expressed that this was the first time that she "felt heard" by the school and that she was hopeful about the process. Additionally, the initial resistance to participate in the process on the part of the school seemed to be replaced by a sense of cooperation. Amanda's physician expressed satisfaction with the direction of the consultation process and reported that Amanda's mother had stated that she was pleased with the services thus far.

Needs Analysis Phase

Content Issues

A CNAI meeting was held to discuss observations of Amanda's behavior regarding compliance with directions at home and seeking help at school. At home, Ms. Reynolds reported that she gave Amanda an average of five prompts for each direction and that Amanda complied with her directions approximately 64% of the time. She stated that she often felt frustrated because she had to repeat her requests several times before Amanda followed through and she occasionally had to step in and complete tasks for her. Based on these baseline observations, a behavioral goal was set to have Amanda comply with a request with only two to three prompts.

A functional assessment of Amanda's behavior and the home environment suggested that Amanda had difficulty attending to directions because she was easily distracted. In addition, there was often no consequence for Amanda if she did not follow through with her mother's directions. Based on this analysis, a plan was developed that included: (a) providing direct commands, (b) eliminating distractions when delivering commands, and (c) providing a consequence for not complying with directions. The consultant provided initial training for Ms. Reynolds in how to deliver direct commands by gaining eye contact, giving only one direction at a time, and issuing a consequence (i.e., loss of privilege) if the direction was not followed after the second command was delivered.

At school, observations of Amanda's help-seeking behavior were recorded by Ms. Garret, Ms. Carter, and one other teacher across five class periods. Baseline observations indicated that over a 4-day period Amanda asked for help once in her resource class with Ms. Garret and she did not ask for assistance in any of her other classes. Ms. Garret also reported that when Amanda asked for help with her assignment she received an 86% on her assignment, compared to a 60% when she did not ask for help. Based on these observations, a goal was set to have Amanda ask for help at least three times a week, across her five classes.

A functional assessment of Amanda's behavior at school revealed that she was more likely to ask for help when in a smaller class and if a general statement was made to the class eliciting questions, such as, "If anyone has a question, please raise your hand." Her teachers also reported that they often checked on her to see if she needed help and, at times, she appeared self-conscious of her peers seeing the teacher stopping to help her. Based on this analysis, it appeared that Amanda avoided seeking help because she did not want to draw attention from her peers. To address this concern, a plan was developed that included: (a) a class-wide system for indicating when a student needed help (indicator cards placed on desktops); (b) teacher proximity control, involving having the teacher circulate throughout the class; and (c) a progress monitoring system by which Amanda could chart her progress with her assignments when she received help. Consultation plan sheets were developed by the consultant (see Figures 5.6 and 5.7) to summarize the goal, outline the plan steps, and rate progress toward goal attainment. The team determined that due to Amanda's comfort level with smaller peer groups, the plan would be implemented in her smaller class (math) initially and then generalized to her other classes at a later time.

In addition to the consultation interventions, the team discussed other common resources that could support Amanda's academic development. Her mother was referred to a university-based academic skills clinic to provide further academic support and skill practice. Since Amanda had participated in this program before with some success (i.e., her mother indicated that it was a good opportunity for Amanda to practice organization and basic academic skills with one-on-one guidance), the consultant arranged for a referral to the clinic and coordinated communication between the clinic therapist and supervisor, consultation team, and physician.

Process Goals and Issues

The goal during the conjoint needs analysis stage was to continue to facilitate respectful communication, consensus building, and collaborative treatment planning. Although the consultation team decided to focus on different behaviors across home and school, the consultant emphasized that by sharing expertise and responsibility across settings consistency across home and school would be enhanced, thereby increasing the effectiveness of the intervention plan. Thus, the consultant provided opportunities for all team members to share observations in regard to both of Amanda's target behaviors, and elicited and validated their opinions and levels of agreement with the developed intervention plans. Additionally, it appeared that Ms. Reynolds, Ms. Garret, and Ms. Carter were feeling more comfortable with the process in that they did not solicit greater support by inviting other members to the meetings.

The consultant shared the observations and interventions with the physician. He stated that Amanda's behaviors were more indicative of learned behaviors rather than symptoms of her developmental disabilities and he was in agreement with the treatment plans developed by the consultation team. In addition, he expressed that he was pleased with the change in communication between home and school because the strained relationships had been a significant barrier in Amanda's educational progress.

Child's Name: Amanda Reynolds
Week of:_____

Consultation Plan

Behavioral Goal:
Amanda will ask for help at least 3 times in a week, in any class.

Plan Summary:
Provide her with a color card to ask for help without raising her hand. Motivate her to use the card by charting her progress with stickers.

Please list the primary steps of the plan on the lines below. Then, each day, please check in the appropriate box in the matrix to the left whether each step was completed.

Mon	Tues	Wed	Thur	Fri

 Plan Steps:

1. Provided color-coded card to ask for help.
2. Amanda used card.
3. Provided sticker.
4. Charted progress with assignment.

Goal Rating

At the end of the week, please use the following scale to rate how closely the above goal was met. The consultant will collect this form each week. Thank you!

-2	-1	0	+1	+2
Situation significantly worse	Situation somewhat worse	No Progress	Goal partially met	Goal fully met

FIGURE 5.6. School consultation plan for Amanda.

Plan Implementation Phase

Content Issues

Ms. Reynolds and Ms. Garret were the primary treatment agents. The consultant maintained continued contact across home and school to assess treatment fidelity and address any questions or concerns. Amanda's mother and teachers continued to collect behavioral observations of Amanda's compliance with directions and help-seeking behavior. Additionally, Ms. Reynolds and Ms. Garret recorded their fidelity with the intervention by using daily treatment

Child's Name: Amanda Reynolds
Week of:_____

Consultation Plan

Behavioral Goal:
Amanda will follow a direction within 2-3 times of being asked.

Plan Summary:
Capture her attention and eliminate distractions.

Please list the primary steps of the plan on the lines below. Then, each day, please check in the appropriate box in the matrix to the left whether each step was completed.

Sun Mon Tue Wed Thu Fri Sat

 Plan Steps:

1. Look Amanda in the eye when giving direction.
2. Eliminate distractions (turn off t.v., take away book).

Goal Rating

At the end of the week, please use the following scale to rate how closely the above goal was met. The consultant will collect this form each week. Thank you!

-2	-1	0	+1	+2
Situation significantly worse	Situation somewhat worse	No Progress	Goal partially met	Goal fully met

FIGURE 5.7. Home consultation plan for Amanda.

integrity checklists. These forms included a list of the treatment plan steps with a box next to each one to check off the steps that were completed on a daily basis (see Figures 5.6 and 5.7). In addition, they also completed a goal attainment scale each week to indicate their perception of Amanda's progress toward the consultation goals. The consultant collected the observation and treatment integrity forms on a regular basis to monitor Amanda's progress and inform her physician. Both Ms. Reynolds and Ms. Garret indicated that the plan was relatively easy to use and fit well into the home and school environments.

During this phase of consultation, Ms. Reynolds informed the team that they would be moving and Amanda would be attending a different school for the next academic year. As a result, Ms. Garret suggested that they schedule a meeting with the special education coordinator from the new school and develop a transition plan. Additionally, because the consultant would no longer be working through the pediatrician's office after the end of the school year, another consultant was brought in to process so that Amanda and Ms. Reynolds could continue to receive consultation services through the transition into the next school year.

Process Goals and Issues

One of the goals for consultation during the plan implementation phase was to reinforce continued mutual respect and collaboration between home and school. The consultant reinforced opportunities for communication between home and school via phone contact or home–school notes to share information regarding Amanda's progress. The consultant also emphasized and built upon the strengths of the team members, such as strong positive relationships with Amanda and consistent behavior management. With each contact, the consultant made a special effort to reinforce the partnership between home and school and emphasize its benefits for Amanda's short- and long-term progress.

Plan Evaluation Phase

Content Issues

After approximately 6 weeks of plan implementation, the team met for a CPEI to discuss Amanda's progress toward her treatment goals. During this time, the school had spring break and several days of school-wide achievement tests. As a result, observations at school were only recorded for 2 weeks.

At home, Ms. Reynolds reported that the number of prompts that she had to give Amanda per direction had reduced from an average of five prompts at baseline to two (range = 1–3 prompts, effect size = 2.83; see Figure 5.8). She also reported that Amanda was complying with directions approximately 50% of the time. Although this indicated a decrease in the percentage of compliance from baseline (64%), this number actually reflected that Ms. Reynolds was more consistently issuing a consequence for Amanda's noncompliance. Amanda was also complying with requests more often with only one to two prompts, which she had not done during baseline. Overall, Amanda's mother reported that she felt the goal was "partially met." The team discussed adding to the treatment plan by including a self-monitoring chart of Amanda's chores to help decrease the number of directions given and increase Amanda's level of compliance with her regularly scheduled responsibilities.

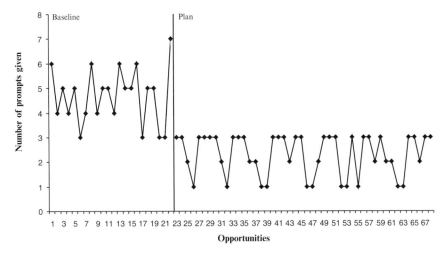

FIGURE 5.8. Number of prompts given to Amanda at home across baseline and intervention phases.

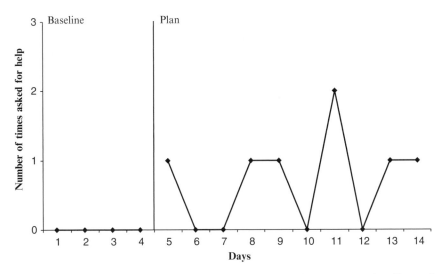

FIGURE 5.9. Amanda's help-seeking behaviors during math class across baseline and intervention phases.

At school, Ms. Garret reported that over a 2-week period of time Amanda asked for help in her math class an average of one time per day (range = 0–2, effect size = 1.04; see Figure 5.9) and had "fully met" her goal of asking for help at least three times a week, one out of 2 weeks. She indicated that the plan was easy to use in her classroom because of her limited number of students. Ms. Garret stated that she planned to talk with Amanda's other teachers to begin to generalize the plan to her other classes.

Overall, Ms. Reynolds and Ms. Garret indicated that they were satisfied with Amanda's progress at home and school and wanted to continue with the intervention plan. Ms. Garret recommended that Amanda's IEP be revised to reflect the goals discussed during the consultation process and include the intervention plan so that Amanda's future teachers could use similar strategies. The team discussed setting up a transition meeting to meet with the Special Education Coordinator of Amanda's new school to address a transition plan. A plan was set to schedule a meeting over the summer.

At this point, the consultation team determined that formal consultation meetings would no longer be held because of the difficulties of scheduling meetings in the last weeks of school. Continued communication regarding Amanda's progress occurred via e-mail, phone, or home–school notes in Amanda's daily planner. The consultant continued to remain in contact via e-mail and phone calls throughout the end of the school year and began to transition the process over to a new CBC pediatric consultant who followed Amanda to her new school.

Process Goals and Issues

At the end of the process, Ms. Garret stated that she was glad to participate in CBC. She reported that initially she was reluctant to get involved because she did not think Amanda was in need of extra support. However, she realized that the process was a "team effort" and that Amanda's needs were impacting her educational and developmental progress. She also offered to work more closely with Ms. Reynolds throughout her transition to a new school process and took responsibility for ensuring that Amanda got the services that she needed in other classes and in her new school. Ms. Reynolds reported that she felt much greater support from the school and she was hopeful about continuing a partnership in the future. Amanda's physician also expressed satisfaction with Amanda's progress and the developed partnership between home and school.

This case study illustrates the utility of the CBC model in addressing the multifaceted needs of children with health-care issues across multiple settings involving various disciplines (i.e., pediatrician, psychologist, general educator, special educator, parent). The strategies used by the consultant emphasizing mutual respect, shared perspective-taking, and joint responsibility fostered a collaborative partnership among the important stakeholders in Amanda's life and significantly impacted her educational and behavioral progress.

Summary

Since its inception in the early 1990s, many studies and reviews have been published on CBC procedures and outcomes in problem-solving situations involving parents and educators across home and school systems. However, the ecological nature of CBC provides flexibility in adapting to various setting characteristics and contextual demands. This chapter provided examples wherein CBC has evolved and adapted to unique professional situations, including school-based teams, Head Start settings, and pediatric medical settings. Inherent in the discussion is the recognition that to practice CBC effectively in unique contexts requires that consultants acquire a knowledge base that is commensurate with the demands of the practice setting (e.g., early childhood, pediatric health, and mental health issues). Furthermore, to be effective in these and other novel settings, consultants need to remain flexible and adaptable to challenging relational and interpersonal issues. Whereas case goals continue to focus on positive child-related outcomes, relational goals such as increasing mutual understanding, enhancing consultee skills and competencies, and creating shared opportunities for decision making are pronounced. The case studies presented here illustrate some of these unique realities. At the same time, positive child outcomes and consultee satisfaction in these cases suggest that the CBC process can meaningfully and effectively adapt to unique context demands to benefit children.

6
Research on Conjoint Behavioral Consultation

Brandy L. Clarke, Jennifer D. Burt, and Susan M. Sheridan

In the first several chapters of this text, theoretical and definitional considerations of CBC were reviewed. Empirical studies of the model have been increasing, with research focusing primarily on outcomes, communication processes, and social validation. Findings have generally provided support of CBC as an effective model for addressing behavioral, academic, and socioemotional concerns. In addition, much has been learned about communication patterns and relational aspects within CBC interactions and perceptions by consumers. These research areas are reviewed in this chapter.

Review of Outcome Research

Numerous studies have been conducted evaluating the efficacy of CBC across home and school settings, in relation to academic, social, and behavioral outcomes, using experimental and case study methodologies. Table 6.1 presents a listing of published studies summarized by authors, sample, target behavior, measures, outcomes, and methodological features (e.g., social validity assessment, fidelity information, and follow-up).

Reviews and Meta-Analyses

The position of CBC within the larger framework of evidence-based interventions related to parent consultation was the focus of a review by Guli (2005), who conducted an extensive search of parent consultation literature using rigorous criteria specified in the Procedural and Coding Manual of the Division16 Task Force on Evidence-based Interventions in School Psychology (Kratochwill & Stoiber, 2002). The majority of the 18 studies identified used single-participant designs, including both within-participant and multiple baseline designs. Each of the studies was subjected to comprehensive and rigorous review of methodological strengths and weaknesses. CBC research was included in this review because of its emphasis on consultation as the structure for service delivery.

TABLE 6.1. Review of CBC outcome studies.

Authors	Samples	Target behaviors	Measures	Results	Methodological features	Limitations
Colton and Sheridan (1998)	N = 3 males, 8–9 years old, diagnosed with ADHD	Cooperative peer interactions	Direct observations Social Skills Rating System Social validity	SSRS-P: Significant pre/post results for child 2 SSRS-T: Significant pre/post results for children 1 and 3	Independent observations Direct observations (participants and peers) Treatment integrity Multiple probe design across participants Social validity assessed	Participant groups not matched Objectivity of behavioral observations Lack of independent observations in home
Galloway and Sheridan (1994)	N = 6, grades 1–3	Math completion and accuracy	Classroom math assignments (completion/accuracy) Social validity Treatment integrity	Math accuracy: Gains for home-note group ranged from 20 to 84% Gains for CBC group ranged from 50 to 144% Math completion: Gains for home-note group ranged from 14 to 99% Gains for CBC group ranged from 39 to 133%	Permanent product measures Social comparison across both groups Treatment integrity Comparison group Social validity assessed	AB design with replications, not true experiment Increasing baseline data points Lack of control over math instruction Generalizability
Gortmaker, Warnes, and	5-year-old male kindergarten	Selective mutism	Direct observations Social validity	Effect size = 1.60	Direct observations Treatment integrity	No reliability data No objective

(Continued)

TABLE 6.1. Review of CBC outcome studies—Cont'd.

Authors	Samples	Target behaviors	Measures	Results	Methodological features	Limitations
Sheridan (2004)	case study		Treatment integrity		Process integrity	treatment integrity data
Illsley and Sladeczek (2001)	$N = 5$	Conduct problem behavior Parenting practices and skills	Direct observations of child behavior Parental knowledge of behavioral principles Video-taped parent–child interactions	Positive change in child behavior 4/5 parents had improvements in parenting skills	Direct observations Manualized approach Parental behavior/ knowledge change measures	Significant variation between parents
Kratochwill, Elliott, Loitz, Sladeszek, and Carlson (2003)	$N = 125$ Head Start preschoolers	Externalizing and internalizing behavior problems	Direct observations *Child Behavior Checklist* (CBCL) Treatment integrity *Responding to Children's Behavior Checklist* (RCB) Social validity	Effect sizes for manual group: Aggression = –.41 Compliance = –.28 Other = .55 Total = –.08 Effect sizes for video group: Aggression = .15 Compliance = .08 Other = –.05 Total = .05	Direct observations Standardized assessments Treatment integrity Random assignment Control group	Statistical power low due to small group size and large variance Two treatment groups not randomly assigned High attrition rate

(Continued)

TABLE 6.1. Review of CBC outcome studies—Cont'd.

Authors	Samples	Target behaviors	Measures	Results	Methodological features	Limitations
Ray, Skinner, and Watson (1999)	5-year-old male diagnosed with Autistic Disorder	Increase compliance with low probability commands	Direct observations	Increased rate of compliance from 15 to 95%	Direct observations	Generalizability Lack of social validity data
Sheridan, Clarke, Knoche, and Edwards (2006)	N = 50 children aged 6 and younger	Academic Social Behavioral	Direct observations Parent-Teacher Relationship Scale-II (PTRS) Social validity	Median effect size home = .97, school = 1.06 Significant improvement in parent-teacher relationship	Process integrity Treatment integrity Direct observation	Reliability of direct observations Quasi-experimental approach No direct measure of treatment integrity
Sheridan and Colton (1994)	6-year-old male	Irrational fear	Direct observations	Stable baseline at 0% Gradual increasing trend with treatment No overlapping data points with baseline Follow-up 100%	Direct observation Follow-up data	No control group Lack of control over extraneous variables Social validity data
Sheridan, Eagle, Cowan, and Mickelson (2001)	N = 52, K–9th grade	Academic Social Behavioral	Direct observations Social validity	Effect sizes for home = 1.08, school = 1.11 Total = 1.10	Direct observations Process integrity Treatment integrity	Reliability of direct observations Limited treatment integrity data

(Continued)

TABLE 6.1. Review of CBC outcome studies—Cont'd.

Authors	Samples	Target behaviors	Measures	Results	Methodological features	Limitations
Sheridan, Eagle, and Doll (2006)	$N = 125$ students with one, more than one, or no forms of diversity	Efficacy of CBC with diverse clients 192 different target behaviors	Direct observations Social validity	Average effect sizes for one form of diversity = 1.21 Average effect sizes for two or more forms of diversity = 1.51	Direct observations Process integrity	Lack of experimental control Nonrandom selection or group assignment
			Demographic measures of diversity	Average effect sizes for no diversity = 1.35		Limited sample size within groups Diversity indicators based on parent reports
Sheridan, Kratochwill, and Elliott (1990)	$N = 4$, 8–9 years old	Social interactions (withdrawn)	Direct observations	Home, social withdrawal behaviors decreased 1–2 SD	Independent observations Direct observations (participants and peers) Treatment integrity Multiple baseline design	Participant groups not matched Objectivity of behavioral observations Lack of independent observations in home
			Behavioral rating scales	School, social withdrawal total internalizing problems decreased 1 + SD		
			Self-report	3 parents reported that assertion/social initiation increased 1 + SD At school, Assertion/ social initiation increased 1 + SD		

(Continued)

TABLE 6.1. Review of CBC outcome studies—Cont'd.

Authors	Samples	Target behaviors	Measures	Results	Methodological features	Limitations
Sheridan, Warnes, Cowan, Schemm, and Clarke (2004)	Case study 4-year-old male in Early Childhood	Tantrumming	Direct observations Social validity	Length of tantrums decreased from 4 to 1.6 minutes	Social validity measures	No effect size reported Case study Generalizability
Weiner, Sheridan, & Jenson (1998)	Special Education $N=5$, grades 7–9	Math homework completion Math accuracy	Permanent products Socialvalidity	Total effect size math completion = .60; accuracy = .67	Multiple baseline design Follow-up data Process integrity Treatment integrity	Lack of stability and variability during baseline Limited treatment integrity data

Source: From Sheridan. S.M.. Clarke, B.L.., & Burt, J.D. (2008). Conjoint behavioral consultation: What do we know and what do we need to know? In W. P. Erchul & S. M. Sheridan (Eds.). *Handbook of research in school consultation: Empirical foundations for the field.* Mahwah, NJ: Lawrence Erlbaum Associates. Reprinted with permission.

Note: Readers are referred to Guli (2005) for additional methodological information and findings related to CBC research.

Based on the Task Force criteria, CBC was found to hold promise as an evidence-based parent consultation model. Specifically, relative to other parent consultation models, CBC provided the strongest evidence for producing significant school-related outcomes. Furthermore, parent consultation studies receiving the highest ratings for key methodological features were those using a model of joint parent–teacher consultation, including CBC. All but one of the highest ratings for both significant outcomes and clinical significance were received by joint models of parent–teacher (i.e., conjoint) consultation.

Sheridan, Eagle, Cowan, and Mickelson (2001) conducted the first large-scale review of CBC outcome research. In this review, the outcomes of 4 years of federally funded CBC studies were reported. Specifically, 30 graduate student consultants provided CBC services to parents and teachers of 52 students with disabilities (such as behavior disorders, learning disabilities, and attention-deficit hyperactivity disorder) or to those who were at risk for becoming eligible for special education services. Target behaviors included noncompliance, encopresis, anxiety, and homework completion, among a host of other typical childhood concerns. Efficacy of CBC was evaluated in each case by computing effect sizes across home and school settings. In addition, a prediction model was tested based on client age, case complexity, and symptom severity. Perceptions of effectiveness, process acceptability, and consultee satisfaction with CBC services were also assessed.

Average case outcomes at home and school were very favorable. Specifically, the average effect size for CBC case outcomes was 1.10 (SD = 1.07), with home- and school-based effect sizes averaging 1.08 (SD = .82) and 1.11 (SD = 1.24), respectively. Confidence intervals computed around effect sizes revealed that the "true" population average effect size related to CBC could be found within the range of .83 and 1.36, with 95% confidence.

Researchers in this study were also concerned with identifying variables predictive of CBC outcomes. Multiple linear regression was used to examine the relationships between client age, case complexity (i.e., number of target behaviors) and severity of symptoms (i.e., rated by parents and teachers prior to CBC), and individual effect sizes. A model fitting client age and symptom severity was found to predict school effect size relatively well ($R^2 = .425$, Adjusted $R^2 = .343$; $p = .008$). Specifically, the older client (11 years of age and older) with less severe symptoms would be predicted to experience higher effect sizes with CBC intervention. On the other hand, the older client with severe symptoms would be predicted to demonstrate a smaller effect size. Similarly, younger clients (ages 5–7) with higher severity ratings prior to CBC services were predicted to experience higher effect sizes than those experiencing less severity, and than older children at all severity levels. Case complexity (i.e., number of target behaviors) was not significant in the models. Likewise, the multiple regression with home effect sizes did not result in any statistically significant model. Thus, client age, symptom severity, and case complexity were not predictive of effects in home settings.

Sheridan, Eagle, and Doll (in press) analyzed the outcomes of CBC with a sample of diverse students (experiencing one, more than one, or no forms of diversity). Behavioral outcomes, attainment of goals, and various forms of social validity (acceptability, satisfaction, and perceptions of efficacy) were measured with 125 students representing varying levels of diversity and 192 target behaviors. Forty-four percent of the clients were diverse in one or more respects. Collectively, 26% of the clients experienced one form of diversity; 18% demonstrated two or more. Approximately 23% of the sample were identified by their parents as racially diverse (nonwhite); 19.5% had only one adult living at home, 15.3% were living in poverty conditions, 6.9% had mothers who had not completed high school, and 4.8% spoke a language other than English in the home.

Findings indicated that CBC interventions yielded high effect sizes regardless of the presence of diversity or the number of diverse characteristics exhibited. Average effect sizes were 1.21, 1.51, and 1.35 for students experiencing one, two or more, and no forms of diversity, respectively. Likewise, parents and teachers of students experiencing diversity were very positive regarding the CBC process and outcomes, indicating favorable results on social validity measures. Social validity measures (i.e., perceptions of goal attainment, effectiveness, acceptability, and satisfaction) yielded very favorable results.

Review of Experimental Studies

In the first empirical study of CBC, Sheridan, Kratochwill, and Elliott (1990) were concerned with increasing the social initiation behaviors of socially withdrawn children. Of particular interest was the demonstration of behavioral generalization to the home setting. Participants in this study were four socially withdrawn children from a rural town in the Midwest (3 girls, 1 boy; ages 8–12). There were two treatment conditions in the study (i.e., CBC and consultation with teachers only). In the CBC condition, teachers and parents worked together with a school psychologist consultant; in the teacher-only condition, parents were not included in consultation. In both experimental conditions, children were exposed to the same behavioral treatment (i.e., goal setting, self-monitoring, and positive reinforcement). In the CBC condition, these same procedures were implemented across home and school settings. In teacher-only consultation, they were instituted at school only.

A multiple baseline across participants design was used to evaluate the effectiveness of the separate consultation interventions. When consultation was undertaken with parents and teachers together, initiations increased in both home and school settings. Baseline performance for each child was approximately 1 initiation per week at school; during the last phase of treatment performances increased to between 30 and 40 initiations per week. At home, baseline levels ranged from approximately 1 initiation per week to approximately 7 per week during the last phase of treatment. However, when consultation was undertaken with teachers only, children's initiations increased at school only. Baseline performance for each child was 0–1 initiation per week at school, with weekly rates of between 6 and 26 during the last phase of treatment. At home, baseline rates were between 0 and 1.5 per week, increasing to between only 1 and 4 per week during the last phase of treatment. Treatment gains at school were maintained for all children in both conditions, but were most notable for those in the CBC condition. Thus, although behavioral consultation with teachers was found to be effective in increasing the social initiation behaviors of socially withdrawn children at school, both generalization and maintenance of treatment effects appeared to be stronger when conjoint behavioral consultation procedures were utilized. Social validity and treatment integrity measures were also included and yielded positive results.

A second outcome study evaluated the effects of CBC combined with a behavioral training and reinforcement program with three boys between the ages of 8 and 9 diagnosed with ADHD and exhibiting performance deficits in their cooperative play behavior (Colton & Sheridan, 1998). A behavioral social skills treatment package was implemented within the context of CBC to address the children's observed social deficits. The behavioral social skills treatment program consisted of four major components: (a) social skills coaching and role play, (b) a home–school communication system, (c) self-monitoring of recess behaviors, and (d) positive reinforcement.

Outcome measures in this study included direct observations of positive interaction behaviors and behavioral rating scales. Specifically, 20-minutes direct (partial interval) observations were conducted one to two times weekly in analogue play situations to assess participants' positive interaction behaviors toward classmates. Behaviors coded in the observations were cooperative interactions with peers, negative aggressive behaviors, and isolative behaviors. The *Social Skills Rating System – Teacher, Parent, and Student* forms (*SSRS*; Gresham & Elliott, 1990) were used as a standardized, norm-referenced measure of social behavior prior to and following CBC.

A multiple baseline across participants design was used to evaluate the effects of the CBC/social skills treatment program on target children's cooperative play behaviors. All participants increased positive play behaviors with peers during treatment phases. Average positive social behaviors increased from 27% during baseline to 61% during treatment. There was little to no overlap in data across baseline and treatment conditions for two of the three participants. Social comparison data (i.e., involving a comparison with same-gender classmates identified by classroom teachers as having adequate social skills) revealed that all participants increased their positive interactions to a level that approached that of "normal" comparison peers.

Acceptability of CBC was assessed on the *BIRS-R* (revised for consultation procedures; Sheridan et al., 2001), completed by parents and teachers (Von Brock & Elliott, 1987). Children's acceptability of the treatment protocol was assessed by the *Children's Intervention Rating Profile* (*CIRP*; Witt & Elliott, 1985). Parents and teachers reported the procedures were acceptable, and child responses suggested that they found the social skills intervention highly acceptable.

Treatment integrity was assessed for CBC procedures by systematic audiotape analysis. Integrity of parents' and teachers' follow-through of treatment procedures was assessed via self-report on the home note. Data indicated that the consultant achieved 98% of consultation objectives across all interviews, and that parents and teachers adhered to treatment components 100% of the time.

A variation of traditional, individualized CBC was evaluated by Weiner, Sheridan, and Jenson (1998), who implemented consultation services in a group format. Parents and teachers of five junior high school (eighth and ninth grades) students with homework concerns served as participants in this study. Given the age of the sample, students also participated in the CPAI and CTEI meetings. A multiple baseline across participants design was used to evaluate the effects of CBC on math homework completion and accuracy. A structured homework intervention program (Olympia, Jenson, & Hepworth-Neville, 1996) was used to standardize strategies across participants. The primary components of the program were self-recording, home-based structure and supervision, and positive reinforcement.

Permanent products of homework completion and accuracy served as the primary dependent variables in the study. On average, students completed 63.2% of their homework (SD = 39.73) during baseline, and 87.2% (SD = 22.87) during treatment conditions. The average effect size for completion was .60. Average accuracy rates increased from 45% (SD = 36.63) at baseline to 69.6% (SD = 28.63) at treatment, with an average effect size of .67, suggesting moderate to high effects.

Perceptions of effectiveness and goal attainment were evaluated using the Effectiveness factor of the *Behavior Intervention Rating Scale* (*BIRS*) and *Goal Attainment Scaling* (*GAS*). On a scale of 1–6, parent and teacher mean item ratings on the *BIRS*-Effectiveness factor (*BIRS*-E) were 4.84 and 4.74, respectively. *GAS* ratings averaged 1.71 (goal mostly met) for parents and 2.0 (goal completely met) for teachers.

Consumer satisfaction with consultation services were assessed in this study, with both teachers and parents responding favorably. On the *CEF*, mean item responses of 5.42 were found for teachers and 6.13 for parents (out of a possible 7). Both consultee and client acceptability were also assessed. Parents and teachers completed the *BIRS*-Acceptability factor (*BIRS*-A) (revised for consultation), and students completed the *CIRP*. Parents and teachers reported high levels of acceptability, with mean item scores of 5.6 and 5.2 (out of a possible 6), respectively. Students' acceptability of the intervention was more neutral than parents or teachers, with mean item ratings on the *CIRP* averaging 2.6 out of a possible 5.

Kratochwill, Elliott, Loitz, Sladeczek, and Carlson (2003) conducted a study of the differential effects of CBC using two methods of consultee intervention support: manual based and video based. Using a pretest–posttest repeated-measures experimental design, the investigators evaluated outcomes of CBC-manual, CBC-video, and control group using multiple measures (*Child Behavior Checklist (CBCL)* [Achenbach, 1991a]; *Teacher Rating Form* [Achenbach, 1991b]; *Social Skills Rating Scale* [Gresham & Elliott, 1990]). The sample was comprised of 125 Head Start children, parents, and teachers. Target behaviors included aggression, compliance, and "other" behaviors such as participating, being on task, and joining a group. Parents' and teachers' goal attainment scores characterized students as meeting their overall behavior goals. Specifically, 75% of parents in the manual group and 95.5% of parents in the video group reported progress toward goal attainment. For teachers, 60% in the manual group and 73.1% in the video group reported similar progress. Reliable change indices (RCI; Gresham & Noell, 1993) were computed for the standardized measures to determine whether reported changes in behaviors pre- to posttest were significant. A RCI of ±1.96 is considered statistically significant (Gresham & Noell, 1993). In the manual and video conditions, an average of 46.08% and 31.37% were deemed statistically significant using RCI. This is in comparison to 25.42% in the control condition. Contrary to these positive findings, effect sizes were negligible. Parents and teachers reported high rates of treatment acceptability and satisfaction with the manual and videotape treatment programs.

Review of Case Studies

Some systematic CBC case studies have also been conducted. In a carefully controlled set of case studies, the model was evaluated with academically underachieving children (Galloway & Sheridan, 1994). Participants were six primary grade students (grades 1–3) who often failed to complete math assignments on time and/or with acceptable levels of accuracy. They all demonstrated performance deficits; they had the skills to complete assignments with accuracy, but often failed to do so.

In two separate sets of case studies, the investigators evaluated the effectiveness of a standard intervention with and without the inclusion of CBC. Both studies involved the use of a manualized home-note system, wherein teachers recorded daily performances in math, as well as process behaviors intended to help them complete work (e.g., pencil ready and papers out). The home note also included a checklist to help remind parents of what to do at home and served as a measure of intervention integrity.

A manual was developed that instructed parents in the use of the home note, including potential reinforcers and ways to handle problems. In the first set of case studies, the manual and home note served as the only interventions. In the second, the home note and manual were used, but were instituted in the context of CBC. Students were also involved in the latter part of consultation (plan implementation and plan evaluation).

The investigators used AB with replication designs to assess outcomes of the home note and CBC interventions. All three children in the home note-only case studies showed improvements in math completion and accuracy. Baseline accuracy scores ranged from 43 to 69%, with posttreatment scores ranging from 67 to 83% (between 20 and 84% gains over baseline). Consistent with the selection criteria, baseline data paths were unstable (i.e., fewer than 80% of the data points were within 15% of the mean level). Furthermore, the data remained variable during plan implementation. Baseline completion levels were variable and ranged from 43 to 74%, with posttreatment completion rates ranging from 86 to 88%. Completion data for two of the three children in the home-note manual condition continued to be variable after treatment.

As in the home-note condition, all children in the home note with CBC condition demonstrated improvements in math completion and accuracy, but the gains were greater and more stable. Specifically, baseline accuracy means ranged from 35 to 57%, with treatment means ranging from 86 to 89% (representing up to a 149% gain over baseline). Although baseline performance was variable, the improved performance during treatment was considered stable for all three children. For work completion, baseline means ranged from 41 to 69%, with treatment means ranging from 95 to 100%. As with the accuracy data, completion data were considered stable. Findings in the CBC case studies also suggested enhanced treatment integrity, maintenance of treatment gains at follow-up, and consumer acceptability. Furthermore, parents in the CBC condition adhered more faithfully to the treatment regimen than did parents in the home note-only case studies, which may be one reason for the greater treatment effects. Parents in the CBC case studies also used home reinforcers more effectively than did parents in the home note-only condition. Teachers in the CBC condition reported greater satisfaction; however, there was no difference in the degree of treatment integrity demonstrated by teachers.

Another case study involved a child displaying irrational fears (Sheridan & Colton, 1994). In this case, a Kindergarten teacher referred a 6-year-old boy who spoke of nightmares repeatedly in school. The boy reported vivid stories of monsters and spiders in his room who often grabbed him at the ankle. He was terrified of sleeping alone and, as a result, slept in his parents' room all night, every night for more than 2 years. The goal for consultation in this case was to get the child to sleep in his own room on a consistent basis.

Treatment involved a fading of environment and positive reinforcement procedure, wherein positive reinforcers were delivered each time the child slept in a spot that moved successively closer to his own room. An AB changing criterion design was used, with the criterion being adequate performance demonstrated over two occasions at each successive level, moving the boy closer to his own room. Dramatic, immediate improvements were observed in this case. Two weeks of baseline showed 0 occasions of sleeping in the boy's own room and 14 occasions of sleeping on the floor of his parents' room. Six steps were identified during treatment, which involved the child moving successively closer to his own room. The child demonstrated immediate effects, with perfect performance at each level until he met the goal of sleeping in his own bed. Likewise, he demonstrated no regression at a 1-month follow-up.

Ray, Skinner, and Watson (1999) implemented CBC in the case of a 5-year-old boy with autism, who demonstrated problem behaviors including aggression and noncompliance. Compliance behaviors appeared to be related to the person issuing the command, with greater levels of compliance associated with his mother than with his teacher. The intervention plan involved the issuance of high-probability command sequences (simple, easy-to-perform tasks) immediately preceding low-probability commands (those typically preceding noncompliance and problem behaviors). As part of consultation, the parent and the teacher received instruction on issuing commands, which included sharing information, modeling, and practicing effective commands. Multiple phases of the intervention were instituted to allow for the transfer of stimulus control from the parent to the teacher in the classroom environment. Across eight intervention phases and a final generalization phase, the child gradually demonstrated high rates of compliance with teacher-issued commands. Compliance with teacher commands increased from 15% during baseline to 95 and 100% during the final intervention and generalization phases, respectively.

Gortmaker, Warnes, and Sheridan (2004) reported the outcomes of a case study of a selectively mute 5-year-old child. An AB case study with follow-up design was used to evaluate the effects of the CBC-mediated intervention. The interventions used in this case included programming common stimuli and positive reinforcement. Since school was the only setting in which the child would not speak, talking was established with the teacher in an alternative location outside of the classroom. Once the child established speech with the teacher outside of the classroom, reinforcers were delivered in the classroom as he gradually elicited speech in the classroom. Upon intervention implementation, a gradual positive trend was seen in the child's speaking behaviors. During the first 3 weeks of intervention, the child immediately increased speech from 0 words at school per day during baseline to an average of 5.3 words per day during treatment. Speaking behaviors continued to increase (with the exception of a decrease following a long school holiday), and maintained at a 2-week follow-up. An effect size of 1.60 was yielded, with 100% nonoverlapping data between baseline and treatment phases. In addition, the child spoke to multiple persons in the school setting (e.g., different teachers and peers) and even spoke in front of groups of peers with seeming comfort. Both the child's teacher and parent reported high levels of acceptability for the process (ratings of 6.0 and 5.73 on a 6-point Likert scale for the teacher and parent, respectively, on the *BIRS*-A). Satisfaction with the consultant was also high, as determined with *CEF* mean item ratings of 6.60 and 6.13 for teacher and parent on a 7-point scale, respectively.

In a paper describing CBC within a context of family-centered services, Sheridan, Warnes, Ellis, Schnoes, and Woods (2006) described a case study of a 4-year-old male attending Early Childhood Special Education (ECSE). The target concern upon CBC referral was tantrumming behavior in the school, home, and public settings, with a specific goal of decreasing the duration of tantrums. The intervention designed to address the concerns of consultees was comprised of antecedent control and differential reinforcement. Specifically, the child was provided with choices for activities and ignored when tantrumming occurred. When he responded appropriately, the child was reinforced through verbal praise and tactile stimulation. Behavioral data indicated that the goal was met quickly upon intervention implementation, with tantrum duration decreasing from an average of 4 minutes during baseline to an average of 1.6 minutes during treatment. The child's parent and the teacher reported that their goals were completely met, as indicated via *GAS*. Both the parent and teacher also reported high levels of acceptability, with *BIRS* acceptability ratings of 5.9 for parent ratings and 5.8 for teacher ratings (out of a possible 6.0). Perceptions of effectiveness, also assessed with the *BIRS*, were high (5.0 and 4.9 for *BIRS* parent and teacher effectiveness ratings, respectively).

Illsley and Sladeczek (2001) reported five case studies of children with significant conduct problems including aggression, noncompliance, and socially inappropriate behaviors. In addition, this series of case studies identified changes in parent knowledge and skill related to effective parenting practices. CBC was found to be effective in producing positive changes in the children's conduct problems at home. All children made significant progress on behaviors targeted for intervention, with decreases in aggressive behavior and increases in compliance and socially appropriate behaviors. As a group, parents tended to demonstrate improvement in their knowledge of child management strategies, increase their use of praise, and express less criticism of their children following CBC. However, much variability in parent outcomes was observed, suggesting that the process was differentially effective across participants. More research is needed to determine child, parent, teacher, or contextual variables that may mediate or moderate the effects of CBC on outcomes.

Review of Process Research

In addition to research investigating the outcomes of CBC on behavioral, social, or academic targets, researchers have explored the interpersonal and communication processes in CBC. Research investigating relational communication, collaborative interactions, and other dimensions of helpfulness within CBC is reviewed next. A summary is given in Table 6.2.

Relational Communication Patterns

Relational coding research, and the coding systems used therein, assesses the connectedness of individuals within a conversation, along with the pragmatic (i.e., control-related) aspects of messages. Erchul et al. (1999) evaluated relational communication patterns that occur between parents, teachers, and

TABLE 6.2. Summary of CBC process research.

Authors	Sample	Dependent variable	Measures	Results	Limitations
Erchul, Sheridan, Ryan, Grissom, Killough, and Mettler (1999)	4 CBC cases 9696 individual messages	Domineeringness Dominance	*Family Relational Communication Control Coding System (FRCCCS)* CBC process integrity	Domineeringness: Overall, consultants displayed higher levels than both parents and teachers Dominance: Parents and teachers displayed the same level and were somewhat higher than consultants	Small sample size Generalizability No established sense for high or low levels of domineeringness or dominance Altered standardized measures No CBC research for optimal relationship dynamics
Grissom, Erchul, and Sheridan (2003)	N = 20 CBC cases N = 16 consultants N = 23 teachers N = 20 parents N = 20 clients	Domineeringness Dominance	*Family Relational Communication Control Coding System (FRCCCS)* Social validity	Overall, all participants shared in the level of influence over the process No significant correlations for domineeringness and outcomes were found Teachers reported lower acceptability when parents were more dominant Parents reported lower perceived effectiveness when they were more dominant	Small sample size Low statistical power Only CPIIs were coded Self-report outcome measures Limited external validity of CBC cases

(Continued)

TABLE 6.2. Summary of CBC process research—Cont'd.

Authors	Sample	Dependent variable	Measures	Results	Limitations
Sheridan, Meegan, and Eagle (2002)	N = 13 consultants N = 19 parents and teachers N = 16 students 8848 speech acts 4986 speech exchanges	Influence Involvement	*Psychosocial Processes Coding Scheme (PPCS)* Direct observations Social validity	Participants displayed higher levels of collaboration followed by obliging statements with minimal controlling or withdrawing comments No significant relationship between speech act exchanges and behavioral outcomes was found	No control of relationship or differences among participants No study of intermediary variables Small sample size All consultants trained by same researcher Lack of reliability data for direct behavioral outcomes Only CPIIs were coded Selection bias

Source: From Sheridan, S. M., Clarke, B. L., & Burt, J. D. (2008). Conjoint behavioral consultation: What do we know and what do we need to know? In W. P. Erchul & S. M. Sheridan (Eds.). *Handbook of research in school consultation: Empirical foundations for the field.* Mahwah, NJ: Lawrence Erlbaum Associates. Reprinted with permission.

consultants in CBC by assessing who is speaking to whom and with what degree of relational control. The *Family Relational Communication Control Coding System* (*FRCCCS*; Heatherington & Friedlander, 1987) was used to analyze domineeringness (an individual's directiveness or *attempt* to define or structure relationships throughout consultation) and dominance (an individual's demonstrated influence or *success* in defining the relationship). Four CBC cases consisting of 12 interviews were audio taped, transcribed, and coded in terms of domineeringness and dominance using the *FRCCCS*. Erchul et al. (1999) found that no single individual attempted to direct or influence the other members at disproportionate levels. Rather, communication patterns tended to be bidirectional and reciprocal, supporting the notion that CBC is a *collaborative* process involving symmetrical and reciprocal relationships.

Aspects of interpersonal control within the context of CBC and their relationship to case outcomes were the focus of investigation by Grissom, Erchul, and Sheridan (2003). Measures of dominance and domineeringness were assessed using the *FRCCCS*. Outcome variables included acceptability and effectiveness of CBC (measured with the *BIRS*), consultant effectiveness (measured with the *CEF*), and attainment of consultation goals (measured with *GAS*). Conjoint Problem Identification Interviews (CPII) for 20 CBC cases were coded on the relational control variables (cf. Erchul & Schulte, 1990). Perceptions of outcomes in CBC were not significantly related to attempts to influence (i.e., domineeringness) and demonstrated influence (i.e., dominance) by consultants and teachers. The relationship between parent domineeringness and outcome measures also was not significant. However, parent dominance was significantly related to two outcome measures. Specifically, as parents influenced the parent–consultant dyadic exchange, teachers' ratings of acceptability/effectiveness was lower. The authors suggested that teachers' lower perceptions of acceptability and effectiveness may be due to unmet expectations for the consultant to be more directive with the process.

In addition, parent dominance within the parent–consultant and parent–teacher dyad was associated with less favorable parental goal attainment ratings. Thus, as parents demonstrated more influence in the CNII, they reported less positive behavioral outcomes for their child. Previous research in behavioral consultation demonstrated similar results with teacher attempts at control over the process relating to less positive outcomes (e.g., Erchul, 1987; Erchul & Chewning, 1990; Witt, Erchul, McKee, & Pardue, 1991). Such findings suggest that control within the consultee-to-consultee and consultant-to-consultee exchange may be an important factor influencing perceptions of case outcomes.

Social Context

Sheridan, Meegan, and Eagle (2002) examined the nature of the social context in CBC and its relationship to case outcomes (i.e., effect sizes, perceived effectiveness/acceptability of consultation procedures, and satisfaction with the consultant). The *Psychosocial Processes Coding Scheme* (*PPCS*; Leaper, 1991) was used to assess two dimensions of communication function within CBC: influence and involvement. Influence was defined as the degree to which a speech act (i.e., a phrase or utterance bound by intonation, pauses, or grammar, which conveyed a single message) attempted to control the task in consultation, or the extent to which a statement directly or indirectly influenced the process. Involvement referred to the degree to which a speech act facilitated or hindered the social relationship. Direct and indirect levels of these two dimensions created four main categories of speech acts: (a) collaborative speech was high in both influence and involvement, (b) controlling speech was high on influence and low on involvement, (c) obliging speech was low on influence and high on involvement, and (d) withdrawing speech was low on both influence and involvement.

Analyses were conducted using 30-minutes segments of 16 CPIIs. Descriptive analysis of the speech acts revealed that individual speech acts among participants were highly collaborative, followed by obliging with negligible amounts of controlling or withdrawing messages. More specifically, when consultants were not making collaborative statements, they were obliging, rather than controlling. These results suggest that the social context of CBC is conducive to the development of collaborative partnerships across home and school settings. In addition, effect sizes were found to be meaningful and positive. Thus, not only were collaborative relationships formed, but the collaborative process was effective in addressing target concerns related to the child.

Review of Social Validity Research

The importance of social validity in consultation outcome research is now well accepted (Elliott, Witt, & Kratochwill, 1991). Kazdin (1977) and Wolf (1978) described social validity as the social significance of the target behavior chosen for treatment, the social appropriateness or acceptability of the treatment procedures, and the resulting behavior change. For consultation outcomes to be considered socially valid, (a) goals should be socially significant, (b) procedures should be considered socially appropriate, and (c) effects should be clinically meaningful. In the consultation literature, the predominant focus of social validity research is centered on treatment acceptability. Treatment acceptability is defined as "judgments of lay persons, clients, and others of whether the procedures proposed for treatment are appropriate, fair, and reasonable for the problem or client" (Kazdin, 1980, p. 493). The meaningfulness of consultation outcomes is often measured through ratings of intervention effectiveness and attainment of consultation goals (e.g., through *GAS*; Kiresuk, Smith, & Cardillo, 1994). The CBC literature has also examined social validity through parent and teacher perceptions of helpfulness. Helpfulness is characterized as responsiveness to client needs, promotion of competency acquisition, and promotion of partnership and collaboration among systems (Dunst, Trivette, Davis, & Cornwell, 1994).

TABLE 6.3. Summary of CBC social validity research.

Authors	Sample	Dependent variable	Measures	Results	Limitations
Freer and Watson (1999)	$N = 111$ parents $N = 61$ teachers	Acceptability ratings between teacher-only consultation, parent-only consultation, and CBC	Problem questionnaire (list of academic, social/ emotional, behavioral problems) *Intervention Rating Profile-15 (IRP-15)*	CBC rated as most preferred approach for all problem types by parents and teachers CBC rated as most acceptable form of consultation by parents and teachers	Low return rate of surveys Lack of variability in characteristics of sample Bias of previous experience with consultation Differences may be explained by other variables Analogue data lacks ecological validity
Sheridan, Erchul, Brown, Dowd, Warnes, Marti, and Eagle (2004)	$N = 137$ parents $N = 122$ teachers $N = 118$ child-clients	Perceptions of helpfulness	*Consultant Evaluation Form* (CEF) *Behavior Intervention Rating Scale-Effectiveness* factor (*BIRS-*E) *Behavior Intervention Rating Scale-Acceptability* factor (*BIRS-*A) *Goal Attainment Scaling* (GAS) Direct observations Congruence between parent and teacher ratings	Nonsignificant relationship between parent and teacher helpfulness ratings Nonsignificant relationship between parent and teacher agreement and effect sizes Significant relationships between difference scores and parent acceptability, teacher acceptability, and parent effectiveness ratings	Reliability of observational data Select consultant sample

(*Continued*)

TABLE 6.3. Summary of CBC social validity research—Cont'd.

Authors	Sample	Dependent variable	Measures	Results	Limitations
Sheridan and Steck (1995)	$N = 409$ School Psychologists	Perceptions of CBC (procedural acceptability, situational acceptability)	Consultation Questionnaire	Procedural acceptability ratings were "highly acceptable" CBC acceptability was greater than other modes of service delivery (teacher consultation, parent consultation, direct service) for academic, behavioral, and social/emotional concerns	Only nationally certified school psychologists sampled Situational acceptability and process acceptability measures may assess different constructs Self-report of attitudes may differ from behavior
Sladeczek, Elliott, Kratochwill, Robertson-Mjaanes, and Stoiber (2001)	Case study 5-year-old pre-school male with conduct problems	Perceptions of goal attainment	*Goal Attainment Scaling* (GAS) Direct observation	*T* score = 64.18, a score above 50 indicating performance above baseline expectations	Generalizability Case study

Source: From Sheridan, S. M., Clarke, B. L., & Burt, J. D. (2008). Conjoint behavioral consultation: What do we know and what do we need to know? In W. P. Erchul & S. M. Sheridan (Eds.), *Handbook of research in school consultation: Empirical foundations for the field*. Mahwah, NJ: Lawrence Erlbaum Associates. Reprinted with permission.

CBC repeatedly has been recognized as acceptable (Freer & Watson, 1999; Sheridan & Steck, 1995; Sladeczek, Elliott, Kratochwill, Robertson-Mjaanes, & Stoiber, 2001) and helpful (Sheridan, Erchul et al., 2004) by parents, teachers, and school psychologists. Several outcome studies reviewed here included measures of social validity as variables of interest (also see Table 6.1). In addition, some studies have used survey methodology to determine acceptability of CBC in a hypothetical sense. Finally, at least two studies considered measures of social validity (i.e., goal attainment and consultant helpfulness) as primary variables of interest. Studies that had as their main focus the social validity of CBC are summarized later and in Table 6.3.

Acceptability Research

Sheridan and Steck (1995) surveyed a national sample of school psychologists to examine their perceptions of the acceptability of CBC as a model of service delivery. The Consultation Questionnaire was developed for this study and used to assess school psychologists' acceptability of CBC. The questionnaire consisted of three sections: (a) demographic and consultant information (i.e., gender, highest degree earned, age of students served, number of years as a practicing school psychologist, and geographic locale of practice); (b) procedural acceptability of CBC (i.e., 15 items from the acceptability factor of *BIRS*); and (c) situational acceptability (i.e., acceptability of 4 methods of service delivery across 21 student problem situations). The purpose of this study was to (a) evaluate practicing school psychologists' perceptions of CBC, (b) investigate variables that influence its acceptability, and (c) examine the desirability of CBC with other behavioral modes of service delivery (i.e., direct intervention, parent-only, and teacher-only consultation).

Practicing school psychologists responding to the survey reported CBC to be an acceptable model of service delivery. Overall, CBC was rated very favorably by respondents, and ratings were positive across different problem types and in comparison to other modes of service delivery. School psychologists rated the mean procedural acceptability of CBC as 5.24 on a 6-point Likert scale, with 6 reflecting high acceptability. The overall mean logistical barriers score was 4.31 on a 6-point Likert scale, with high scores reflecting a lack of logistical barriers. Although school psychologists rated CBC as acceptable, they also reported that logistical barriers, such as lack of time and administrative/organization support, impacted the overall acceptability of the model. Age of students served, theoretical orientation, and number of years in practice had no influence on the acceptability ratings.

School psychologists also found CBC to be more acceptable than other modes of service delivery across all problem types (i.e., academic, behavioral, and social-emotional). Further, CBC was rated similarly by school psychologists across all age groups, with the exception of secondary-school psychologists rating CBC and direct service as equally acceptable. These findings suggest that CBC is perceived by practicing school psychologists as generally more applicable than other modes of service delivery.

Parent and teacher perceptions of the acceptability of different approaches to behavioral consultation (i.e., teacher-only consultation, parent-only consultation, and conjoint behavioral consultation) were examined by Freer and Watson (1999). A total of 111 parents of elementary-aged children and 61 elementary and secondary teachers participated. Each participant received a packet containing the "Problem Questionnaire" and the *Intervention Rating Profile-15* (*IRP-15*; Witt & Elliott, 1985). The author-developed Problem Questionnaire consisted of a list of 17 common academic (e.g., reading), behavioral (e.g., high distractibility), and social emotional (e.g., trouble making friends) problems. Respondents were asked to select one consultation approach that was most appropriate for each given problem, and rated the overall acceptability of each consultation model on the *IRP-15*.

Both parents and teachers found CBC to be a very acceptable model of consultation. The respondents consistently selected CBC as the most preferred consultation approach for academic, behavioral, and social emotional problems. Regarding overall acceptability, both parents and teachers rated CBC as the most acceptable model of behavioral consultation (overall mean CBC = 78.88, parent-only consultation = 63.31, teacher-only consultation = 60.45). These results are consistent with those of Sheridan and Steck (1995), who found that school psychologists, parents, and teachers find CBC to be an acceptable model of service delivery. However, this research was conducted using survey methodology, assessing acceptability of analogue situations rather than actual cases. Thus, the results of these studies are based on hypothetical acceptability, not actual experience with the model.

CBC outcome studies have extended the social validity literature base to include treatment acceptability measurements from field-based case work. A 4-year study examining the effectiveness of 52 CBC cases demonstrated parents and teachers found the CBC process to be acceptable (Sheridan et al., 2001). Specifically, ratings on the acceptability factor of the *BIRS-R* demonstrated that CBC was a highly acceptable process. Parents' mean item ratings of the acceptability of CBC yielded an average of 5.44 (on a scale of 1–6, with 6 reflecting high acceptability), and teachers' mean item ratings averaged 5.45. These results are not unique to this outcome study. Multiple CBC studies have investigated the acceptability of CBC and have found it to be rated as highly acceptable by parents and teachers alike. The reader is referred to Table 6.1 for a complete list of outcome studies that measured social validity.

Goal Attainment

Sladeczek et al. (2001) investigated participants' perceptions of client goal attainment as program evaluation procedure within the context of a CBC case study. Specifically, a kindergarten teacher referred a 5-year-old preschool boy for conduct problems. The teacher reported that the child frequently screamed when angry and disrupted other children. His mother indicated that he demanded her attention by clinging to her. The initial goal for consultation was to increase the child's appropriate behaviors (i.e., decrease screaming behavior at school and decrease clinging behavior at home).

During the CPAI, baseline data were discussed, intervention goals were identified, and intervention strategies were developed. Baseline data indicated that the boy had between 6 and 17 screaming incidents per day at school and 17–20 clinging episodes per day at home. The *GAS* worksheet was used to identify clear goals for the target behaviors, with anchors on the *GAS* associated with frequency of screaming incidents at school and clinging behaviors at home. *GAS* represented an average frequency of the target behavior on a weekly basis and provided the teacher and parent with a common language to communicate the effectiveness of the intervention. During the last few weeks of the intervention, both the child's parents and teacher consistently rated his progress toward the intervention goals at +2 ("goal fully met"). Translating *GAS* scores into T-scores (Cardillo & Smith, 1994) resulted in a postintervention T-score of 64.18 (with scores greater than 50 suggesting performance above what is expected from baseline), indicating positive outcomes for the intervention package implemented within the context of CBC. Both the consultant and consultees found CBC to be enhanced by the use of *GAS*. Despite the positive outcomes of this case study, caution should be exercised when generalizing outcomes given the small sample size and inexact ability of the *GAS* to establish an absolute level of functioning.

Previous outcome studies have also used *GAS* to assess parent and teacher perceptions of consultation goals. A 4-year investigation by Sheridan et al. (2001) examined the effectiveness of 52 CBC cases. Goal attainment reports indicated that 100% of parents and 94% of teachers rated goals as partially or fully met.

Helpfulness Research

Congruence among home and school systems has been identified as an important variable related to a child's academic performance (Hansen, 1986; Hill, 2001). Similarly, congruence between consultants and consultees related to their respective roles is related to positive outcomes of consultation (Erchul, Hughes, Meyers, Hickman, & Braden, 1992). Sheridan, Erchul et al. (2004) furthered the examination of congruence by investigating the congruence of parent and teacher perceptions of the helpfulness of CBC and its relationship to case outcomes. Specifically, Sheridan and colleagues assessed (a) congruence in the degree to which parents and teachers found the CBC consultant to be helpful and (b) the relationship between parent and teacher agreement on social validity and behavioral outcomes.

Participants included 118 children, 137 parents, 122 teachers, and 53 graduate consultants. Thirty-nine percent of the child clients were considered diverse on one or more variables (i.e., one parent living at home, nonwhite, living in poverty, mother did not have a high school degree, speaking a language other than English in the home). The Acceptability factor of the *BIRS-R* was used to assess parent and teacher acceptability of CBC. *GAS* provided an assessment of parents' and teachers' perceptions of efficacy through their rating of the degree to which consultation goals were achieved. In addition, the *CEF* (Erchul, 1987) measured parents' and teachers' ratings of the consultant's effectiveness. Individual child outcomes were measured via permanent products and direct behavioral observations throughout the implementation of CBC with effect sizes computed using a "no assumptions approach" (Busk & Serlin, 1992).

To assess the congruence between parents' and teachers' perceptions of helpfulness, a Pearson correlation was computed between parents' and teachers' total scores on the *CEF*. The resulting correlation was nonsignificant. Correlations between parent and teacher agreement scores (i.e., absolute difference score between parent and teacher *CEF* scores) and effect sizes were also nonsignificant. The results suggest that parents' and teachers' perspectives of the helpfulness of the consultant are not necessarily related to one another. However, negative correlations were found between parent and teacher agreement scores (i.e., *CEF* difference scores) and social validity outcomes (i.e., teacher acceptability, parent acceptability, and parent effectiveness ratings). Thus, as differences between parents and teachers regarding the helpfulness of CBC increased, the acceptability of the model appeared to decrease. For parents only, as differences among parents and teachers increased, their perceptions of the efficacy of CBC decreased. Thus, the identification of means to promote congruence and agreement related to aspects of CBC appears worthy of further investigation.

Summary

CBC outcome research has demonstrated that the model provides an effective mechanism for addressing the needs of children who are at risk for academic, behavioral, and/or social difficulties. Furthermore, research on processes within CBC suggests that processes establish a collaborative context for joint planning, decision making, and problem solving. Numerous small and meta-analytic studies, utilizing both hypothetical and naturalistic methods, have found that parents, teachers, and school psychologists identify CBC to be an acceptable model of service delivery.

There continues to be a need for empirical investigation of both outcomes and processes of CBC. Future research is needed to identify (a) conditions under which CBC is effective, (b) variables within settings or participants that may mediate or moderate the relationship between process and outcome, (c) the effects of CBC on consultee variables such as behavioral management skills or partnering practices, (d) the effects of CBC on family–school or adult–child relationships, (e) long-term maintenance effects of CBC outcomes, and (f) the utility of CBC as a prevention model. These research issues may be best addressed through new and sophisticated research designs such as those that model change over time, randomly assign participants to varying experimental conditions, and use mixed methods (including qualitative and quantitative) to address complex research questions.

References

Abikoff, H., & Gittelman, R. (1985). Classroom observation code: A modification of the Stony Brook code. *Psychopharmacology Bulletin, 21,* 901–909.

Achenbach, T.M. (1991a). *Manual for the Child Behavior Checklist/4–18 and 1991 Profile.* Burlington: Department of Psychiatry, University of Vermont.

Achenbach, T.M. (1991b). *Manual for the Teacher's Report Form and 1991 Profile.* Burlington: Department of Psychiatry, University of Vermont.

Adelman, H.S., & Taylor, L. (1998). Mental health in the schools: Moving forward. *School Psychology Review, 27,* 175–190.

Alexander, K., & Entwisle, D.R. (1988). Achievement in the first two years of school: Patterns and processes. *Monographs of the Society for Research in Child Development, 53*(2, Serial No. 218).

Ames, C. (1993). How school-to-home communications influence parent beliefs and perceptions. *Equity and Choice, 9,* 44–49.

August, G.J., Anderson, D., & Bloomquist, M.L. (1992). Competence enhancement training for children: An integrated child, parent, and school approach. In S.L. Christenson & J.C. Conoley (Eds.), *Home–school collaboration: Enhancing children's academic and social competence* (pp. 175–192). Silver Spring, MD: National Association of School Psychologists.

Barton, P.E., & Coley, R.J. (1992). *America's smallest school: The family.* Princeton, NJ: Educational Testing Service.

Batsche, G., Elliot, J., Schrag, J., & Tilly, W. D. (2005, October). *Response to intervention: The opportunity and the reality.* Paper presented to the Annual Conference of the National Association of State Directors of Special Education, Minneapolis, MN.

Bempechat, J. (1998). *Against the odds: How "at-risk" students exceed expectations.* San Francisco: Jossey-Bass.

Bergan, J.R., & Kratochwill, T.R. (1990). *Behavioral consultation and therapy.* New York: Plenum Press.

Bergan, J.R., & Tombari, M.L. (1975). The analysis of verbal interactions occurring during consultation. *Journal of School Psychology, 13,* 209–226.

Bergan, J.R., & Tombari, M.L. (1976). Consultant skill and efficacy and the implementation and outcome of consultation. *Journal of School Psychology, 14,* 3–14.

Blechman, E.A., Taylor, C.J., & Schrader, S.M. (1981). Family problem solving versus home notes as early intervention with high-risk children. *Journal of Consulting and Clinical Psychology, 49,* 919–926.

Bradley, R.H., Caldwell, B.M., & Rock, S.L. (1988). Home environment and school performance: A ten year follow-up and examination of three models of environmental action. *Child Development, 59,* 852–867.

Bronfenbrenner, U. (1977). Toward an experimental ecology of human development. *American Psychologist, 32*, 513–531.

Bronstein, P., Duncan, P., Clauson, J., Abrams, C.L., Yannett, N., Ginsburg, G., & Milne, M. (1998). Preventing middle school adjustment problems for children from lower-income families: A program for aware parenting. *Journal of Applied Developmental Psychology, 19*, 129–152.

Brown, D. (1997). Implications of cultural values for cross-cultural consultation with families. *Journal of Counseling and Development, 76*, 29–35.

Brown-Chidsey, R. (Ed.). (2005). *Assessment for intervention: A problem-solving approach*. New York: Guilford Press.

Brown-Chidsey, R., & Steege, M.W. (2006). *Response to intervention: Principles and strategies for effective instruction*. New York: Guilford Press.

Busk, P., & Serlin, R. (1992). Meta-analysis for single-case research. In T.R. Kratochwill & J. Levin (Eds.), *Single-case research design and analysis* (pp. 187–212). Hillsdale, NJ: Lawrence Erlbaum Associates.

Cardillo, J.E., & Smith, A. (1994). Psychometric issues. In T.J. Kiresuk, A. Smith, & J.E. Cardillo (Eds.), *Goal attainment scaling: Applications, theory, and measurement* (pp. 173–241). Hillsdale, NJ: Lawrence Erlbaum Associates, Inc.

Carlson, C., & Christenson, S.L. (2005). Evidence-based parent and family interventions in school psychology: Overview and procedures. *School Psychology Quarterly, 20*, 345–351.

Cataldo, M.F. (1984). Clinical considerations in training parents of children with special problems. In R.E. Dangel & R.A. Polster (Eds.), *Parent training* (pp. 329–357). New York: Guilford Press.

Cavell, T.A., & Hughes, J.N. (2000). Secondary prevention as context for studying change processes in aggressive children. *Journal of School Psychology, 38*, 199–235.

Christenson, S.L. (1995). Families and schools: What is the role of the school psychologist? *School Psychology Quarterly, 10*, 118–132.

Christenson, S.L. (2004). *Parent–teacher partnerships: Creating essential connections for children's reading and learning*. Unpublished training manual.

Christenson, S.L., & Hirsch, J. (1998). Facilitating partnerships and conflict resolution between families and schools. In K.C. Stoiber & T.Kratochwill (Eds.), *Handbook of group interventions for children and families* (pp. 307–344). Boston: Allyn & Bacon.

Christenson, S.L., & Sheridan, S.M. (2001). *Schools and families: Creating essential connections for learning*. New York: Guilford Press.

Colton, D., & Sheridan, S.M. (1998). Conjoint behavioral consultation and social skills training: Enhancing the play behavior of boys with attention deficit-hyperactivity disorder. *Journal of Educational and Psychological Consultation, 9*, 3–28.

Comer, J.P. (1995). *School power: Implications of an intervention project*. New York: Free Press.

Conoley, J.C., & Gutkin, T.B. (1986). School psychology: A reconceptualization of service delivery realities. In S. Elliott & J. Witt (Eds.), *Delivery of psychological services in schools: Concepts, processes, issues* (pp. 393–424). New York: Erlbaum.

Creer, T.L., & Bender, B.G. (1995). Pediatric asthma. In M.C. Roberts (Ed.), *Handbook of pediatric psychology* (2nd ed., pp. 219–240). New York: Guilford Press.

Dauber, S.L., & Epstein, J.L. (1993). Parents' attitudes and practices of involvement in inner city elementary and middle schools. In N.F. Chavkin (Ed.), *Families and schools in a pluralistic society* (pp. 53–72). Albany: State University of New York Press.

Dempsey, I., & Dunst, C.J. (2004). Help-giving styles as a function of parent empowerment in families with a young child with a disability. *Journal of Intellectual and Developmental Disability, 29*, 50–61.

Dunst, C., & Deal, A. (1994). A family-centered approach to developing individualized family support plans. In C. Dunst, C. Trivette, & A. Deal (Eds.), *Supporting and strengthening families: Vol. 1. Methods, strategies and practices* (pp. 73–89). Cambridge, MA: Brookline Books.

Dunst, C.J., & Trivette, C.M. (1987). Enabling and empowering families: Conceptual and intervention issues. *School Psychology Review, 16*, 443–456.

Dunst, C.J., Trivette, C.M., Davis, M., & Cornwell, J.C. (1994). Characteristics of effective help-giving practices. In C.J. Dunst, C.M. Trivette, & A.G. Deal (Eds.), *Supporting and strengthening families. Vol. 1. Methods, strategies and practices* (pp. 171–186). Cambridge, MA: Brookline Books.

Dunst, C., Trivette, C., & Deal, A. (1988). *Enabling and empowering families: Principles and guidelines for practice.* Cambridge, MA: Brookline Books.

Duvall, S.F., Delquadri, J.C., Elliott, M., & Hall, R.V. (1992). Parent tutoring procedures: Experimental analysis and validation of generalization in oral reading across passages, settings, and time. *Journal of Behavioral Education, 2*, 281–303.

Edens, J.H. (1997). Home visitation programs with ethnic minority families: Cultural issues in parent consultation. *Journal of Educational and Psychological Consultation, 8*, 373–383.

Elliott, S.N., Sladeczek, I.E., & Kratochwill, T.R. (1995). *Goal attainment scaling: Its use as a progress monitoring and outcome effectiveness measure in behavioral consultation.* Poster session presented at the annual meeting of the American Psychological Association, New York.

Elliott, S.N., Witt, J.C., & Kratochwill, T.R. (1991). Selecting, implementing, and evaluating classroom interventions. In G. Stoner, M.R. Shinn, & H.M. Walker (Eds.), *Interventions for achievement and behavior problems* (pp. 99–135). Silver Spring, MD: National Association of School Psychologists.

Entwisle, D.R., Alexander, K.L., Cadigan, D., & Pallas, A. (1986). The schooling process in first grade: Two samples a decade apart. *American Educational Research Journal, 23*, 587–613.

Erchul, W.P. (1987). A relational communication analysis of control in school consultation. *Professional School Psychology, 2*, 113–124.

Erchul, W.P., & Chewning, T.G. (1990). Behavioral consultation from a request-centered relational communication perspective. *School Psychology Quarterly, 5*, 1–20.

Erchul, W.P., Hughes, J.N., Meyers, J., Hickman, J.A., & Braden, J.P. (1992). Dyadic agreement concerning the consultation process and its relationship to outcome. *Journal of Education and Psychological Consultation, 3*, 119–132.

Erchul, W.P., & Schulte, A.C. (1990). The coding of consultation verbalizations: How much is enough? *School Psychology Quarterly, 5*, 256–264.

Erchul, W.P., Sheridan, S.M., Ryan, D.A., Grissom, P.F., Killough, C.E., & Mettler, D.W. (1999). Patterns of relational communication in conjoint behavioral consultation. *School Psychology Quarterly, 14*, 121–147.

Frank, J.L., & Kratochwill, T.R. (2008). School-based problem-solving consultation: Plotting a new course for evidence-based research and practice in consultation. In W.P. Erchul & S.M. Sheridan (Eds.), *Handbook of research in school consultation: Empirical foundations for the field.* (pp. 13–32) Mahwah, NJ: Lawrence Erlbaum Associates.

Freer, P., & Watson, T.S. (1999). A comparison of parent and teacher acceptability ratings of behavioral and conjoint behavioral consultation. *School Psychology Review, 28*, 672–684.

Friend, M., & Cook, L. (1992). *Interactions: Collaboration skills for school professionals.* New York: Longman.

Funderburk, B.W., Eyberg, S.M., Newcomb, K., McNeil, C.B., Hembree-Kigin, T., & Capage, L. (1998). Parent–child interaction therapy with behavior problem children: Maintenance of treatment effects in the school setting. *Child and Family Behavior Therapy, 20*, 17–38.

Gadow, K.D., Nolan, E.E., Paolicelli, L.M., & Sprafkin, J. (1991). A procedure for assessing the effects of methylphenidate on hyperactive children in public school settings. *Journal of Clinical Child Psychology, 20*, 268–276.

Gadow, K.D., Sprafkin, J., & Nolan, E.E. (1996). *ADHD school observation code.* Stony Brook, NY: Checkmate Plus.

Galloway, J., & Sheridan, S.M. (1994). Implementing scientific practices through case studies: Examples using home–school interventions and consultation. *Journal of School Psychology, 32*, 385–413.

Garbarino, J. (1982). *Children and families in the social environment.* New York: Aldine.

Gettinger, M., & Waters-Guetschow, K. (1998). Parental involvement in schools: Parent and teacher perceptions of roles, efficacy, and opportunities. *Journal of Research and Development in Education, 32*, 38–52.

Gortmaker, V., Warnes, E.D., & Sheridan, S.M. (2004). Conjoint behavioral consultation: Involving parents and teachers in the treatment of a child with selective mutism. *Proven Practice, 5*, 66–72.

Gresham, F.M. (1989). Assessment of treatment integrity in school consultation and prereferral intervention. *School Psychology Review, 18*, 37–50.

Gresham, F.M., & Elliott, S.N. (1990). *Social skills rating system manual.* Circle Pines, MN: American Guidance Service.

Gresham, F.M., & Noell, G.H. (1993). Documenting the effectiveness of consultation outcomes. In J. Zins, T. Kratochwill, & S. Elliott (Eds.), *Handbook of consultation services for children* (pp. 249–273). San Francisco: Jossey-Bass.

Grissom, P.F., Erchul, W.P., & Sheridan, S.M. (2003). Relationships among relational communication processes and perceptions of outcomes in conjoint behavioral consultation. *Journal of Educational and Psychological Consultation, 14*, 157–180.

Grolnick, W.S., Benjet, C., Kurowski, C.O., & Apostoleris, N.H. (1997). Predictors of parent involvement in children's schooling. *Journal of Educational Psychology, 89*, 538–548.

Guli, L.A. (2005). Evidence-based parent consultation with school-related outcomes. *School Psychology Quarterly, 20*, 455–472.

Guralnick, M. (1989). Recent developments in early intervention efficacy research: Implications for family involvement in PL 99-457. *Topics in Early Childhood Special Education, 9*, 1–17.

Gutkin, T.B. (1999). The collaboration debate: Finding our way through maze: Moving forward into the future: A response to Erchul (1999). *Journal of School Psychology, 37*, 229–241.

Gutkin, T.B. (Ed.). (2002). Evidence-based interventions in school psychology: The state of the art and future directions [Special issue]. *School Psychology Quarterly, 17*, 339–340.

Gutkin, T.B., & Curtis, M.J. (1999). School-based consultation theory and practice: The art and science of indirect service delivery. In C.R. Reynolds & T.B. Gutkin (Eds.), *The handbook of school psychology* (3rd ed., pp. 598–637). New York: John Wiley & Sons.

Gutkin, T.B., & Curtis, M.J. (1982). School-based consultation: Theory and techniques. In C.R. Reynolds & T.B. Gutkin (Eds.), *The handbook of school psychology* (pp. 796–828). New York: Wiley.

Hansen, D.A. (1986). Family–school articulations: The effects of interaction rule mismatch. *American Educational Research Journal, 23*, 643–659.

Harris, K.C. (1991). An expanded view on consultation competencies for educators serving culturally and linguistically diverse exceptional students. *Teacher Education and Special Education, 14*, 25–29.

Harry, B. (1992). *Cultural diversity, families, and the special education system: Communication and empowerment.* New York: Teachers College Press.

Hayes, S.C., Barlow, D.H., & Nelson-Gray, R.O. (1999). *The scientist practitioner: Research and accountability in the age of managed care* (2nd ed.). Needham Heights, MA: Allyn & Bacon.

Heatherington, L., & Friedlander, M.L. (1987). *Family relational communication control coding system coding manual.* Unpublished manuscript, Psychology Department, Williams College, Williamstown, MA.

Heller, L.R., & Fantuzzo, J.W. (1993). Reciprocal peer tutoring and parent partnership: Does parent involvement make a difference? *School Psychology Review, 22*, 517–534.

Hembree-Kigin, T., & McNeil, C.B. (1995). *Parent–child interaction therapy.* New York: Plenum Press.

Henderson, A.T., & Mapp, K.L. (2002). *A new wave of evidence: The impact of school, family, and community connections on student achievement.* Austin, TX: Southwest Educational Development Laboratory.

Henning-Stout, M. (1994). Thoughts on being a White consultant. *Journal of Educational and Psychological Consultation, 5*, 269–273.

Hernandez, D.J. (2004). Demographic change and the life circumstances of immigrant families. *The Future of Children, 14*(2), 17–47. http://www.futureofchildren.org/usr_doc/hernandez.pdf. Accessed 07.05.07.

Hill, N.E. (2001). Parenting and academic socialization as they relate to school readiness: The roles of ethnicity and family income. *Journal of Educational Psychology, 93*, 686–697.

Hoagwood, K., Burns, B.J., Kiser, L., Ringeisen, H., & Schoenwald, S.K. (2001). Evidence-based practice in child and adolescent mental health services. *Psychiatric Services, 52*, 1179–1189.

Hobbs, N. (1975). *The futures of children.* San Francisco: Jossey-Bass.

Hook, C.L., & DuPaul, G.J. (1999). Parent tutoring for students with attention deficit/hyperactivity disorder: Effects on reading performance at home and school. *School Psychology Review, 28*, 60–75.

Hoover-Dempsey, K.V., Bassler, O.C., & Brissie, J.S. (1992). Explorations in parent–school relations. *Journal of Education Research, 85*, 287–294.

Hoover-Dempsey, K.V., & Sandler, H.M. (1995). Parental involvement in children's education: Why does it make a difference? *Teachers College Record, 92*, 310–331.

Hoover-Dempsey, K.V., & Sandler, H.M. (1997). Why do parents become involved in their children's education? *Review of Educational Research, 67*, 3–42.

Husen, T. (1969). *Talent, opportunity and career.* Stockholm: Almqvist & Wiksell.

Illsley, S.D., & Sladeczek, I.E. (2001). Conjoint behavioral consultation: Outcome measures beyond the client level. *Journal of Educational and Psychological Consultation, 12,* 397–404.

Individuals with Disabilities Education Act of 1997, Pub. L. No. 105–17, 111 Stat. 37 (1997) (codified at 20 U.S.C. §§ 1400–1487).

Individuals with Disabilities Education Act of 1999, 20 U.S.C. § 1400 *et seq.*

Ingraham, C.L. (2000). Consultation through a multicultural lens: Multicultural and cross-cultural consultation in schools. *School Psychology Review, 29,* 320–343.

Ingraham, C.L. (2008). Studying multicultural aspects of consultation. In W.P. Erchul & S.M. Sheridan (Eds.), *Handbook of research in school consultation: Empirical foundations for the field.* (pp. 269–292) Hillsdale, NJ: Lawrence Erlbaum Associates.

Jayanthi, M., Sawyer, V., Nelson, J.S., Bursuck, W.D., & Epstein, M.H. (1995). Recommendations for homework-communication problems: From parents, classroom teachers, and special education teachers. *Remedial and Special Education, 16,* 212–225.

Johnson, S.M., Bolstad, O.D., & Lobitz, G.K. (1976). Generalization and contrast phenomena in behavior modification with children. In E.J. Mash, L.A. Hamerlynck, & L.C. Handy (Eds.), *Behavior modification and families.* New York: Brunner/Mazel.

Kazdin, A.E. (1977). Assessing the clinical or applied significance of behavior change through social validation. *Behavior Modification, 1,* 427–452.

Kazdin, A.E. (1980). Acceptability of alternative treatments for deviant child behavior. *Journal of Applied Behavior Analysis, 13,* 259–273.

Kazdin, A.E. (1982). *Single case experimental designs: Methods for clinical and applied settings.* New York: Oxford University Press.

Kazdin, A.E., Esveldt-Dawson, K., French, N.H., & Unis, A.S. (1987). Problem-solving skills training and relationship therapy in the treatment of antisocial child behavior. *Journal of Consulting and Clinical Psychology, 55,* 76–85.

Kazdin, A.E., Siegel, T.C., & Bass, D. (1992). Cognitive problem-solving skills training and parent management training in the treatment of antisocial behavior in children. *Journal of Consulting and Clinical Psychology, 60,* 733–747.

Kellaghan, T., Sloane, K., Alvarez, B., & Bloom, B.S. (1993). *The home environment and school learning: Promoting parental involvement in the education of children.* San Francisco: Jossey-Bass.

Kiresuk, T.J., Smith, A., & Cardillo, J.E. (Eds.). (1994). *Goal attainment scaling: Applications, theory, and measurement.* Hillsdale, NJ: Lawrence Erlbaum Associates.

Kline, F.M., & Rubel, L. (2001). Why this book? In F.M. Kline, L.B. Silver, & S.C. Russell (Eds.), *The educator's guide to medical issues in the classroom.* (pp. 1–12) Baltimore: Paul H. Brookes Publishing Co.

Kratochwill, T.R. (1985a). Case study research in school psychology. *School Psychology Review, 14,* 204–215.

Kratochwill, T.R. (1985b). Selection of target behaviors in behavioral consultation. *Behavioral Assessment, 7,* 49–61.

Kratochwill, T.R. (in press). Best practices in school-based problem solving consultation. In A. Thomas and J. Grimes (Eds.), *Best practices in school psychology-V.* Washington, DC: National Association of School Psychologists.

Kratochwill, T.R., Albers, C.A., & Shernoff, E.S. (2004). School-based interventions. *Child and Adolescent Psychiatric Clinics of North American, 13,* 885–903.

Kratochwill, T.R., & Bergan, J.R. (1990). *Behavioral consultation in applied settings: An individual guide.* New York: Plenum Press.

Kratochwill, T.R., Clements, M.A., & Kalymon, K.M. (2007). Response to intervention: Conceptual and methodological issues in implementation. In S.R. Jimmerson, M.K. Burns, & A.M. VanDerHeyden (Eds.), *The handbook of response to intervention: The science and practice of assessment and intervention.* New York: Springer.

Kratochwill, T.R., Elliott, S.N., & Carrington Rotto, P.C. (1995). Best practices in school-based behavioral consultation. In A. Thomas, & J. Grimes (Eds.), *Best practices in school psychology-III* (pp. 519–538). Washington, DC: National Association of School Psychologists.

Kratochwill, T.R., Elliott, S.N., Loitz, P.A., Sladeczek, I.E., & Carlson, J. (2003). Conjoint consultation using self-administered manual and videotape parent–teacher training: Effects on children's challenging behaviors. *School Psychology Quarterly, 18,* 269–302.

Kratochwill, T.R., Hoagwood, K.E., White, J., Levitt, J.M., Romanelli, L.H., & Saka, N. (in press). Evidence-based interventions and practices in school psychology: Challenges and opportunities for the profession. In T. Gutkin & C. Reynolds (Eds.), *Handbook of school psychology* (4th ed.). Hoboken, NJ: John Wiley & Sons.

Kratochwill, T.R., & Pittman, P. (2002). Defining constructs in consultation: An important training agenda. *Journal of Educational and Psychological Consultation, 13,* 69–95.

Kratochwill, T.R., & Shapiro, E.S. (2000). Conceptual foundations of behavioral assessment in schools. In E.S. Shapiro & T.R. Kratochwill (Eds.), *Behavioral assessment in schools: Theory, research and clinical foundations* (2nd ed., pp. 3–8). New York: Guilford Press.

Kratochwill, T.R., & Shernoff, E.S. (2004). Evidence-based practice: Promoting evidence-based interventions in school psychology. *School Psychology Review, 33,* 34–48.

Kratochwill, T.R., & Stoiber, K.C. (2002). Evidence-based interventions in school psychology: Conceptual foundations of the procedural and coding manual of Division 16 and the Society for the Study of School Psychology Task Force. *School Psychology Quarterly, 17,* 341–389.

Ladd, J.M., & Price, J.M. (1987). Predicting children's social and school adjustment following the transition from preschool to kindergarten. *Child Development, 58,* 1168–1189.

Lareau, A. (1987). Social class differences in family–school relationships: The importance of cultural capital. *Sociology of Education, 60,* 73–85.

Lareau, A. (1989). *Home advantage.* Philadelphia: Falmer Press.

Leaper, C. (1991). Influence and involvement in children's discourse: Age, gender, and partner effects. *Child Development, 62,* 797–811.

Leitch, M.L., & Tangri, S.S. (1988). Barriers to home–school collaboration. *Educational Horizons, 66,* 70–74.

Locke, D.C. (1992). *Increasing multicultural understanding (multicultural aspects of counseling series 1).* Newbury Park, CA: Sage.

Lopez, E. (2000). Conducting instructional consultation through interpreters. *School Psychology Review, 29,* 378–388.

Lynch, E.W., & Hanson, M.J. (1993). Changing demographics: Implications for early intervention. *Infants and Young Children, 6,* 50–55.

Lynch, E.W., & Hanson, M.J. (1998). *Developing cross-cultural competence: A guide for working with young children and their families* (2nd ed.). Baltimore: Paul H. Brookes Publishing Co.

Marti, D.C., Bevins, K., & Sheridan, S.M. (2005). *Culturally sensitive services using CBC: A case illustration.* Paper presented at the annual meeting of the National Association of School Psychologists, Atlanta, GA.

Marti, D.C., Burt, J.D., Sheridan, S.M., Clarke, M.A., & Rohlk, A.M. (2004). *Culturally sensitive services using CBC: A case illustration.* Paper presented at the annual meeting of the National Association of School Psychologists, Dallas, TX.

Marx, E., & Wooley, S.F. (Eds.). (1998). *Health is academic: A guide to coordinated school health programs.* New York: Teachers College Press.

McConaughy, S.H., Kay, P.J., & Fitzgerald, M. (1998). Preventing SED through parent teacher action research and social skills instruction: First year outcomes. *Journal of Emotional and Behavioral Disorders, 6,* 54–98.

McConaughy, S.H., Kay, P.J., & Fitzgerald, M. (1999). The achieving, behaving, caring project for preventing ED: Two-year outcomes. *Journal of Emotional and Behavioral Disorders, 7,* 224–239.

McKay, M., & Bannon, W. (2004). Evidence update: Engaging families in child mental health services. *Child and Adolescent Psychiatric Clinics of North America, 40,* 1–17.

McKay, M., Nudelman, R., & McCadam, K. (1996). Involving inner-city families in mental health services: First interview engagement skills. *Research on Social Work Practice, 6,* 462–472.

McNeil, C.B., Eyberg, S.M., Eisenstadt, T.H., Newcomb, K., & Funderburk, B.W. (1991). Parent–child interaction therapy with young behavior problem children: Generalization of treatment effects to the school setting. *Journal of Clinical Child Psychology, 20,* 140–151.

McWilliam, R.A., Tocci, L., & Harbin, G.L. (1998). Family-centered services: Service providers' discourse and behavior. *Topics in Early Childhood Special Education, 18,* 206–221.

Mehrabian, A., & Ferris, S.R. (1967). Inference of attitudes from nonverbal communication in two channels. *Journal of Consulting Psychology, 31,* 248–252.

Mehran, M., & White, K.R. (1988). Parent tutoring as a supplement to compensatory education for first-grade children. *Remedial and Special Education, 9,* 35–41.

Merriam-Webster's Collegiate® Dictionary, Tenth Edition. (2004). Partner. [Electronic version]. Springfield, MA: Merriam-Webster Inc.http://www.m-w.com/cgi-bin/dictionary?book=Dictionary&va=partner&x=0&y=0 Accessed 23.01.06.

Miller, G.A. (1969). Psychology as a means of promoting human welfare. *American Psychologist, 24,* 1063–1075.

Miranda, A.H. (1993). Consultation with culturally diverse families. *Journal of Educational and Psychological Consultation, 4,* 89–93.

Mitrsomwang, S., & Hawley, W. (1993). *Cultural adaptation and the effects of family values and behavior on the academic achievement and persistence of Indochinese students.* Final report (#R117E00045) to OERI. Washington, DC: U.S. Department of Education.

Moles, O.C. (1993). *Building school–family partnerships for learning: Workshops for urban educators.* Washington, DC: Office of Educational Research and Improvement (OERI), US Department of Education.

Morrow, L.M., & Young, J. (1996). *Parent, teacher, and child participation in a collaborative family literacy program: The effects on attitude, motivation, and literacy achievement Reading Research Report no. 64.* College Park, MD: National Reading Research Center.

Morrow, L.M., & Young, J. (1997). A family literacy program connecting school and home: Effects on attitude, motivation, and literacy achievement. *Journal of Educational Psychology, 89,* 736–742.

Nastasi, B.K., Bernstein Moore, R., & Varjas, K. (2004). *School-based mental health service: Creating comprehensive and culturally specific programs.* Washington, DC: American Psychological Association.

National Institute of Mental Health. (2005). *Children's mental health: An overview and key considerations for health system stakeholders.* Washington, DC: National Institute for Health Care Management.

No Child Left Behind Act of 2001, Pub. L. No. 107–110, 115 Stat. 1425 (2002).

Noell, G.H. (2008). Research examining the relationships among consultation process, treatment integrity, and outcomes. In W. P. Erchul & S. M. Sheridan (Eds.), *Handbook of research in school consultation: Empirical foundations for the field.* (pp. 323–342) Mahwah, NJ: Lawrence Erlbaum Associates.

Olympia, D., Jenson, W., & Hepworth-Neville, M. (1996). *Homework partners: Sanity savers for parents: Tips for tackling homework.* Longmont, CO: Sopris West.

Pelham, W.E. (1993). Pharmacotherapy of children with attention deficit hyperactivity disorder. *School Psychology Review, 22,* 199–227.

Pelham, W.E., Greiner, A. R., & Gnagy, E.M. (1998). *Children's summer treatment program manual.* Buffalo, NY: Author.

Peng, S.S., & Lee, R.M. (1992). *Home variables, parent–child activities, and academic achievement: A study of 1988 eighth graders.* Paper presented at the annual meeting of the American Educational Research Association, San Francisco, CA.

Phelan, P., Davidson, A.L., & Yu, H.C. (1998). *Adolescents' worlds: Negotiating family, peers, and school.* New York: Teachers College Press.

Phillips, V., & McCullough, L. (1990). Consultation-based programming: Instituting the collaborative ethic. *Exceptional Children, 56,* 291–304.

Pianta, R., & Walsh, D.B. (1996). *High-risk children in schools: Constructing sustaining relationships.* New York: Routledge.

Power, T., DuPaul, G.J., Shapiro, E.S., & Kazak, A.E. (2003). *Promoting children's health: Integrating school, family, and community.* New York: Guilford Press.

Power, T.J. (2003). Promoting children's mental health: Reform through interdisciplinary and community partnerships. *School Psychology Review, 32,* 3–16.

Power, T.J., DuPaul, G.J., Shapiro, E.S., & Parrish, J.M. (1995). Pediatric school psychology: The emergence of a subspecialty. *School Psychology Review, 24,* 244–257.

Power, T.J., DuPaul, G.J., Shapiro, E.S., & Parrish, J.M. (1998). Role of the school-based professional in health-related services. In L. Phelps (Ed.), *Health-related disorders in children and adolescents: A guidebook for understanding and educating.* (pp. 15–28) Washington, DC: American Psychological Association.

Program Performance Standards for the Operation of Head Start Programs. (2006). 45 CFR 1304.40. http://www.access.gpo.gov/nara/cfr/waisidx_05/45cfr1304_05.html Accessed 07.07.06.

Quinn, M. (2001a). *Collecting data while teaching, and other circus acts.* http://cecp.air.org/present/default.asp Accessed 20.05.06.

Quinn, M. (2001b). *Using data to determine intervention: Removing the guesswork.* http://cecp.air.org/present/default.asp Accessed 20.05.06.

Ramirez, S.Z., Lepage, K.M., Kratochwill, T.R, & Duffy, J.L. (1998). Multicultural issues in school-based consultation: Conceptual and research considerations. *Journal of School Psychology, 36*, 479–509.

Rappaport, J. (1981). In praise of paradox: A social policy of empowerment over prevention. *American Journal of Community Psychology, 9*, 1–25.

Rathvon, V. (2003). *Effective school interventions: Strategies for enhancing academic achievement and social competence.* New York: Guilford Press.

Ray, K.P., Skinner, C.H., & Watson, T.S. (1999). Transferring stimulus control via momentum to increase compliance in a student with autism: A demonstration of collaborative consultation. *School Psychology Review, 28*, 622–628.

Reid, J.B., & Patterson, G.R. (1992). Early prevention and intervention with conduct problems: A social interactional model for the integration of research and practice. In G. Stoner, M.R. Shinn, & H.M. Walker (Eds.), *Interventions for achievement and behavior problems* (pp. 715–739). Silver Spring, MD: National Association of School Psychologists.

Reynolds, A.J. (1991). Early schooling of children at risk. *American Educational Research Journal, 28*, 392–422.

Rhoades, M.M., & Kratochwill, T.R. (1998). Parent training and consultation: An analysis of a homework intervention program. *School Psychology Quarterly, 13*, 241–264.

Rhode, G., Jenson, W.R., & Reavis, H.K. (1992). *The tough kid book: Practical classroom management strategies.* Longmont, CO: Sopris West.

Rhode, G., Jenson, W.R., & Reavis, H.K. (1996). *The tough kid handbook.* Longmont, CO: Sopris West.

Roach, A.T., & Elliott, S.N. (2005). Goal attainment scaling: An efficient and effective approach to monitoring student progress. *Teaching Exceptional Children, 37*, 8–17.

Rogers, M.R. (1998). The influence of race and consultant verbal behavior on perceptions of consultant competence and multicultural sensitivity. *School Psychology Quarterly, 13*, 265–280.

Sanetti, L.H., & Kratochwill, T.R. (2005). Treatment integrity assessment within a problem-solving model. In R. Brown-Chidsey (Ed.), *Problem-solving based assessment for educational intervention* (pp. 304–325). New York: Guilford Press.

Santa-Barbara, J., Woodward, C.A., Levin, S., Streiner, D.L., Goodman, J.T., & Epstein, N.B. (1977). Interrelationships among outcome measures in the McMaster family therapy study. *Goal Attainment Review, 3*, 47–58.

Sayger, T.V., Horne, A.M., Walker, J.M., & Passmore, J.L. (1988). Social learning family therapy with aggressive children: Treatment outcome and maintenance. *Journal of Family Psychology, 1*, 261–285.

Shapiro, E.S. (2004). *Academic skills problems workbook* (rev. ed.). New York: Guilford Press.

Shapiro, E.S., & Kratochwill, T.R. (Eds.). (2000). *Behavioral assessment in schools: Theory, research, and clinical foundations* (2nd ed.). New York: Guilford Press.

Shellenberger, S., & Couch, K.W. (1984). The school psychologist's pivotal role in promoting the health and well-being of children. *School Psychology Review, 13*, 211-215.

Sheridan, S.M. (2000). Considerations of multiculturalism and diversity in behavioral consultation with parents and teachers. *School Psychology Review, 29*, 344–353.

Sheridan, S.M. (2004). *Family–school partnerships: Creating essential connections for student success.* Keynote presented at the Resource Teacher: Learning and Behaviour Conference, Christchurch, New Zealand.

Sheridan, S.M., Clarke, B.L., & Burt, J.D. (2008). Conjoint behavioral consultation: What do we know and what do we need to know? In W.P. Erchul & S.M. Sheridan

(Eds.), *Handbook of research in school consultation: Empirical foundations for the field.* (pp. 171–202) Mahwah, NJ: Lawrence Erlbaum Associates.

Sheridan, S.M., Clarke, B.L., Knoche, L.L., & Edwards, C.P. (2006a). The effects of conjoint behavioral consultation in early childhood settings. *Early Education and Development, 17,* 593–617.

Sheridan, S.M., & Colton, D.L. (1994). Conjoint behavioral consultation: A review and case study. *Journal of Educational and Psychological Consultation, 5,* 211–228.

Sheridan, S.M., Eagle, J.W., Cowan, R.J., & Mickelson, W. (2001). The effects of conjoint behavioral consultation: Results of a four-year investigation. *Journal of School Psychology, 39,* 361–385.

Sheridan, S.M., Eagle, J.W., & Doll, B. (2006b). An examination of the efficacy of conjoint behavioral consultation with diverse clients. *School Psychology Quarterly, 21,* 396–417.

Sheridan, S.M., Eagle, J.W., & Dowd, S.E. (2005). Families as contexts for children's adaptation. In S. Goldstein & R. Brooks (Eds.), *Handbook of resiliency in children* (pp. 165–179). New York: Kluwer/Plenum Press.

Sheridan, S.M., Erchul, W.P., Brown, M.S., Dowd, S.E., Warnes, E.D., Marti, D.C., et al. (2004). Perceptions of helpfulness in conjoint behavioral consultation: Congruity and agreement between teachers and parents. *School Psychology Quarterly, 19,* 121–140.

Sheridan, S.M., & Gutkin, T.B. (2000). The ecology of school psychology: Examining and changing our paradigm for the 21st century. *School Psychology Review, 29,* 485–502.

Sheridan, S.M., & Kratochwill, T.R. (1992). Behavioral parent–teacher consultation: Conceptual and research considerations. *Journal of School Psychology, 30,* 117–139.

Sheridan, S.M., Kratochwill, T.R., & Bergan, J.R. (1996). *Conjoint behavioral consultation: A procedural manual.* New York: Plenum Press.

Sheridan, S.M., Kratochwill, T.R., & Elliott, S.N. (1990). Behavioral consultation with parents and teachers: Delivering treatment for socially withdrawn children at home and school. *School Psychology Review, 19,* 33–52.

Sheridan, S.M., & McCurdy, M. (2005). Ecological variables in school-based assessment and intervention planning. In R. Brown-Chidsey (Ed.). *Assessment for intervention: A problem-solving approach* (pp. 43–64). New York: Guilford Press.

Sheridan, S.M., Meegan, S., & Eagle, J.W. (2002). Exploring the social context in conjoint behavioral consultation: Linking processes to outcomes. *School Psychology Quarterly, 17,* 299–324.

Sheridan, S.M., & Steck, M. (1995). Acceptability of conjoint behavioral consultation: A national survey of school psychologists. *School Psychology Review, 24,* 633–647.

Sheridan, S.M., Warnes, E.D., Cowan, R.J., Schemm, A.V., & Clarke, B.L. (2004). Family-centered positive psychology: Building on strength to promote student success. *Psychology in the Schools, 41,* 7–17.

Sheridan, S.M., Warnes, E.D., Ellis, C., Schnoes, C., & Woods, K.E. (2006c). *Conjoint behavioral consultation: Collaboration among family, school, and pediatric systems in the provision of services for children and adolescents with ADHD.* Manuscript submitted for publication.

Shivack, I.M., & Sullivan, C.W. (1989). Use of telephone prompts at an inner-city outpatient clinic. *Hospital & Community Psychiatry, 40,* 851–853.

Shuck, A., Ulsh, F., & Platt, J.S. (1983). Parents encourage pupils (PEP): An inner city parent involvement reading project. *Reading Teacher, 36,* 524–528.

Singh, N., Parmelee, D., Sood, B., & Katz, R.C. (1993). Collaboration of disciplines. In J. Matson (Ed.), *Hyperactivity in children: A handbook.* Boston: Allyn & Bacon.

Sladeczek, I.E., Elliott, S.N., Kratochwill, T.R., Robertson-Mjaanes, S., & Stoiber, K.C. (2001). Application of goal attainment scaling to a conjoint behavioral consultation case. *Journal of Educational and Psychological Consultation, 12*, 45–59.

Soo-Hoo, T. (1998). Applying frame of reference and reframing techniques to improve school consultation in multicultural settings. *Journal of Psychological and Educational Consultation, 9*, 325–335.

Sue, D.W., Bingham, R.P., Porche–Burke, L., & Vasquez, M. (1999). The diversification of psychology: A multicultural revolution. *American Psychologist, 54*, 1061–1069.

Swick, K.J. (1988). Parental efficacy and involvement: Influences on children. *Childhood Education, 65*, 37–38.

Tarver Behring, S., Cabello, B., & Kushida, D. (2000). Cultural modifications to current school-based consultation approaches reported by culturally diverse beginning consultants. *School Psychology Review, 29*, 354–367.

Tarver Behring, S., & Gelinas, R.T. (1996). School consultation with Asian American children and families. *The California School Psychologist, 1*, 13–20.

Tarver Behring, S., & Ingraham, C.L. (1998). Culture as a central component to consultation: A call to the field. *Journal of Educational and Psychological Consultation, 9*, 57–72.

Thorp, E.K. (1997). Increasing opportunities for partnership with culturally and linguistically diverse families. *Intervention in School and Clinic, 32*, 261–269.

Troiano, R.P., Flegal, K.M., Kuczmarski, R.J., Campbell, S.M., & Johnson, C.L. (1995). Overweight prevalence and trends for children and adolescents: The National Health and Nutrition Examination Surveys, 1963 to 1991. *Archives of Pediatrics and Adolescent Medicine, 149*(10), 1085–1091.

U.S. Department of Education. (2001). *Twenty-third annual report to congress on the implementation of the individuals with disabilities education act*. Washington, DC: Author.

Vernberg, E.M., & Reppucci, N.D. (1986). Behavioral consultation. In F.V. Mannino, E.J. Trickett, M.F. Shore, M.G. Kidder, & G. Levin (Eds.), *Handbook of mental health consultation* (pp. 49–80). Rockville, MD: National Institute of Mental Health.

Von Brock, M.B., & Elliott, S.N. (1987). Influence of treatment effectiveness information on the acceptability of classroom interventions. *Journal of School Psychology, 25*, 131–144.

Vosler-Hunter, R.W. (1989). *Changing roles, changing relationships: Parent and professional collaboration on behalf of children with emotional disabilities*. Portland, OR: Portland State University, Research and Training Center on Family Support and Children's Mental Health.

Wahler, R.G., & Fox, J.J. (1981). Setting events in applied behavior analysis: Toward a conceptual and methodological expansion. *Journal of Applied Behavior Analysis, 14*, 327–338.

Walberg, H.J. (1984). Families as partners in educational productivity. *Phi Delta Kappan, 65*, 397–400.

Walker, J.M.T., Wilkins, A.S., Dallaire, J.R., Sandler, H.M., & Hoover-Dempsey, K.V. (2005). Parental involvement: Model revision through scale development. *The Elementary School Journal, 106*, 85–104.

Webster, M. (1981). *Webster's new collegiate dictionary*. Springfield, MA: G&C Merriam Company.

Webster-Stratton, C. (1998). Preventing conduct problems in head start children: Strengthening parenting competencies. *Journal of Consulting and Clinical Psychology, 66*, 715–730.

Webster-Stratton, C. (2003). Aggression in young children: Services proven to be effective in reducing aggression. In. R.E. Trembly, R.G. Barr, & R.DeV. Peters (Eds.), *Encyclopedia on early childhood development* [online] (p. 1–6). Montreal, Quebec: Centre of Excellence for Early Childhood Development. http://www.excellence-earlychildhood.ca/documents/Webster-StrattonANGxp.pdf. Accessed 07.05.07.

Webster-Stratton, C., Reid, M.J., & Hammond, M. (2001). Preventing conduct problems, promoting social competence: A parent and teacher training partnership in head start. *Journal of Clinical Child Psychology, 30*, 283–302.

Weiner, R., Sheridan, S.M., & Jenson, W.R. (1998). Effects of conjoint behavioral consultation and a structured homework program on math completion and accuracy in junior high students. *School Psychology Quarterly, 13*, 281–309.

Weiss, H.M., & Edwards, M.E. (1992). The family–school collaboration project: Systemic interventions for school improvement. In S.L. Christenson & J.C. Conoley (Eds.), *Home–school collaboration: Enhancing children's academic and social competence* (pp. 215–243). Silver Spring, MD: National Association of School Psychologists.

Weissberg, R.P., & Greenberg, M.T. (1998). School and community competence-enhancement and prevention programs. In W. Damon (Series Ed.) & I.E. Sigel & K.A. Renninger (Vol. Eds.), *Handbook of child psychology: Vol. 4. Child psychology in practice* (5th ed., pp. 877–954). New York: John Wiley & Sons.

Welch, M., & Sheridan, S.M. (1995). *Educational partnerships: Serving students at risk*. San Antonio, TX: Harcourt Brace.

West, J.F. (1990). Educational collaboration in the restructuring of schools. *Journal of Educational and Psychological Consultation, 1*, 23–40.

White, J.L., & Kratochwill, T.R. (2005). Practice guidelines in school psychology: Issues and directions for evidence-based interventions in practice and training. *Journal of School Psychology, 43*, 99–115.

Witt, J.C., Daly, E. J., III, & Noell, G.H. (2000). *Functional assessments: A step-by-step guide to solving academic and behavior problems*. Longmont, CO: Sopris West.

Witt, J.C., & Elliott, S.N. (1985). Acceptability of classroom management strategies. In T.R. Kratochwill (Ed.), *Advances in school psychology* (Vol. 4, pp. 251–288). Hillsdale, NJ: Lawrence Erlbaum Associates.

Witt, J.C., Erchul, W.P., McKee, W.T., & Pardue, M.M. (1991). Conversational control in school-based consultation: The relationship between consultant and consultee topic determination and consultation outcome. *Journal of Educational and Psychological Consultation, 2*, 101–117.

Wolf, M.M. (1978). Social validity: The case for subjective measurement or how applied behavior analysis is finding its heart. *Journal of Applied Behavior Analysis, 11*, 203–314.

Woodward, C.A., Santa-Barbara, J., Streiner, D.L., Goodman, J.T., Levin, S., & Epstein, N.B. (1981). Client, treatment, and therapist variables related to outcome in brief, systems-oriented family therapy. *Family Process, 20*, 189–197.

Wright, J. (2006). *Curriculum-based assessment list builder*. http://www.lefthandlogic.com/htmdocs/tools/cbaprobe/cba.shtml Accessed 07.07.06.

Ysseldyke, J.E., & Christenson, S.L. (1993). *The instructional environment scale—II*. Longmont, CO: Sopris West.

Ysseldyke, J.E., & Christenson, S.L. (2002). *Functional assessment of academic behavior: A system for assessing individual student's instruction environments*. Longmont, CO: Sopris West.

Appendix A

Objectives, definitions, and examples of conjoint needs identification interview.

Objectives	Definitions	Examples
Social opening	Establish a friendly supportive atmosphere	Position chairs in such a way that parents and teachers are close to each other and can make eye contact easily Smile Use nonverbal communication to convey interest in parents and teachers
	Demonstrate interest in the consultees	"How is your new job going, Ms. Gyen?" "I thought about you last night when I was watching your college team play football!"
Open up dialogue	Establish the attitude that everyone's information is vital Use inclusive language	"I am so glad that you are here! Your knowledge about your son is so important to us in helping him do his best in school!" "Let's talk about some of the things that we noticed about Julia's interactions with other children" "I see we have similar concerns at home and at school"
	Emphasize the expertise of everyone involved	"You know Karla better than anyone, Mr. Olson. Your input will be invaluable!" "Ms. O'Brien, you have first-hand information on what triggers Karla's crying episodes. Your observations are critical to helping us decide what to do"
	Discuss the importance and roles of each participant (i.e., provide information, collect/ set-up assessment and observations)	"It will be very helpful for everyone to share their observations and ideas. This will give us the best opportunity to help Stanley" "There will be opportunities for each of you to keep track of what you see and observe. There will also be some expectations that you will work on specific plans for Allie once we set them up. Everyone will have an important role and responsibility, and that will help Allie meet her goals most effectively"
	Discuss steps of the meeting	"The main things we will be talking about are listed on this meeting agenda. Feel free to keep this so you know where we are at in the meeting"

(Continued)

Objectives, definitions, and examples of conjoint needs identification interview—Cont'd.

Objectives	Definitions	Examples
Discuss child, family, and teacher strengths	Discuss things that the child does well	"What are some of Jamie's strengths?" "Please share with us some of the things that Kevin does well"
	Discuss likes and dislikes	"What kinds of things does Jose like to do?" "How does Stacy spend her free time?"
	Establish importance of building upon strengths of all when addressing priorities	"Knowing what Pedro's strengths are will help us use his talents to build up some of his weaknesses" "Once we understand the kinds of things that Maria enjoys, we can use those to address our concerns"
Discuss goals and desires	Discuss goals, aspirations, and desires for the child in the short and long term	"In general, what do we hope to see Jamie accomplish?" "Regarding Fran's friendships, what are some long-term goals you have for her, as her parent and teacher?"
	Share information regarding developmental appropriateness of expectations, if necessary	"It is important for Callie to look at books and begin reading words. At her age, it is also important to start by repeating or naming objects that she sees in pictures on the page"
Select needs and concerns	Discuss what might interfere with the child's learning and development	"What are some concerns that you have about Andrea's language?"
	Explore general concerns	"Describe some of the things that interfere with Jorge's performance"
Select a priority	Discuss importance of selecting one priority	"I see you are concerned that Patrice does the best that she can do in several areas. It will be very important to narrow in on one specific area as a start. This will help us make sure that the focus is manageable, and allow us to evaluate closely how well Patrice responds to our plan before moving on"
	Select a priority	"Which of these behaviors is causing the most difficulty for Joey?" "I hear you saying that Zach's inability to deal with frustration interferes with his interactions with peers, and could be a place to start. Is that correct?"
Define the priority	Define the priority in concrete, observable terms	"It will be important for us to define exactly what we mean by 'getting into fights with peers.' Let's try to define this using clear and specific examples of what Elle does when she gets into fights"
Select a focus/setting	Discuss importance of focus	"Having a place or time in mind allows us to observe and measure exactly what is going on in a specific and focused way"

(*Continued*)

Objectives, definitions, and examples of conjoint needs identification interview—Cont'd.

Objectives	Definitions	Examples
		"This will let us to manage what we are focusing on without being overwhelmed with all of Jacob's difficulties throughout the day. When we find something that works, we can transition to other times or places"
	Address where and when the priority behavior occurs in specific terms	"Where or when is Bobby's talking back to adults most problematic?" "What subject is causing Ellen the most difficulty in getting her work done?"
	Select a focus or a place to start	"Great! We will start by focusing on Patty's lack of social interactions during the noon recess"
Determine what works and what does not	Discuss what has already been tried to address the concern	"I know you have tried certain things to deal with Jackson's difficulties identifying sight words. What have you tried so far?"
	Point out strengths from what has already worked to be used later in coming up with a plan	"So it sounds like you have figured out that giving Cammie choices works better than demanding her to do things your way. That's a great idea!"
	Emphasize strengths of consultees	"You've worked really hard on this. I can tell you care a lot about Josh"
Collect information	Discuss the rationale for collecting information	"It will be very helpful to get a good idea of exactly how often Eric is wetting his pants. This will give us an idea of what is occurring now, and allow us to measure any changes in his behavior once we start an intervention"
	Select a specific time, place, and procedure	"During morning circle time, please watch Franco's behavior and mark on the masking tape how often he gets up and runs to other places in the room. Afterwards, please place the masking tape on the chart in the row corresponding to the correct day"
	Provide consultees with charts to record information	"Can you keep track on this chart, and indicate when Evan yells out?"
	Discuss rationale of watching what happens before and after the priority behavior, as well as specific patterns that occur	"Please also note what happens before and what happens after Jessica cries so we can begin looking for patterns"
	Establish times for consultant to observe	"It would be really helpful if I could come in and observe Juanita's behaviors with peers. What is a good day and time, when I can see many of the things we are talking about?"

(Continued)

Objectives, definitions, and examples of conjoint needs identification interview—Cont'd.

Objectives	Definitions	Examples
Meet again	Discuss steps of the next meeting, establish time and place to meet	"At the next meeting we will look at the information you bring in. That will be very important for our next steps of understanding possible reasons the behavior is occurring, and suggest a focus for a plan to address it"
Closing	Summarize what was accomplished at the meeting, emphasizing consultees' expertise, strengths, and how this information will help the child to be successful	"Today we identified a specific area to focus on to help Austin. We discussed some of his strengths that can help him be more successful, and how we will collect information on the concern we share around his difficulty identifying letters"
	Exchange phone numbers and e-mail addresses	"I will write down my phone number and email address. Please contact me right away if you have any questions. Please also write yours down so everyone knows how to stay in touch"
	Inform parents and teachers that they are free to contact you with questions and concerns and remind them you will check in to see how information gathering is going	"I'll call you Wednesday after school to see how the data collection is going. Please get in touch with me if you have any questions or concerns. Thank you!"

Appendix B

Conjoint Needs Identification Interview (CNII)

Child's Name: _____   Date: _____

Parent's Name: _____   Age: _____

Teacher's Name: _____   Grade: _____

School: _____

Consultant's Name: _____

Consultant note: The goals of the CNII are to:

Behavioral goals:

- Jointly identify and define child's priorities in behavioral terms
- Jointly establish a procedure to collect baseline data across setting

Relationship-building goals:

- Identify strengths of the child, family, and school
- Establish joint responsibility in goal setting and decision making
- Establish/improve working relationships between parents and teachers, and between the consultant and consultees
- Validate shared goals of supporting the child
- Increase communication and knowledge regarding the child, goals, concerns, and culture of family and school

Consultant and case goals for interview:

_____

_____

_____

_____

_____

_____

_____

_____

_____

_____

_____

_____

_____

_____

_____

Conjoint Needs Identification Interview (CNII)
Social Opening

Establish a friendly supportive atmosphere (e.g., position of the chairs, non-verbal communication); demonstrate interest for the consultee (e.g., ask about past events)

Notes:

Open Up Dialogue

Establish the attitude that everyone's information is vital; use inclusive language; emphasize the expertise of everyone involved; discuss the importance and roles of each participant (i.e., provide information, collect/set-up assessment and observations); discuss steps of the meeting

Notes:

Discuss Child, Family, and Teacher Strengths

Discuss things that are going well; discuss likes and dislikes; establish importance of building upon strengths of all when addressing priorities

Notes:

Discuss Goals and Desires

Discuss goals, aspirations, and desires for the child in the short and long term; emphasize importance of consultees' identified goals and sharing of information regarding developmental appropriateness of expectations

Notes:

Select Needs

Discuss what might get in the way of the goals and desires; explore general concerns

Notes:

Summarize/Validate goals and needs. Begin building a bridge for shared goals and cross-setting similarities

Select/Define the Priority

Discuss importance of selecting one priority; select a priority based on goals and desires; define the priority in concrete, observable terms

Notes:

Summarize/Validate the definition of the priority

Select a Focus/Setting

Discuss importance of focus; answer where and when the priority behavior occurs in specific terms; select a focus or a place to start

Notes:

What Works/What Doesn't?

Discuss what has already been tried; point out strengths from what has already worked to be used later in coming up with a plan; emphasize strengths of consultees

Notes:

Collect Information

Discuss the rationale for collecting information; select a specific time, place, and procedure; provide consultees with charts to record information; discuss rationale of watching what happens before and after the priority behavior, as well as specific patterns that occur; establish times for consultant to observe

Notes:

	Home	School
What will be observed?		
Where will observation occur?		
How will it be recorded?		
When will observation begin?		

Provide parents and teachers with data collection forms
Summarize/Validate data collection procedures

Meet Again

Discuss steps of the next meeting, establish time and place to meet

Closing

Summarize what was accomplished at the meeting, emphasizing consultees' expertise, strengths, and how this information will help the child to be successful; exchange phone numbers and e-mail addresses; let parents and teachers know they are free to contact you with questions and concerns and remind them you will check in to see how information gathering is going

Notes:

Appendix C

Consultation Behavior Record

Child's Name: _____
Person Recording: _____
Dates of Recording: _____

 "Target" behavior -- <u>what</u> we are focusing on:

"Target" setting -- <u>where</u> we will focus:

"Target" time -- <u>when</u> information will be collected:

Pointers -- <u>how</u> information will be recorded:

Day/Date Time, Etc.	Behavior Occurrence	What Happened Before?	What Happened After?	What Else Was Going On?

More data collection on reverse side…

Day/Date Time, Etc.	Behavior Occurrence	What Happened Before?	What Happened After?	What Else Was Going On?

Appendix D

Objectives, definitions, and examples of conjoint needs analysis interview.

Objectives	Definitions	Examples
Social opening	Establish a friendly supportive atmosphere	Position chairs in such a way that parents and teachers are close to each other and can make eye contact easily. Smile Use nonverbal communication to convey interest in parents and teachers
	Demonstrate interest for the consultee	"How is the new baby, Ms. Martinez?" "I heard you've had the flu. How are you feeling now?"
Open up dialogue	Re-emphasize the attitude that everyone's input is vital	"Thanks for coming back in today. I'm really hopeful that together we will come up with some great ideas!"
	Continue to use inclusive language	"We talked about a lot of Kimmie's strengths and some of her difficulties at home and school. We agreed that our main concern was her difficulty following instructions the first time given, and that happens at both home and school"
	Discuss steps of the meeting	"Today we will look at the information you have been collecting, discuss what may be contributing to Pablo's difficulties, and work together to come up with a plan to help him"
Discuss information collected/set goals	Restate the definition of the priority	"The concern that we are dealing with is Jorge not completing homework at home, and not turning it in on time. We defined 'completing homework' as 'finishing all assigned problems or projects and placing them into his backpack at least one night before they are due.' We defined 'turning in homework' as 'placing completed homework pages on Mr. Montgomery's desk on time, the day it is due'"
	Discuss information collected	"Thanks for collecting the information we discussed. Let's take a look at what you saw at home"

(Continued)

Objectives, definitions, and examples of conjoint needs analysis interview—Cont'd.

Objectives	Definitions	Examples
		"I see that Cixin argued with you each morning before school, but Monday there were 4 arguments, whereas other days there were one or two"
	Set jointly determined, developmentally appropriate goals based on information collected	"It seems as though Jason is getting into fights on the playground approximately 4 times per week. At home, he initiates a fight with his brother at least once each day. What would be a reasonable goal for him? The goal should be one that is achievable and within his control"
Determine other events occurring in the environment (antecedents, consequences, sequential events)	Discuss what is happening before and after the priority behavior, as well as specific patterns that occur, during the focused time/setting	"What did you notice that happened before Steven started crying on these days?" "Oftentimes we see patterns in what might be 'setting off' certain behaviors, such as people the child is with, time of day, day of the week, certain academic subjects, or other patterns that are common. Sometimes we can identify predictable things that happen before or after behaviors that are important. What patterns did you notice related to Sam's tantrum behavior?"
	Emphasize this information will help to understand why this behavior is happening and how changes can be made	"If we can uncover some patterns related to Casey's anger outbursts, we will be in a better position to know how to structure an intervention plan to address them"
Determine hypotheses for the behavior	Summarize information gathered, as well as what happens during the focused time/setting (organize and summarize relevant information such as attention that is given, key people that affect the occurrence of the behavior, skills needed to perform the desired behavior)	"One common thing that you observed at home and school is that Erin has more problems controlling her temper when she is overly tired" "Tammie rarely starts her work when instructed by her teacher, and takes several minutes to start homework at home. In the classroom, her peers ask her if they can help, and at home, she receives one on one attention from one of her parents"
	Discuss reasons why the priority behavior is happening	Given what we discussed about the common situations or patterns to Pepe's noncompliance, why do you think he's having difficulty following instructions? "It seems like Kat's delays starting work gains a lot of attention from her peers and from her parents. Do you agree?"
Determine actions/ intervention strategies	Select a focus for change based on why the priority behavior is happening	"Since Ricardo's challenges with comprehension seem related to his limited fluency in oral reading, it would make sense to focus on increasing his fluency and accuracy"

(Continued)

Objectives, definitions, and examples of conjoint needs analysis interview—Cont'd.

Objectives	Definitions	Examples
		"Austin does not speak at school and seems to get his needs met through gestures and head nods. It will be helpful to focus on the way that people respond to his nonverbal requests as one way to encourage speech at school"
	Restate child, teacher, and family strengths	"Charley is a good athlete and really likes playing sports! That could be helpful when we are developing a plan to help him with social skills" "You spend a lot of time reading with Stephanie. That will really help her"
	Jointly develop a plan across home and school, building on these strengths	"What if we used Jon's interest in sports in a program where he could earn 5 extra minutes to play basketball for using self-control on the playground? At home, we could try something similar. What might work at home?"
	Write down a summary of steps of the plan for parents and teachers	"I'll write down the steps on this form. It might be very helpful for you to look at this everyday, and possibly even place a check mark on the line next to the step whenever you complete it"
	Provide an opportunity for parents and teachers to ask questions	"What questions do you have about the plan?"
	Model plan procedures if necessary (either immediately during the interview, or at a time and place that is agreeable to the consultees)	"This is what 'effective commands' look like. Why don't you pretend to be Joey and I'll demonstrate" "Would it be helpful for me to come into the classroom and demonstrate how to use dialogic reading with a small group of students?"
Collect information	Re-emphasize the rationale for collecting information	"It will be important to continue keeping track of the time it takes for Austin to complete his homework. In this way, we can see how he is doing with the plan compared to before the plan was put into place, and evaluate the progress he is making toward his goal"
	Provide parents and teachers with charts to record information	"You can use the same forms and procedures as you have been using. Here are some extra copies"
Meet again	Discuss steps of the next meeting; establish time and place to meet	"When would be a convenient time for us to meet again, to review how the plan is working?"

(Continued)

Objectives, definitions, and examples of conjoint needs analysis interview—Cont'd.

Objectives	Definitions	Examples
Closing	Summarize what was accomplished at the meeting, emphasizing consultees' expertise, strengths, and how this information will help the child to be successful	"We accomplished a lot today! We developed a plan to read to Jesse every night at home, using prompts and questions about the pages. At school, you will do rhymes, word games, and songs to focus on sound awareness. This should help her increase her vocabulary and understanding of basic sounds, as she develops early reading skills"
	Inform consultees that they are free to contact you with questions and concerns and remind them you will communicate frequently to see how the plan is going	"Please feel free to call me anytime with questions. I will touch base at the end of this week to see how it is going"

Appendix E

Conjoint Needs Analysis Interview (CNAI)

Child's Name: _____   Date: _____

Parent's Name: _____   Age: _____

Teacher's Name: _____   Grade: _____

School: _____

Consultant's Name: _____

Consultant note: The goals of the CNAI are to:

Behavioral goals:

- Evaluate information collected across home and school
- Collaboratively develop developmentally appropriate goals for priority behavior across home and school
- Discuss what is happening before and after the priority behavior, as well as specific patterns that occur, during the focused time/setting
- Collaboratively develop a plan built upon strengths and competencies to address the priority behavior across home and school
- Reaffirm information collection procedures

Relationship-building goals:

- Use inclusive language to strengthen partnerships between home and school
- Encourage and validate sharing of parents' and teachers' perspectives of the priority behavior
- Foster an environment that facilitates "give-and-take" communication across settings
- Promote collaborative decision making and shared responsibility for plan development

Consultant and case goals for interview:

_____
_____
_____
_____
_____
_____
_____
_____
_____
_____
_____
_____

Conjoint Needs Analysis Interview (CNAI)

Social Opening

Establish a friendly supportive atmosphere (e.g., position of the chairs, non-verbal communication); demonstrate interest for the consultee (e.g., ask about past events)

Notes:

Open Up Dialogue

Re-emphasize the attitude that everyone's input is vital; continue to use inclusive language; discuss steps of the meeting

Notes:

Discuss Information Collected/Set Goals

Restate the definition of the priority; discuss information collected; set jointly determined, developmentally appropriate goals based on information collected

Notes:

Summarize information collected and connect to goals set

What's Happening?

Discuss what is happening before and after the priority behavior, as well as specific patterns that occur, during the focused time/setting; emphasize this information will help to understand why this behavior is happening and how changes can be made

Before

Notes:

After

Notes:

Other Patterns

Notes:

Why Is It Happening?

Summarize information gathered, as well as what's happening during the focused time/setting (organize and summarize relevant information such as attention that is given, key people that affect the occurrence of the priority behavior, skills needed to perform the desired behavior); discuss reasons why the priority behavior is happening

Notes:

What to Do?

Select a focus for change based on why the priority behavior is happening; restate child, teacher and family strengths; jointly develop a plan across home and school, building on these strengths; write down a summary of steps of the plan for parents and teachers; provide an opportunity for parents and teachers to ask questions; model plan procedures, if necessary

Notes:

Summarize Plan
Provide parents and teachers with plan worksheet

Collect Information

Re-emphasize the rationale for collecting information; select a specific time, place, and procedure; provide parents and teachers with charts to record information

Notes:

	Home	**School**
What will be observed?		
Where will observation occur?		
How will it be recorded?		
When will observation begin?		

Summarize/Validate data collection procedures
Provide parents and teachers with data collection form

Meet Again

Discuss steps of the next meeting; establish time and place to meet

Closing

Summarize what was accomplished at the meeting, emphasizing consultees' expertise, strengths, and how this information will help the child to be successful; let consultees know they are free to contact you with questions and concerns and remind them you will communicate frequently to see how the plan is going

Notes:

Appendix F
Behavioral Functions Chart
for Parents and Teachers

Behavioral Functions

Behavioral Excesses: Too much of a behavior

- Attention
- Escape
- Obtain objects/activities
- Sensory stimulation

Skill Development

Behavioral Deficits: Inability to adequately perform a behavior

- Lack of motivation
- Not enough practice
- Not enough guidance/help
- Lack of exposure
- Too difficult

Appendix G

Consultation Plan

Behavioral Goal:
_____
_____

Plan Summary:
_____
_____
_____

Please list the primary steps of the plan on the lines below. Then, each day, please check in the appropriate box in the matrix to the left whether each step was completed.

Sun	Mon	Tue	Wed	Thu	Fri	Sat

✔ Plan Steps:

1. _____

2. _____

3. _____

4. _____

5. _____

Goal Rating

At the end of the week, please use the following scale to rate how closely the above goal was met. The consultant will collect this form each week. Thank you!

-2	-1	0	+1	+2
Situation significantly worse	Situation somewhat worse	No progress	Goal partially met	Goal fully met

Appendix H
Sample Manualized Home and School Intervention for Increasing Compliance

Miguel's Plan for Success at Home

Manual developed by Michelle Swanger, M.A. Reproduced with permission.

Priority behavior: Following directions

Definition of following directions: When Miguel is given a direction, he will initiate or complete the task without a reminder or reprimand in a reasonable amount of time.

GOAL: Miguel will follow directions at home fifty percent of the time.

Where and when: The plan will focus on the time period before school.

Reason for behavior: Miguel is allowed to escape activities that he does not want to do and he is not motivated to do.

Plan Step 1: Use Morning Checklist

1. Introduce the checklist to Miguel.

2. Give effective commands (see Step 2).

3. When Miguel completes a job he then checks it off.

4. If Miguel completes 50% of the tasks without reminders or reprimands, he will earn a reward. (See effective rewards, Step 3.)

5. Praise the behaviors that he is doing correctly. Praise in detail. For example, "Miguel I like the way you got right out of bed."

*SEE CHECKLIST

Plan Step 2: Give Effective Commands

1. <u>Say *start* instead of *stop*</u>: Tell Miguel to start an appropriate behavior ("Miguel please brush your teeth.") Make fewer stop demands, such as "Don't argue with me!" Decide what you want to see and build on that! Encourage appropriate behaviors.

2. <u>Use a clear directive, not a question</u>: Say "Please brush your teeth," rather than "Can you or will you brush your teeth?"

3. <u>Make eye contact.</u>

4. <u>Shorten the distance</u>: Move close to Miguel (about an arms length away).

5. <u>Use a soft but firm voice.</u>

6. <u>Give a few easy commands to build momentum</u>: Tell Miguel to do easy, fun tasks like touch his finger to his nose and praise him for following directions.

7. <u>Give descriptive directions</u>: Tell him what you expect. "Put your toys into the closet" is more descriptive than "Clean your room," which he might not understand.

8. <u>Demand the possible</u>: Make sure what you ask of Miguel is something he can do. You may want to divide a large job like cleaning a room into small steps like first pick up the toys.

9. <u>Wait 10 seconds</u>: After you say a command wait. Do not talk to him, do not argue, ignore excuses.

10. <u>Only request something twice</u>: Tell Miguel what you want him to do only two times. He should only need one command and one reminder.

11. <u>Remain calm.</u>

12. <u>Reinforce or reward compliance</u>: See Step 3.

Plan Step 3: Effective Rewards

1. When Miguel meets his goal of following directions 50% of the time without more than one reminder, he will be able to choose a reward from a reward menu BEFORE school.
2. Rewards can be:
   a. Natural—They already exist at home.
   b. Edible.
   c. Material—Material rewards or a tangible item for good behavior (e.g., sticker).
   d. Social rewards—A social behavior that the parent does to increase good behavior (e.g., smile, praise, point out a job well done).
3. Select a reward:
   a. Ask Miguel what he likes.
   b. Make a reward menu with Miguel.
   c. Make sure the reward is ALWAYS given after the desired behavior.
4. Golden Rules:
   a. Any reward should not cost a lot of money or take a lot of time. It should be natural whenever possible.
   b. These rewards should not be given to Miguel when he does not follow directions. He should not receive the reward at other times in the day.

- LET'S THINK OF SOME REWARDS!

Plan Steps 4 and 5: Fill Out Home—School Note and Read Home—School Note

Home-School Notes are:

- Periodically completed by you and Ms. Curtis
- An assessment of academic and/or behavioral progress.
- Returned to school.
- Paired with praise and tangible rewards so that the positive information conveyed in the home note will result in rewards at home.

Your Home—School Note:

1. If Migual meets his morning goal of following directions 50% of the time before school, write this in the comment section of the note.
2. Send the note to school.
3. After you pick up Miguel from school, read the note and initial it.

4. See if Miguel made his goal of following directions 80% of the time during independent work time at school.

5. If he met his goal, praise him and let him choose a reward from his reward menu.

6. Repeat steps the next morning.

- If you have any questions feel free to call the consultant.

GOOD LUCK!!!!

Miguel's Plan for Success at School

Priority behavior: Following directions.

Definition of following directions: When Miguel is given a direction, he will initiate or complete the task with no more than one reminder or reprimand in a reasonable amount of time. (Usually the time limit is about 10 sec.)

Goal: Eighty percent of the time, Miguel will follow directions at school during independent work time.

Where and when: The plan will focus on independent work time at school (9:00 to 9:40 AM and 10:00 to 11:00 AM)

Reason for behavior: Miguel is allowed to escape activities that he does not want to do and he is not motivated to do.

Plan Step 1: Home Note

See Steps 6 and 7 in home-note section.

Plan Step 2: Use Work Time Checklist

1. Introduce the checklist to Miguel.

2. Give effective commands (see Step 3).

3. When Miguel completes a job, he checks it off.

4. If he completes 80% of the tasks with no more than one reminder or reprimand, then he will earn a reward. (See effective rewards Steps 4 and 5.)

5. Praise the behaviors that he is doing correctly. Praise in detail. For example, say "Miguel I like the way you are completing your math worksheet."

*SEE CHECKLIST

Plan Step 3: Give Effective Commands

1. _Say start instead of stop_: Tell Miguel to start an appropriate behavior (e.g., "Miguel please start your writing."). Make fewer stop demands, such as "Don't look around the room!" Decide what you want to see and build on that! Encourage appropriate behaviors.

2. Use a clear directive, not a question: Say "Please start writing your story," rather than "Can you or will you write your story?"

3. Make eye contact.

4. Shorten the distance: Move close to Miguel (about an arms length away).

5. Use a soft but firm voice.

6. Give a few easy commands to build momentum: Tell Miguel to do easy, fun tasks like touch his finger to his nose and praise him for following directions.

7. Give descriptive directions: Tell Miguel what you expect. A statement such as "Miguel please pick up your pencil and start writing" is more descriptive than "It is writing time."

8. Demand the possible: Make sure what you ask of Miguel is something he can do. You may want to divide a large job (e.g., write a story) into small steps (e.g., like first write down your title to the story).

9. <u>Wait 10 seconds</u>: After you say a command wait. Do not talk to him, do not argue, ignore excuses.

10. <u>Only request something twice</u>: Tell Miguel what you want him to do only two times. He should only need one command and one reminder.

11. <u>Remain calm</u>.

12. <u>Reinforce or reward compliance</u>: See Step 4.

Plan Steps 4 and 5: Effective Rewards

1. When Miguel meets his goal of following directions 80% of the time without more than one reminder, he will be able to choose a reward from a reward menu AFTER EACH INDEPENDENT WORK TIME.

2. <u>Rewards can be</u>:
    a. Natural—They already exist at home.
    b. Edible.
    c. Material—Material rewards or a tangible item for good behavior (e.g., sticker).
    d. Social rewards—A social behavior that you the parent does to increase good behavior (e.g., smile, praise, point out a job well done).

3. <u>Select a reward</u>:
    a. Ask Miguel what he likes.
    b. Make a reward menu with Miguel.
    c. Make sure the reward is ALWAYS given after. the desired behavior.

4. <u>Golden Rules</u>:
    a. Any reward should not cost a lot of money or take a lot of time. It should be natural whenever possible.
    b. These rewards should not be given to Miguel when he does not follow directions. He should not receive the reward at other times in the day.

* LET'S THINK OF SOME REWARDS!

Plan Steps 6 and 7: Fill Out Home—School Note and Read Home—School Note

Home—School Notes are:
- Periodically completed by you and the parents.
- An assessment of academic and/or behavioral progress.
- Returned to school.
- Paired with praise and tangible rewards so that the positive information conveyed in the home note will result in rewards at home.

Your Home—School Note:
1. Get the home-school note in the morning.
2. If Miguel meets his morning goal of following directions 50% of the time in the morning, praise this progress.
3. At the end of the day, write down what percentage of the time Miguel followed directions.
4. Send the note home.

- If you have any questions feel free to call the consultant.

GOOD LUCK!!!!

Appendix I

Objectives, definitions, and examples of conjoint plan evaluation interview.

Objective	Definitions	Examples
Social opening	Establish a friendly supportive atmosphere (e.g., position of the chairs, nonverbal communication)	"Hello again! It's great to have the chance to see you again!"
	Demonstrate interest for the consultee (e.g., ask about past events)	"I've been wondering how things are going with Patti. I see her at school and she seems really happy!"
Open up dialogue	Re-emphasize the attitude that everyone's input is vital	"Your involvement in this process has been very helpful. It's so important to Hector that we work together"
	Continue to use inclusive language	"What kinds of things have we seen at home and school?"
	Discuss steps of the meeting	"Today we will look at the data that you collected and see how Kyle is doing in relation to his goals. We will decide if the plan is working, and whether we may want to keep it going, make small or large adjustments, or stop the plan altogether"
Determine outcomes of plan	Restate the plan and the goals	"We worked together on coming up with a plan to increase Nick's positive initiations toward peers. We were hoping that he would use these skills and demonstrate at least 3 initiations per morning"
	Discuss how the plan worked and if the goals were met	"I charted the data after I collected it from you yesterday. We can compare Jade's math performance now to his performance before we began. I also drew in a goal line so we can see how closely we are coming to helping Jade meet her goal"

(*Continued*)

Objectives, definitions, and examples of conjoint plan evaluation interview.—Cont'd.

Objective	Definitions	Examples
		"It looks like Miguel did a good job finishing his chores without being prompted 4 out of 6 days this week. At school, he took out his books and began working within 1 minute of being instructed to do so 4 out of 5 days. That is right where we wanted him to be!"
	Decide where to go from here (e.g., modify plan, set a new goal, use plan in another setting, end consultation)	"Alex has not quite met his goal of identifying all of the colors on his color chart. What do you think we should do with the plan, given that Alex is making some progress?"
Determine need to change plan	Discuss what worked and what didn't, emphasizing strengths of the plan	"Let's talk about what parts of the plan seemed to work. What did not work as well?"
	Re-evaluate what is happening before and after, as well as specific patterns, and why the priority behavior is occurring (if necessary)	"What did you notice that we might have missed before? Were there things that seemed to make it difficult to Kristy to get her work done?"
Continue the plan	Discuss how to continue positive changes over time (if appropriate)	"Carlo seems very proud of his accomplishments! How can we make sure he continues doing so well with his self-control?"
	Discuss continuing the plan (e.g., other times and settings) or gradually removing the plan	"Kevin is showing better organization at getting the right materials home and back to school the next day. Shall we continue this daily home-note system for another few weeks, and then fade it to every few days or weekly prompts?"
Discuss need for future meetings	Discuss if a formal meeting is necessary	"What is your preference about meeting again?" "Shall we meet in a few weeks to make sure that Stacy is still doing well complying with instructions?"
	Discuss informal methods (e.g., e-mail, phone calls, home–school notes) to remain in touch, emphasizing the value of continued communication	"Since email worked so well for our communication throughout this process, can we continue to touch base that way over the next couple of months to make sure things are still going well with Pamela's behaviors with her brother and peers at school?" "Working together on this plan and communicating frequently about how things were going really seemed to make a difference for Anna. That communication will still be very important as we move forward"

Objectives, definitions, and examples of conjoint plan evaluation interview.—Cont'd.

Objective	Definitions	Examples
	Discuss plan for follow-up and provide caregivers and teachers with extra plan worksheets and data collection forms	"The careful attention to Tomas' lack of talking at school made a big difference in encouraging his speech. As we wind down the plan, how can we make sure that he continues to talk at school?"
Discuss satisfaction/ social validity	Discuss what caregivers and teachers thought about why the behavior changed, as well as what worked and what didn't with the plan and the process	"What about the plan worked? What pieces should we continue to keep in place? What did not work as well?" "What about the plan seemed to make a difference? How did our working together seem to go?"
	Discuss if caregivers and teachers were satisfied with the results	"How do you feel about the progress that Alexandra is making? How did it compare to what you hoped for Alexandra?"
Plan for future collaboration and home– school partnership	Summarize the plan and the partnership building process, emphasizing collaborative decision making, strengths, expertise, and home–school communication	"We did a lot of work together making plans and decisions for Keely's learning. Sharing observations, information, and ideas was really key to helping her make progress. Staying in contact and communication with each other, across the classroom and home, was particularly important. Great work!"
	Discuss how you might use similar ideas to address future needs, emphasizing specific plans to address priorities, as well as the collaborative decision-making process	"What might we do in the future if Erin has more difficulties?" "We found out how important it is for us to work together, across home and school, to really help Frank. Is this something that we can continue to do as necessary, to keep things on track?"
End consultation	Discuss ways to keep in touch with the consultant and with each other	"Please call me or email me whenever you would like, if I can be of help. It will probably be very helpful for you, Mr. Morrow and Ms. Evans, to stay in touch with each other. You have figured out a good system – keep up the good work!"

Appendix J

Conjoint Plan Evaluation Interview (CPEI)

Child's Name: _____ Date: _____

Parent's Name: _____ Age: _____

Teacher's Name: _____ Grade: _____

School: _____

Consultant's Name: _____

Consultant note: The goals of the CPEI are to:

Behavioral goals:

- Determine if the goals for the priority behavior have been met
- Evaluate what worked and what didn't
- Discuss continuation or termination of plan
- Schedule additional interview if necessary, or terminate consultation

Relationship-building goals:

- Continue to promote open communication and collaborative decision making across the home and school settings
- Reinforce joint efforts in addressing needs
- Discuss caregivers' and teachers' perceptions of the plan and process
- Reinforce caregivers' and teachers' strengths and competencies for addressing future needs for the child
- Establish means for caregivers and teachers to continue to partner in the future

Consultant and case goals for interview:

_____
_____
_____
_____
_____
_____
_____
_____
_____
_____
_____
_____

Conjoint Plan Evaluation Interview (CPEI)

Social Opening

Establish a friendly supportive atmosphere (e.g., position of the chairs, non-verbal communication); demonstrate interest for the consultee (e.g., ask about past events)

Notes:

Open Up Dialogue

Re-emphasize the attitude that everyone's input is vital; continue to use inclusive language; discuss steps of the meeting

Notes:

How Did It Work/What Happened?

Restate the plan and the goals; discuss how the plan worked and if the goals were met; decide where to go from here (e.g., modify plan, set a new goal, use plan in another setting, end consultation)

Notes:

Change Plan

Discuss what worked and what didn't, emphasizing strengths of the plan; it may be necessary to re-evaluate what is happening before and after, as well as specific patterns, and why the priority behavior is occurring; refer to previous interview forms

Notes:

Continue the Plan

Discuss how to continue positive changes over time; discuss continuing the plan (e.g., other times and settings) or gradually removing the plan

Notes:

Discuss Need for Future Meeting

Discuss if a formal meeting is necessary; discuss informal methods (e.g., e-mail, phone calls, home school notes), emphasizing the value of continued communication; discuss plan for follow-up and provide caregivers and teachers with extra plan worksheets and data collection forms

Notes:

What Worked/What Didn't

Summarize the plan and the partnership-building process, emphasizing collaborative decision making, strengths, expertise, and home school communication; discuss what caregivers and teachers thought about why the behavior changed, as well as what worked and what didn't with the plan and the process; discuss how you might use similar ideas to address future needs, emphasizing specific plans to address priorities, as well as the collaborative decision-making process; discuss if caregivers and teachers were satisfied with the results

Notes:

End Consultation

Discuss ways to keep in touch with the consultant and with each other

Appendix K
Forms for Meeting Agendas

INTRODUCTION AND ORIENTATION MEETING

At this meeting, we will be answering the following questions, and any additional ones that you may have. You are welcome to take notes on this page:

Introductions

What is conjoint behavioral consultation?

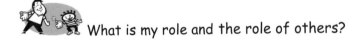What is my role and the role of others?

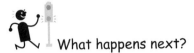What happens next?

 _____ (consultant) will call me:

Date:

Time:

_____

Adapted and reprinted with permission from Brandy L. Clarke.

MEETING 1
BUILDING ON STRENGTHS

At this meeting, we will be answering the following questions, and any additional ones that you may have. You are welcome to take notes on these pages:

 What does _____ do well, what does he/she like?

What is getting in the way of him/her doing well? What are your main concerns at home and at school?

What concern do we want to focus on?

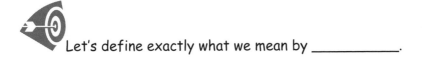 Let's define exactly what we mean by _____.

What time and place do we want to focus on first?

What are our goals for _____ ?

What has already been tried to help _____ meet this goal?

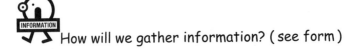 How will we gather information? (see form)

Phone number to call with questions: _____

Email addresses: _____

MEETING 2
PLANNING FOR SUCCESS

At this meeting, we will be addressing the following points, and any additional ones that you may have. You are welcome to take notes on these pages:

 Review information collected. What would be an appropriate goal?

What is happening before, during, and after the behavior?

Why is the behavior happening? (Think about patterns that have been observed, before and after the behavior)

Discuss possible plans (See plan summary sheets).

Let's talk about how these plans will look in your home/classroom and the tools we will need.

 How do we carry out the plan?

Discuss ways to continue collecting information.

Decide when the group can come together for the next meeting.

Phone number to call with questions: _____

Email addresses: _____

MEETING 3
CHECKING AND RECONNECTING

At this meeting, we will be addressing the following questions and discussion items, and any additional ones that you may have. You are welcome to take notes on these pages:

   Did _____ meet his/her goals?

Goal:

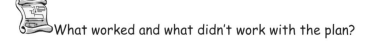   Review information collected at home and at school.

What worked and what didn't work with the plan?

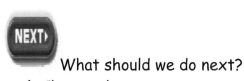 What should we do next?

1. Change plan

2. Continue plan

3. Pick new focus

 Identify ways to keep in touch!

Phone numbers: _____

Email addresses: _____

Index

A

Acceptability research, 149–150
Anger management skills, 103
Attention deficit hyperactivity disorder
　　(ADHD), 61, 117–118

B

Behavioral assessment, 31
　and contrast, 62
Behavioral data
　of culturally diverse student, 95–96
　interpretation of, 40
Behavioral excesses and deficits, 42
Behavioral functions
　and chart for parents and teachers,
　　185
Behavioral intervention options, 43
Behavioral record
　in clinical work and research, 37
Behavioral "side effects," 62
Behavioral social skills treatment
　　program, 137
Behavioral theory
　assumptions of, 6–7
　ecological-behavioral approach and, 7
　limitations of, 6
Behavioral training and reinforcement
　　program, 137
Behavior Intervention Rating Scale
　　(BIRS), 138, 142
BIRS-Acceptability factor (*BIRS*-A),
　　138, 141, 147
　for teacher and parent scales, 94
BIRS-Effectiveness factor (*BIRS*-E),
　　94, 138

C

CAR. *See* Consultation Analysis
　　Record
Case-centered consultation, 21
CBC. *See* Conjoint behavioral
　　consultation
CEF. *See* Consultant Evaluation Form
Challenging situations, management
　　of, 73, 74
Child assessment to ecological
　　assessment, 35. *See also* Conjoint
　　behavioral consultation
Child-care professionals, goal for, 106
Children's learning and behavior, 7
Child's needs, addressing, 61
Child's prenatal and early life
　　experiences, 63
Classroom behaviors, operational
　　definitions for, 34
Clinical and educational professionals,
　　115
CNAI. *See* Conjoint Needs Analysis
　　Interview
CNII. *See* Conjoint Needs
　　Identification Interview
Collaboration, 29, 115
　equality and parity, 4
　modeled by consultants, 62–63
Collaborative relationships, 2
Communication patterns, relational,
　　141
Communication skills, 64
　in CBC, 59
　enhancement of, 83–85
　guidelines and practices for, 65

Communication skills (*continued*)
  minimal encouragers, 67
  nonverbal cues, 66
  open questions, 67
  paraphrase/summarize, 68
  reflection, 68
  tips for effective, 60
Compliance behaviors, 141
  across baseline and treatment
    conditions, 93–94
Conflict management, 72
  focus on mutual goals, 73
  nonverbal language, 74
  provide structure, 74
  reframe, 74
Congruent worlds, students experiences
    and, 11
Conjoint behavioral consultation
  acceptability and effectiveness of,
    145
  case studies review, 139–142
  characteristics/assumptions of, 27
  competency acquisition, 28
  conceptual model of, 24, 25
  diversity and, 79
  efficacy of, 135
  experimental studies, review of,
    136–139
  goals and objectives of, 26–27
  in head start settings, 105
  interventions, 136, 140
  literature, 146
  meetings, 54–55
  with outcomes and processes, 27–28
  outcome studies, review of, 130–134
  partnership-centered, 27
  principles, application of, 98
  relational objectives in, 57–59
  research, 129
  responsive to consumers needs, 28
  reviews and meta-analyses, 129–135
  school psychologists' perceptions
    of, 149
  service delivery, 54
  stages of, 29
  in teaming context, 97
Conjoint needs analysis
  functional/skills assessments, 39–42
  intervention plans, 42–45

  objectives of, 39
  problem-solving/content issues,
    89–90
  process goals and issues, 90–91
Conjoint Needs Analysis Interview,
    89, 120
  content issues, 102, 110
  definitions of, 177–180
  goals during, 90, 181
  objectives of, 39
Conjoint needs identification
  data collection procedures, 33
  objectives of, 30
  prioritizing needs, 30–32
  problem solving/content issues,
    87–88
  process goals and issues, 88–89
  target concerns, 32
Conjoint Needs Identification Interview,
    30, 100, 108
  behavioral and relationship-building
    goals, 171
  content issues, 87, 89
  data collection procedures,
    determination of, 33
  focus and settings, 173
  goals of, 171
  information collection, 174
  need and goal selection, 172
  objectives and definitions, 167–170
  social opening and open up dialogue,
    172
  target behavior for consultation
    process, 118
Conjoint plan evaluation, 47–51
  problem-solving/content issues, 91
  process goals and issues, 95
Conjoint Plan Evaluation Interview,
    91–92, 204
  content issues in, 103, 112, 124
  definitions of, 201–203
  goals of, 204
  objectives of, 47–48, 201–203
Conjoint plan implementation, 45
Conjoint problem identification
    interviews, 145
Conjoint problem solving, 53
Consultant Evaluation Form,
    141, 147

consultant effectiveness measured
  with, 145
difference scores, 152
satisfaction with CBC consultant, 94
Consultation Analysis Record, 64
Consultation behavior record, 175–176
Consultation evaluation and case
  studies, 48–49
Consultation plan, 191
Consultation practice, 22, 23
  direct assessment in, 35–36
Consultation services, traditional and
  revised core characteristics of, 23
Consultee–mediator consultation
  relationships, 21–23
Consultees
  contributions, 71
  diversity among, 71
  similar experiences between, 70
CPEI. *See* Conjoint Plan Evaluation
  Interview
CPII. *See* Conjoint problem
  identification interviews
Cross-cultural communication, 83
Cross-cultural competence, 78
Cross-system partnerships, 25
Cultural guide, 83
Cultural learning process, 82
Culturally sensitive CBC services,
  consultant practices for, 80
Cultural sensitivity, 81
Culture and diversity, 78
Curriculum-based measurement, 109
"Curriculum of home," 10

D

Data collection procedures, 33
Decision making, 59, 63
Diverse families
  case study of, 86
  CBC practices with, 81
  culturally sensitive services for, 80
  trusting relationships with, 82
Diversity issues, 82–83

E

Ecological–behavioral theory, 7, 19
Ecological conceptual model, 5
Ecological theory, 4–6

Educational goals, shared commitment
  to, 62
Effective partnerships development,
  framework for, 12–16
Emotional disturbance, 98
Empowerment, 75
Ethnographic study of diverse
  adolescents, 11
Evidence-based interventions and
  procedures, 43
Evidence-based parent consultation
  model, 135
Exosystem, 5
Expertise, diversity of, 63

F

FAAB. *See* Functional Assessment of
  Academic Behavior
Family-based interventions, 17
Family-centered approach, 85
Family-centeredness elements
  existing family strengths use, 9
  family empowerment, 7–8
  family-identified needs, 8
  new skills and competencies
    acquisition, 8
  strengthening social supports, 9
Family-centered services, goals of, 7–9
Family empowerment, 7
"Family-friendly" communities, 14
Family-identified needs, 8
Family members
  and child's educators, relationship
    between, 61
  roles of, 10
  and teachers' perspectives, 60
Family process variables, in relationship
  with student learning, 10
Family Relational Communication
  Control Coding System, 145
Family-school partnerships. *See*
  Partnerships
Family strengths and abilities, 9
FCS. *See* Family-centered services
FRCCCS. *See* Family Relational
  Communication Control Coding
  System
Functional Assessment of Academic
  Behavior, 35

G

Goal Attainment Scaling (GAS), 50,
    138, 142, 149–150
  CBC efficacy and, 94
  ratigs, development and utilization,
    51
  target behaviors, goals for, 150–151
Growth-producing behaviors, 8

H

Head Start Program Performance
    Standards, 106
Head Start setting, 105
  case study of, 107
    needs analysis phase, 110–111
    needs identification phase, 108–110
    plan evaluation phase, 112–114
    plan implementation phase,
      111–112
  parental participation in, 106
Helpfulness research, 151
Help-seeking behaviors, 120
  across baseline and intervention
    phases, 125
Home consultation plan, 123
Home-school partnerships
  behavioral theory, 6–7
  collaborative relationships, 2–4
  ecological theory, 4–6
  evidence-based models of, 16–18
  family-centeredness, 7–9
  framework for development of, 12–16
  goals and purposes of, 10–12
  meaning of, 1–4
  shared responsibility, 4

I

Individualized Educational Plan (IEP),
    117–118
Individuals with Disabilities Education
    Act (IDEA), 97
Interaction with families, 12
Interdisciplinary pediatric model, 115
Interpersonal and relational skills, 64
Interpersonal contexts, 61
Intervention
  child's immediate response to, 47
  determining effects of, 47–48
  ideas, sources for, 45

  integrity, 45
  options, based on behavior
    functions, 44
Intervention plan implementation, 45
  problem-solving/content issues, 91
  process goals and issues, 91
Intervention plan worksheet, 46
Introductory and orientation
    meetings, 208
  building on strengths, 209–210
  checking and reconnecting, 213–214
  planning for sucess, 211–212

M

Macrosystem, 5
Maintenance interviews, 51
Meeting agendas forms, 208
Mesosystem, 5, 6
Microsystems
  for children's development, 61
  in child's life, 4–5
Miguel's plan for sucess
  at home, 187–193
  at school, 194–200
Motivational beliefs, 15
Multisystemic collaborative
    approach, 115

N

Needs identification phase, 100
No Child Left Behind (NCLB), 97
Nondeficit approach, 69
Nonverbal Cues, 66

O

Organizational consultation, 21

P

Parental involvement, 15
Parental self-efficacy, 15, 72
Parent–child relationships, 12
Parenting role, 15
Parents and teachers
  communication between, 83–85
  consultation, 135
  meaningful roles for, 71–73
Parents and teachers perceptions
  of CBC, 150
  congruence of, 151, 152

Partnership building, 70–72.
    See also Patnerships
Partnerships
    characteristics of, 1, 3
    and collaboration, 29
    evidence-based models of, 16–18
    four A's of
        actions, 14
        approach, 12
        atmosphere, 14
        attitudes, 13
    framework for developing effective,
        12–15
    goals and purposes of, 10–12
    parent benefits with, 12
    theories underlying, 4
    versus traditional orientations, 2
    values and perceptions, 13
Pediatric healthcare systems, 114
    case study, 117
        needs analysis phase, 120–122
        needs identification phase,
            118–120
        plan evaluation phase, 124–126
        plan implementation phase,
            122–124
    roles of CBC consultant, 116
"Performance deficits," 41
Perspective taking skills, 60, 69
PPCS. *See* Psychosocial Processes
        Coding Scheme
Priority behavior, 188
Problem-solving process, 2
Problem-solving teaming context, 98
Process research, review of, 142–144
Psychological variables, to parental
        behaviors, 15–16
Psychosocial Processes Coding Scheme,
    146

R
RCI. *See* Reliable change indices
Relational communication patterns,
        142, 145
Relationship-building strategies, 85
Reliable change indices, 139
Response covariation, 32
Response to Intervention (RtI), 51
    and conjoint problem solving, 53

dependent and independent variables
        in, 52
    implementation of, 53

S
School atmosphere, 14
School-family relationships, 13.
        See also partnerships
School-based teaming approach, 98
School consultation plan, 122
School-linked consultants, 116
School psychologists' perceptions,
        of CBC, 149
Shared ownership and joint
        responsibility, 59
Shared responsibility
    children's progress and, 4
    for educational outcomes, 12
    for learning outcomes, 14
Silence and pauses, in communication,
        66
"Skill deficits," 41
Skill development, 185
Skills and competencies, acquisition
        of, 8
Social context, 145, 146
Social initiation behaviors, 136
Social Skills Rating System, 137
Social supports, strengthening of, 9
Social validity, 49
    research, review of, 145–148
Speech acts, categories of, 146
SSRS. *See* Social Skills Rating System

T
Tantrumming behaviors, 103–104
Target concerns
    guidelines for, 31
    specifying and operationalizing, 32
Task Force on Evidence-Based
        Interventions in School
        Psychology, 17
Team-based relationship building, 99
    case study
        conjoint plan evaluation, 103–105
        needs analysis phase, 100–102
        plan implementation phase,
            102–103
    problem-solving process, 101

Team-based service models, 98
Team format, 98
Technology training consultation, 21
Tourette syndrome, 117
Treatment acceptability, defined as,
    146, 150

U
U.S. Department of Education, 72, 77

V
Validate, Assess, Interpret–Link
    to intervention (VAIL), 40

Printed in the United States of America

 Springer